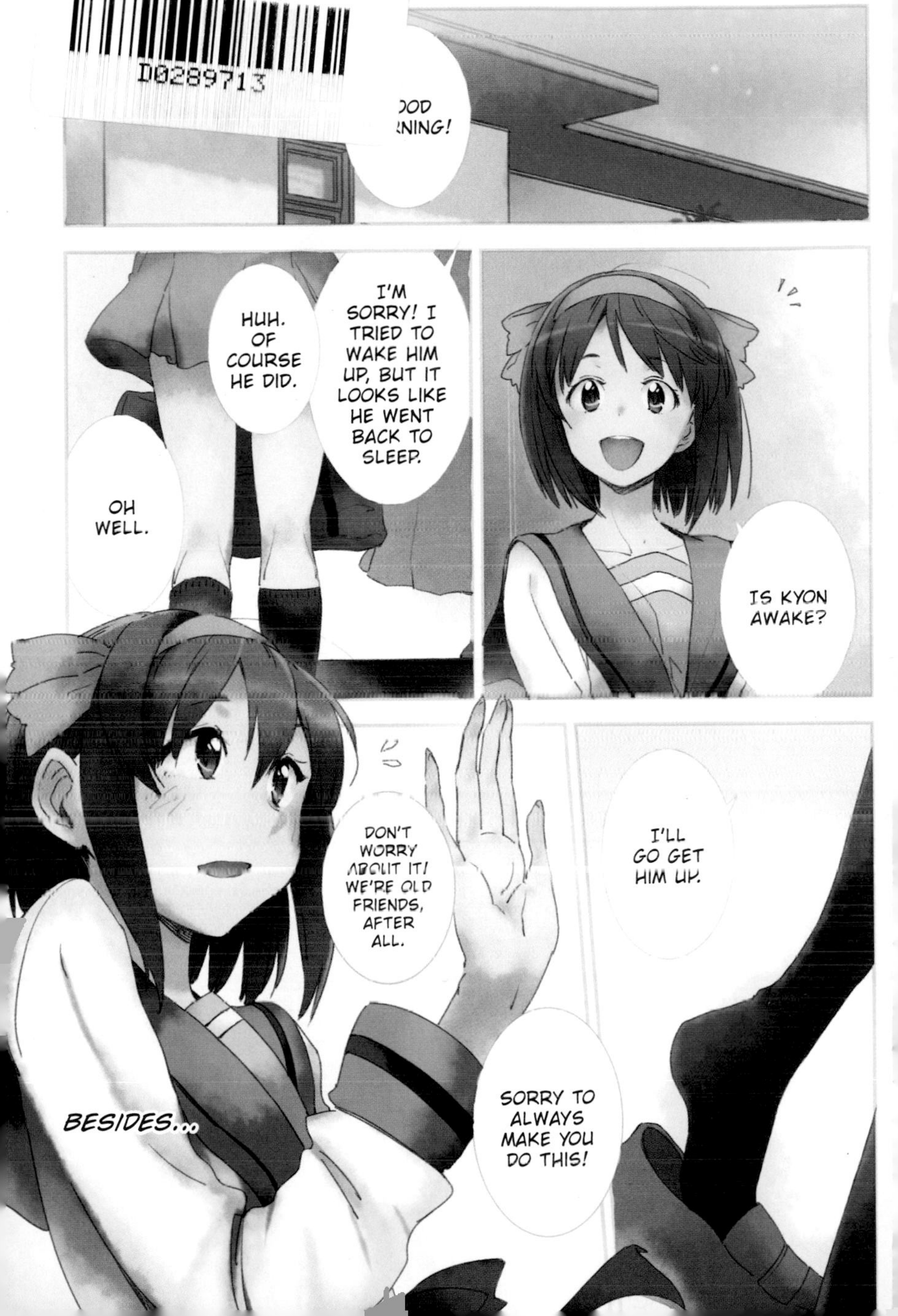
OOD
RNING!
IS KYON AWAKE?
I'M SORRY! I TRIED TO WAKE HIM UP, BUT IT LOOKS LIKE HE WENT BACK TO SLEEP.
HUH. OF COURSE HE DID.
OH WELL.
I'LL GO GET HIM UP.
SORRY TO ALWAYS MAKE YOU DO THIS!
DON'T WORRY ABOUT IT! WE'RE OLD FRIENDS, AFTER ALL.
BESIDES...

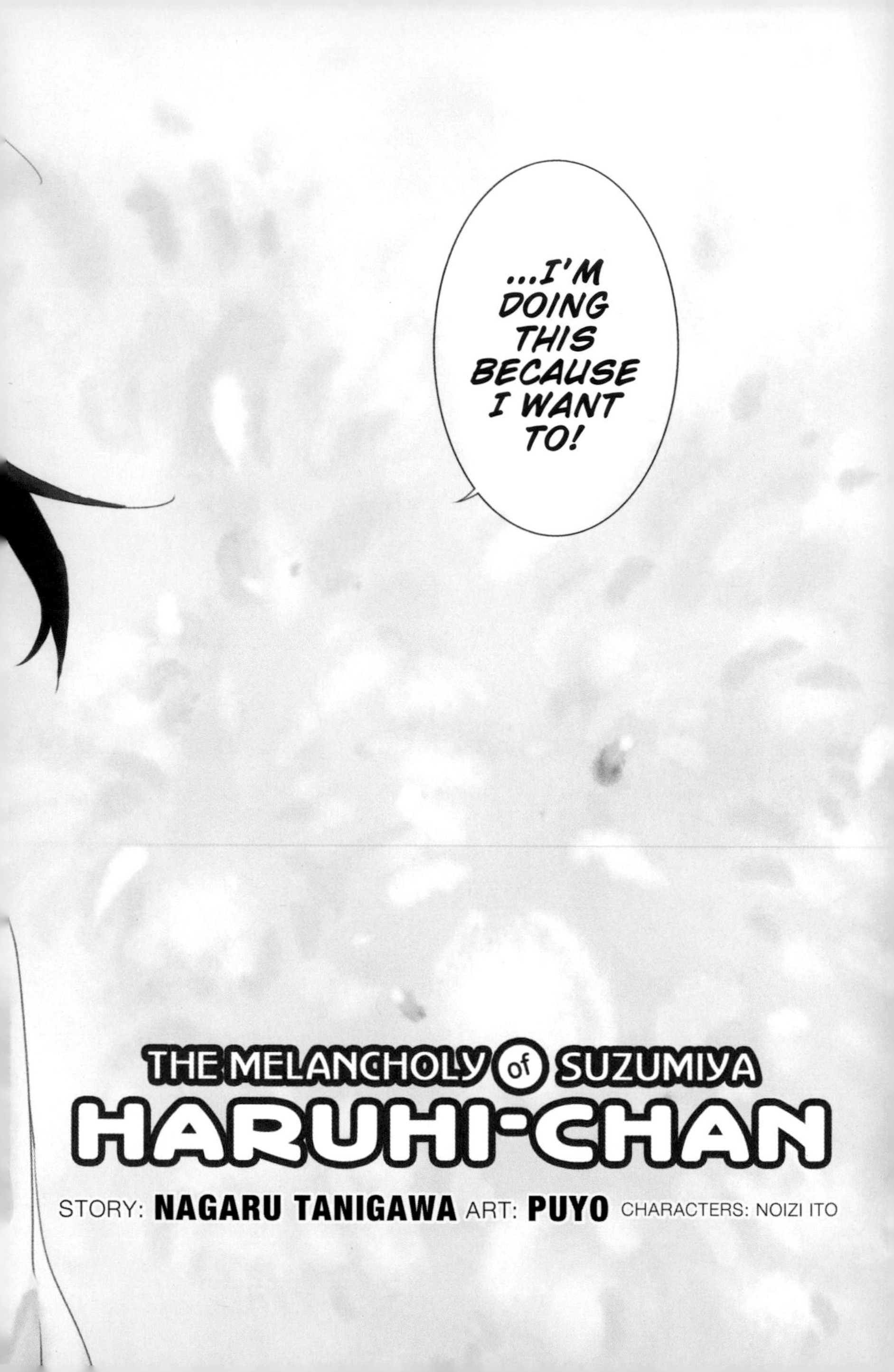
...I'M DOING THIS BECAUSE I WANT TO!
THE MELANCHOLY of SUZUMIYA
HARUHI-CHAN
STORY: NAGARU TANIGAWA ART: PUYO CHARACTERS: NOIZI ITO

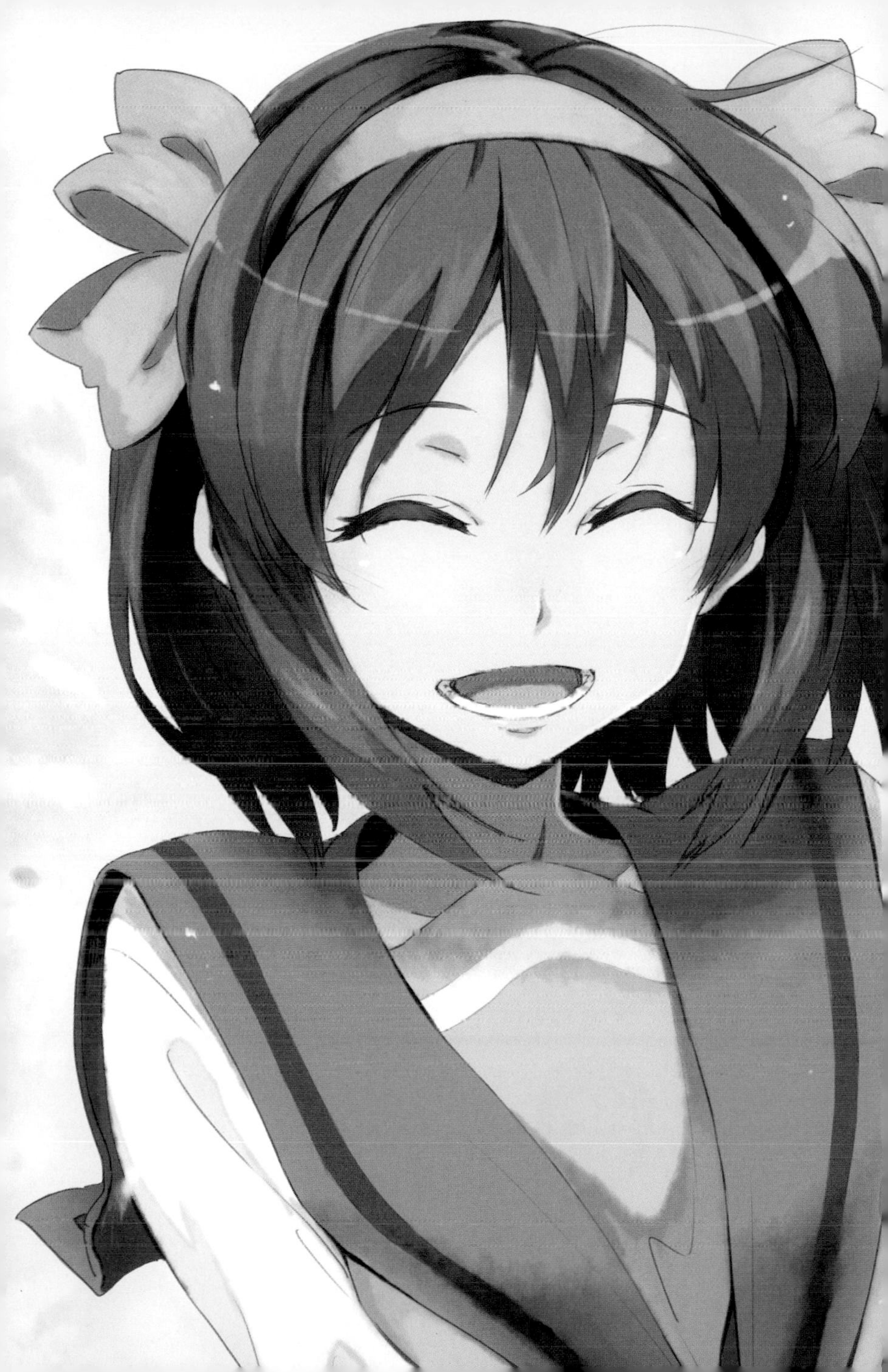

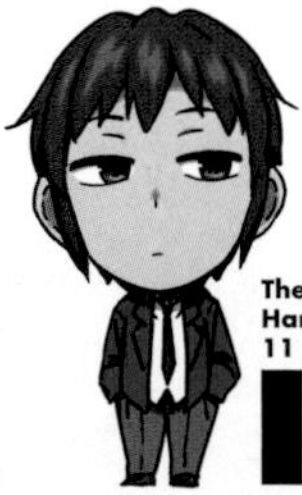

The Melancholy of Suzumiya Haruhi-chan 11

INDEX

THE MELANCHOLY of SUZUMIYA
HARUHI-CHAN
The Untold Adventures of the SOS Brigade

THIS WORLD IS A FICTION...

INDEED...

...IT IS WHOLLY IMAGINARY...

STORY: **NAGARU TANIGAWA** ART: **PUYO** CHARACTERS: NOIZI ITO

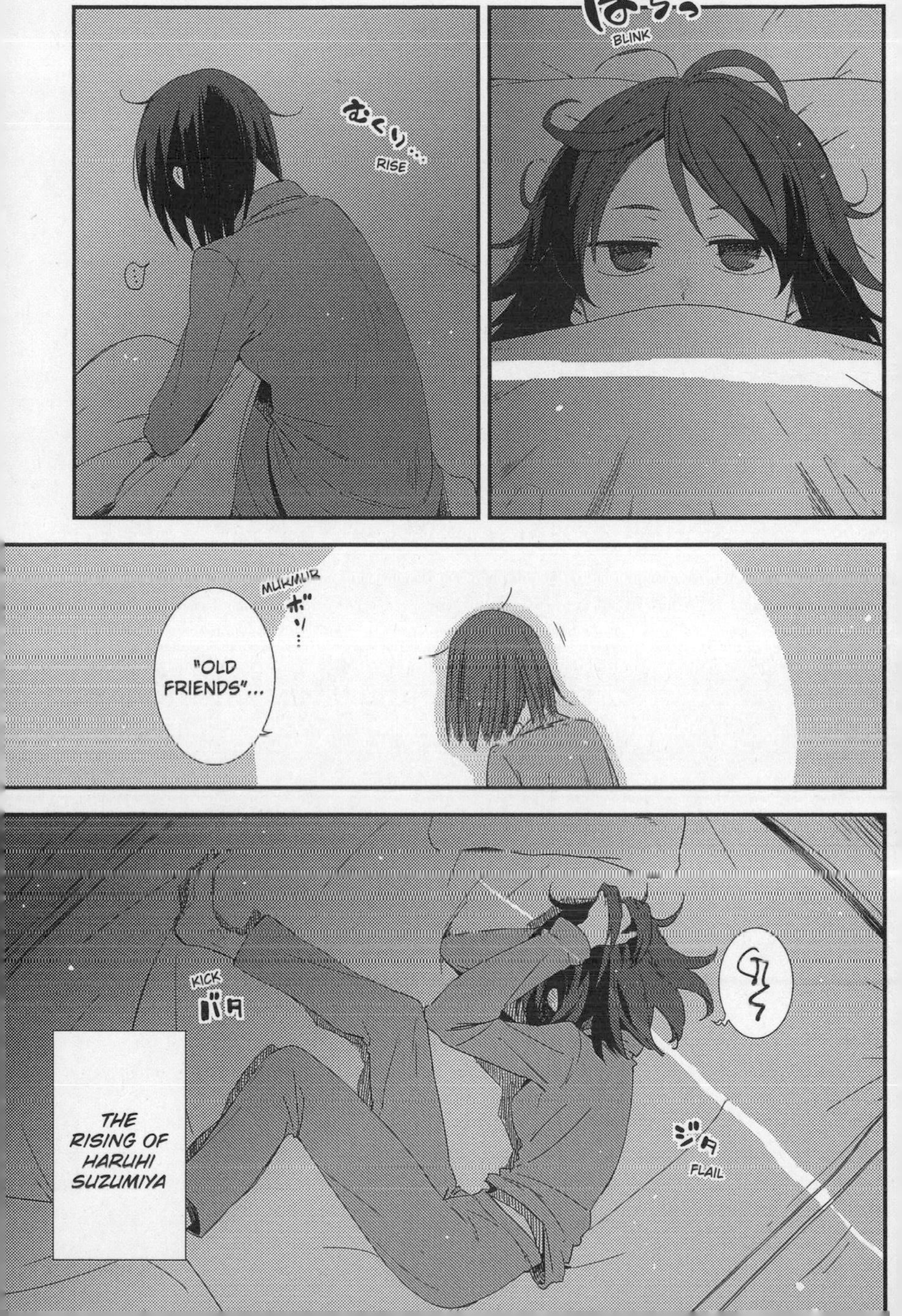
ぱちっ
BLINK
むくり…
RISE
…
MUMUR
ボソ…
"OLD FRIENDS"…
GRR
ジタ
FLAIL
KICK
バタ
THE RISING OF HARUHI SUZUMIYA

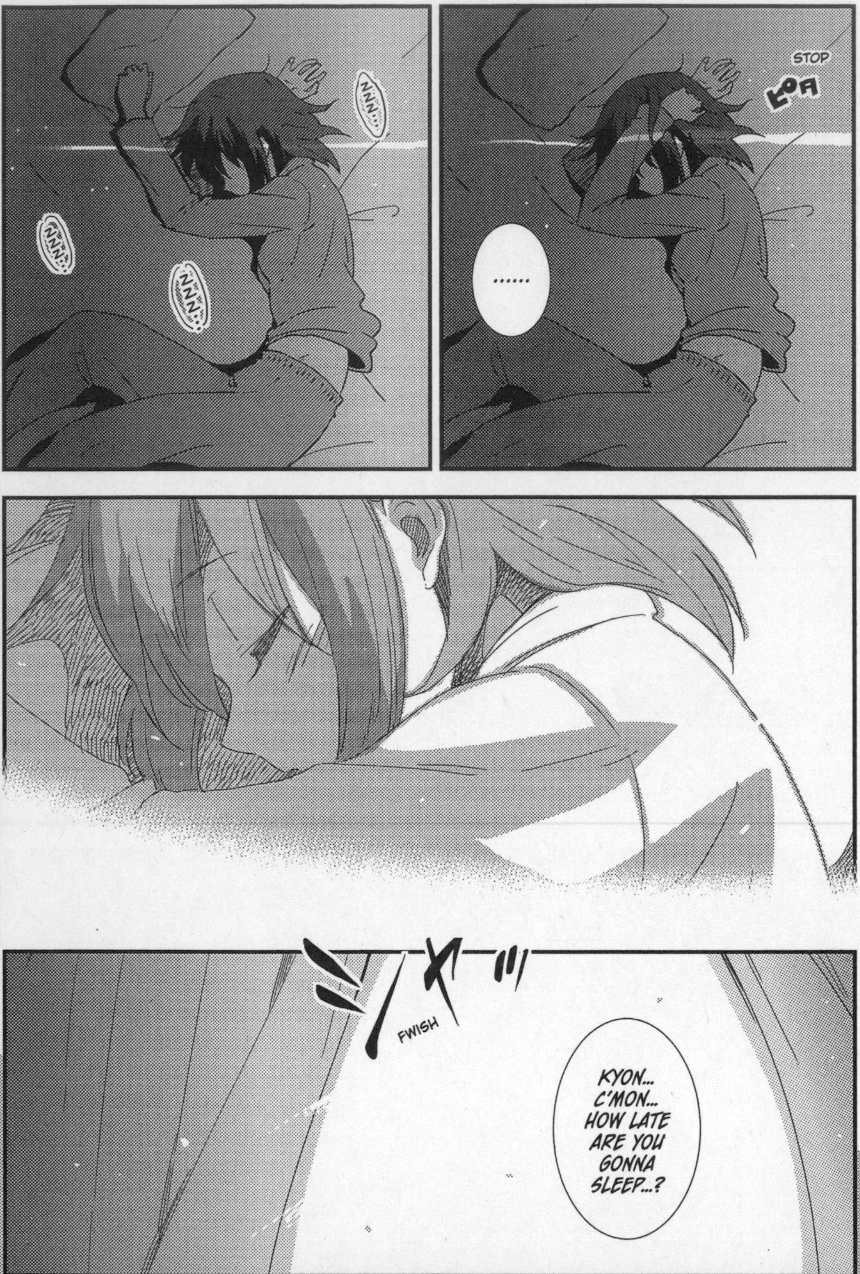
STOP
......
NNN...
NNN...
NNN...
FWISH
KYON... C'MON... HOW LATE ARE YOU GONNA SLEEP...?

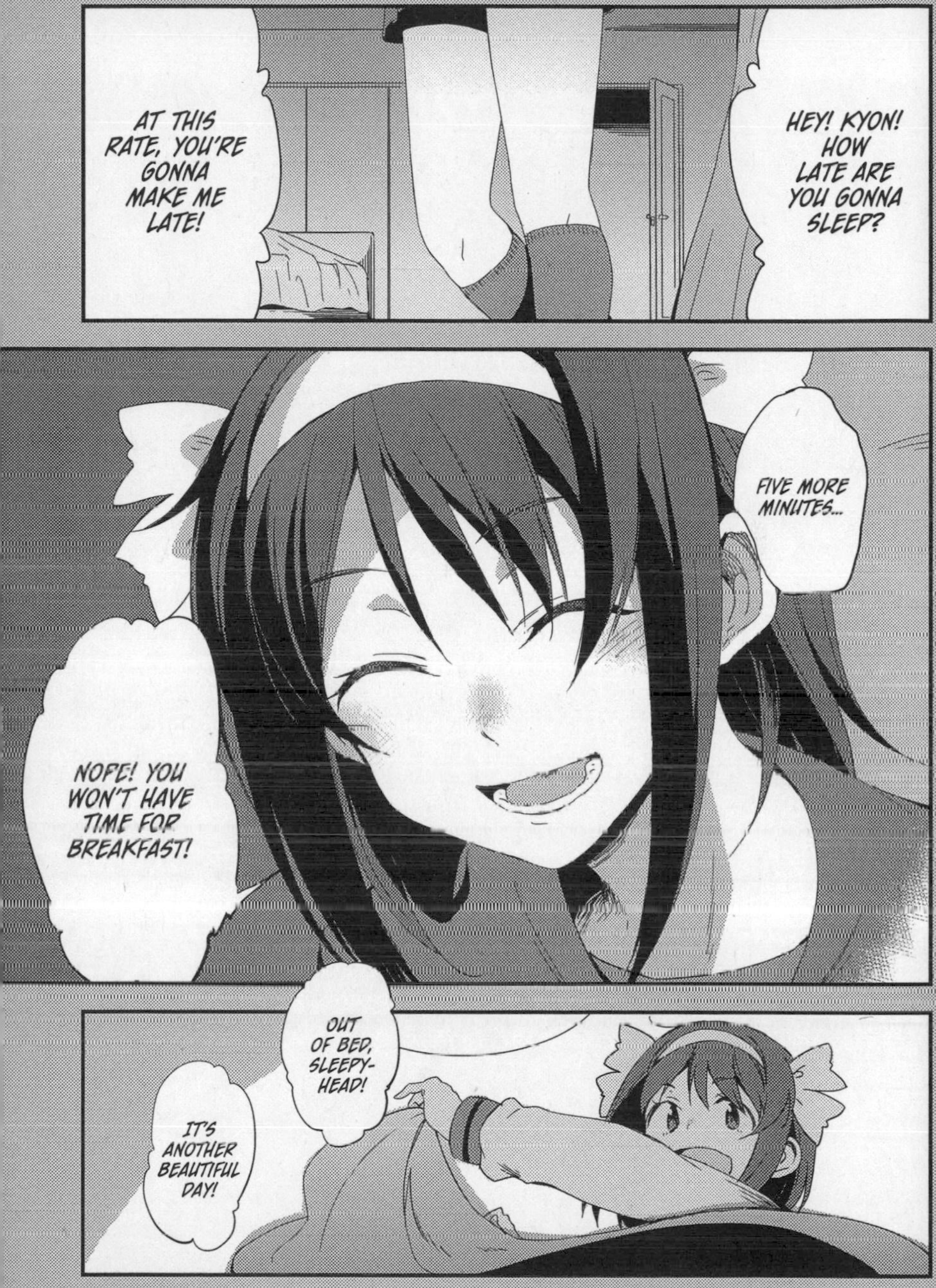
HEY! KYON! HOW LATE ARE YOU GONNA SLEEP?
AT THIS RATE, YOU'RE GONNA MAKE ME LATE!
FIVE MORE MINUTES...
NOPE! YOU WON'T HAVE TIME FOR BREAKFAST!
OUT OF BED, SLEEPY-HEAD!
IT'S ANOTHER BEAUTIFUL DAY!

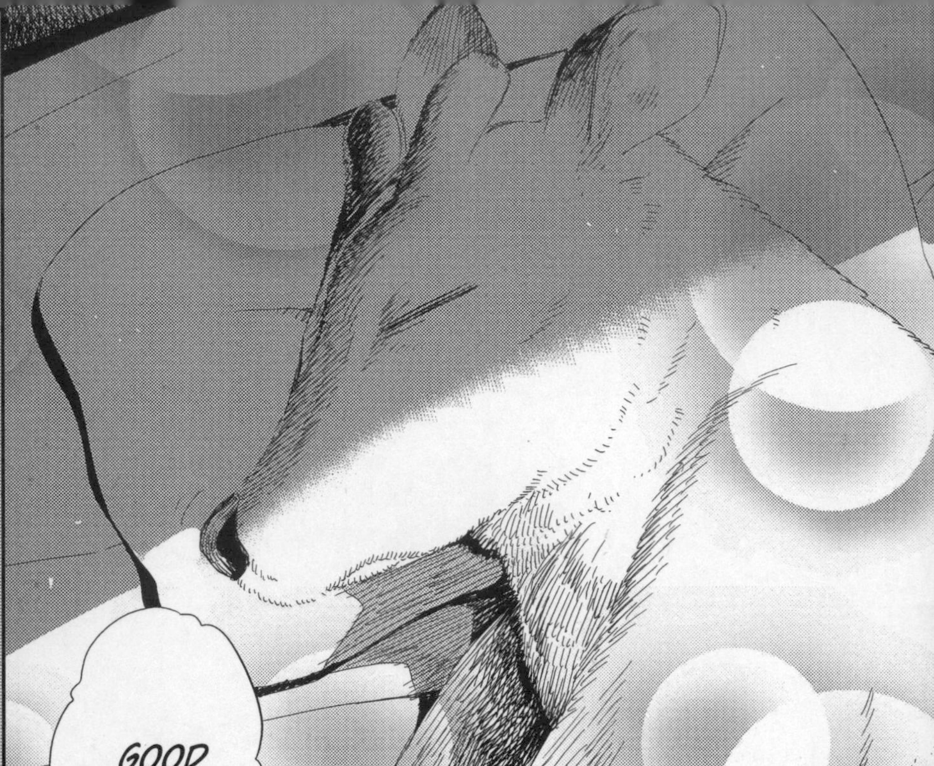
GOOD MORNING, KYON!

NOTE: "KYON" IS ALSO THE JAPANESE WORD FOR THE REEVES'S MUNTJAC, A SPECIES OF SMALL DEER NATIVE TO CHINA.

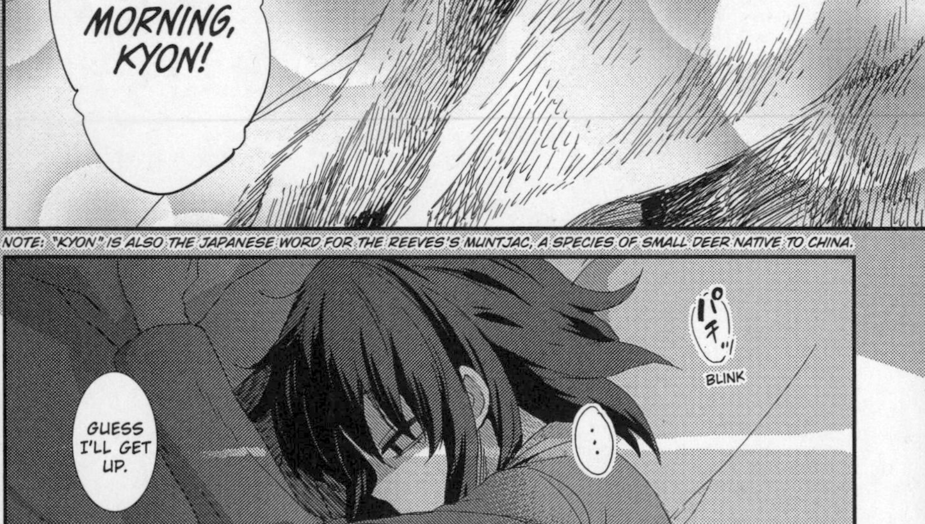
パチッ
BLINK
...
GUESS I'LL GET UP.

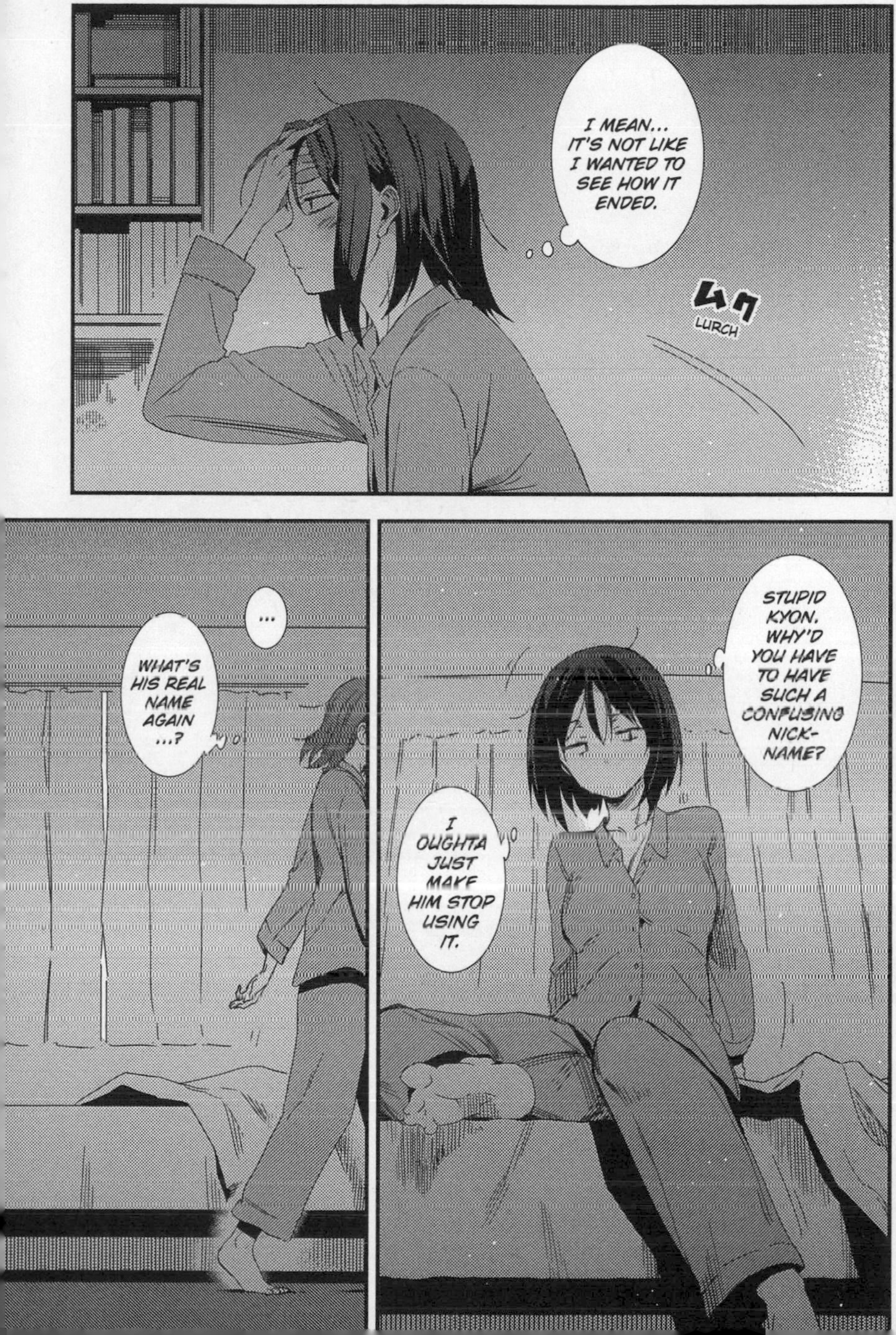
I MEAN... IT'S NOT LIKE I WANTED TO SEE HOW IT ENDED.
LURCH
STUPID KYON. WHY'D YOU HAVE TO HAVE SUCH A CONFUSING NICK-NAME?
I OUGHTA JUST MAKE HIM STOP USING IT.
...
WHAT'S HIS REAL NAME AGAIN...?

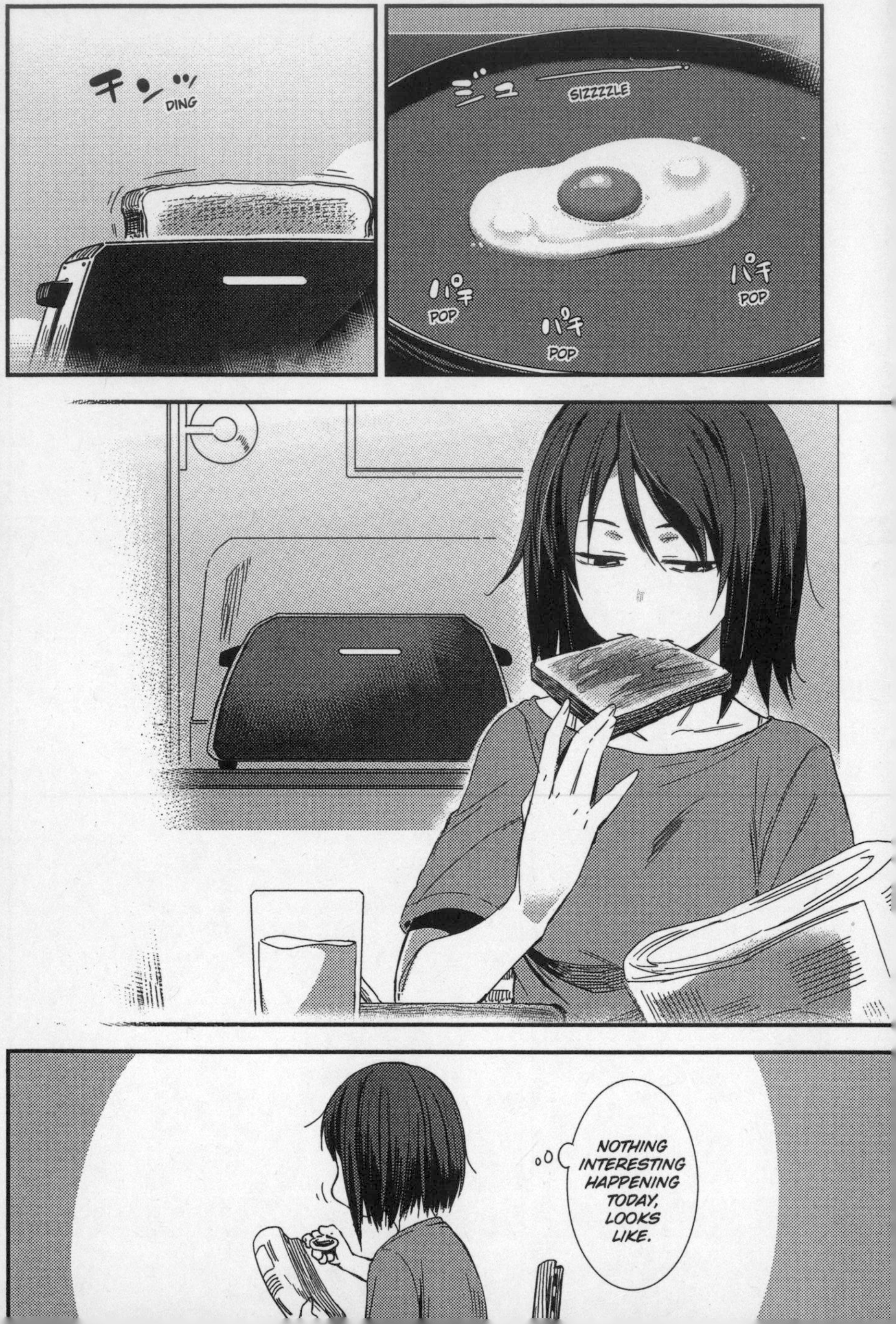
ジュ
SIZZZZLE
パチ
POP
パチ
POP
パチ
POP
チンッ
DING
NOTHING INTERESTING HAPPENING TODAY, LOOKS LIKE.

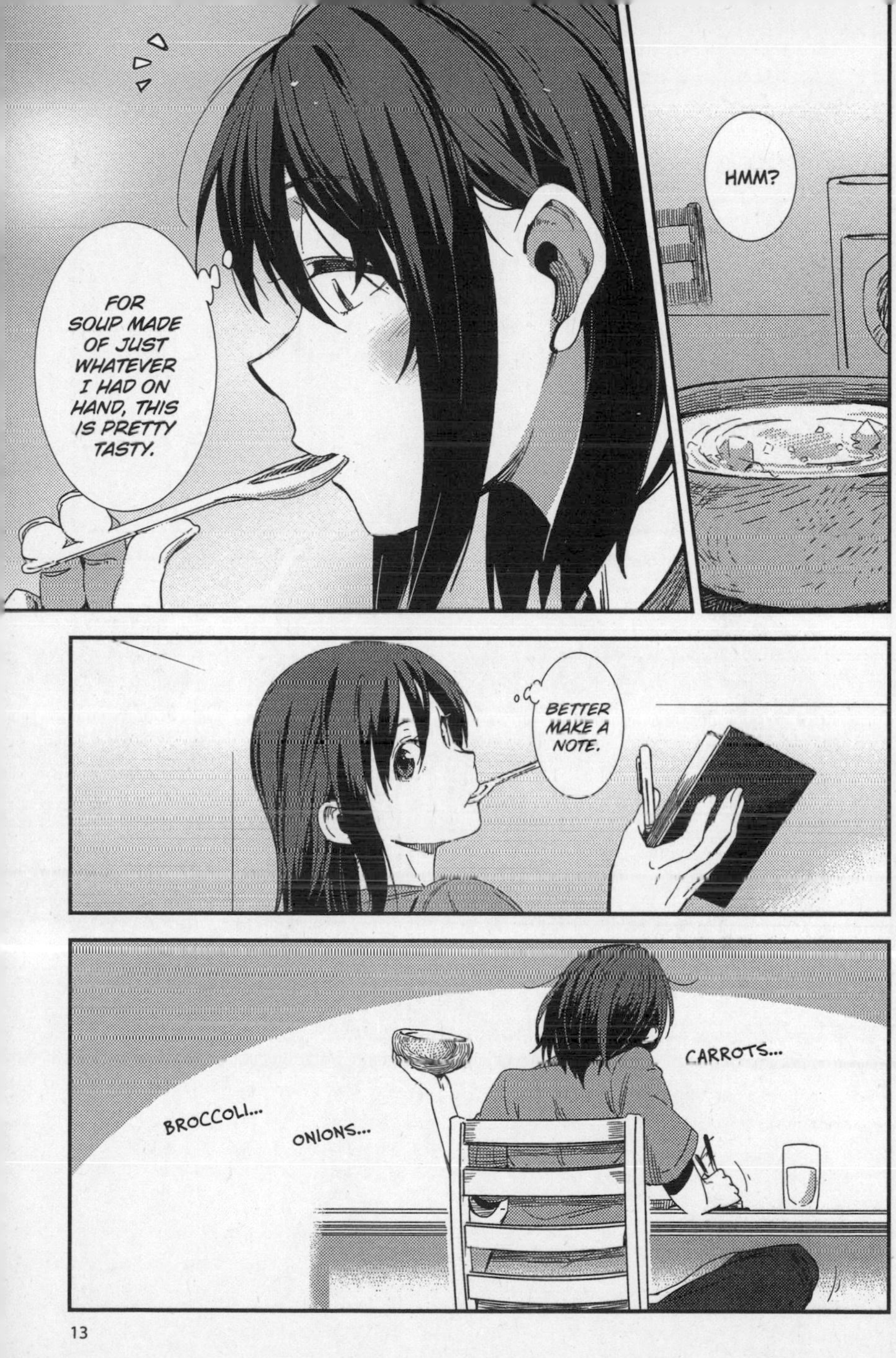
HMM?
FOR SOUP MADE OF JUST WHATEVER I HAD ON HAND, THIS IS PRETTY TASTY.
BETTER MAKE A NOTE.
CARROTS...
ONIONS...
BROCCOLI...

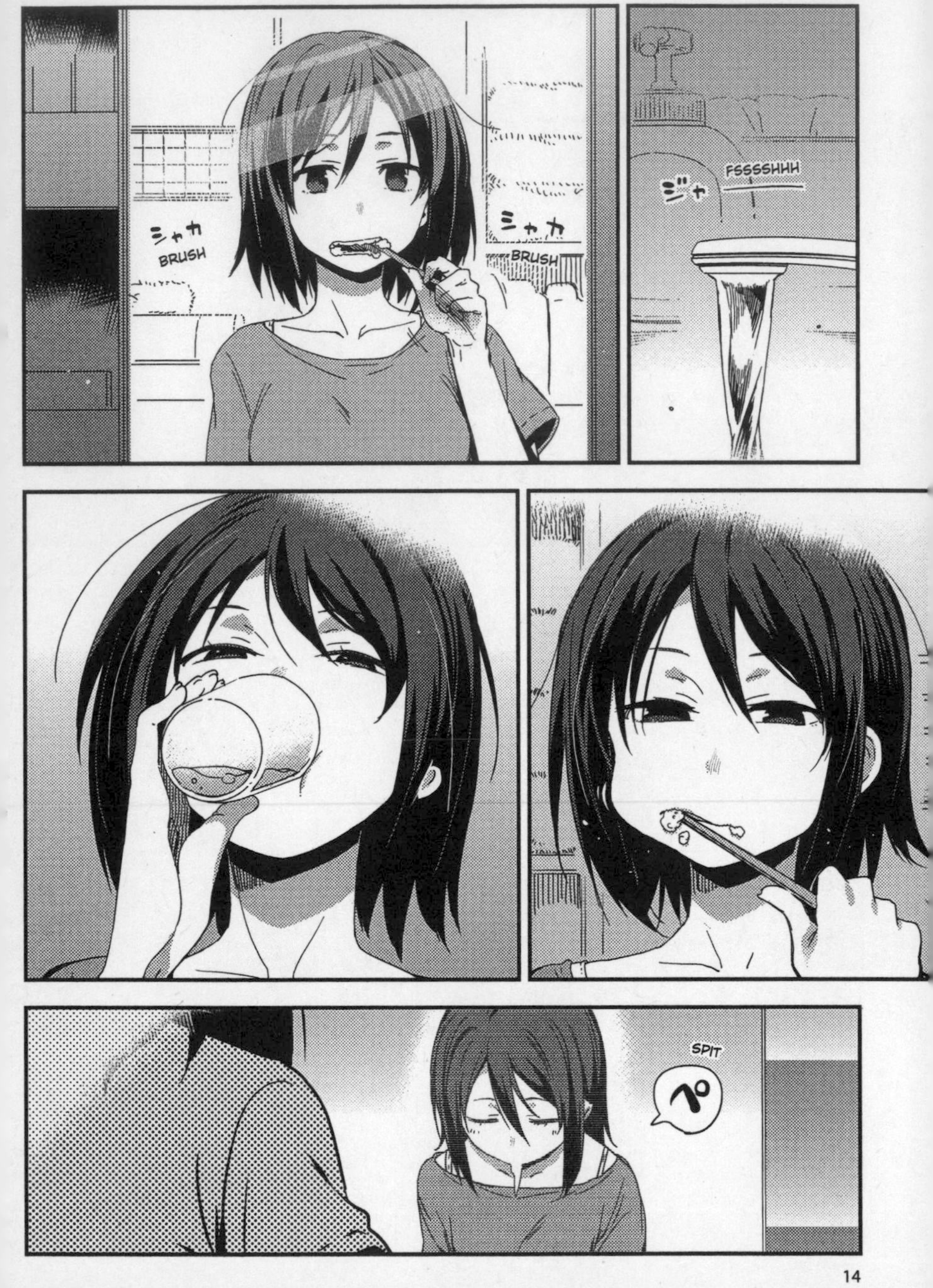
ジャ
FSSSSHHH
シャカ
BRUSH
シャカ
BRUSH
ぺ
SPIT

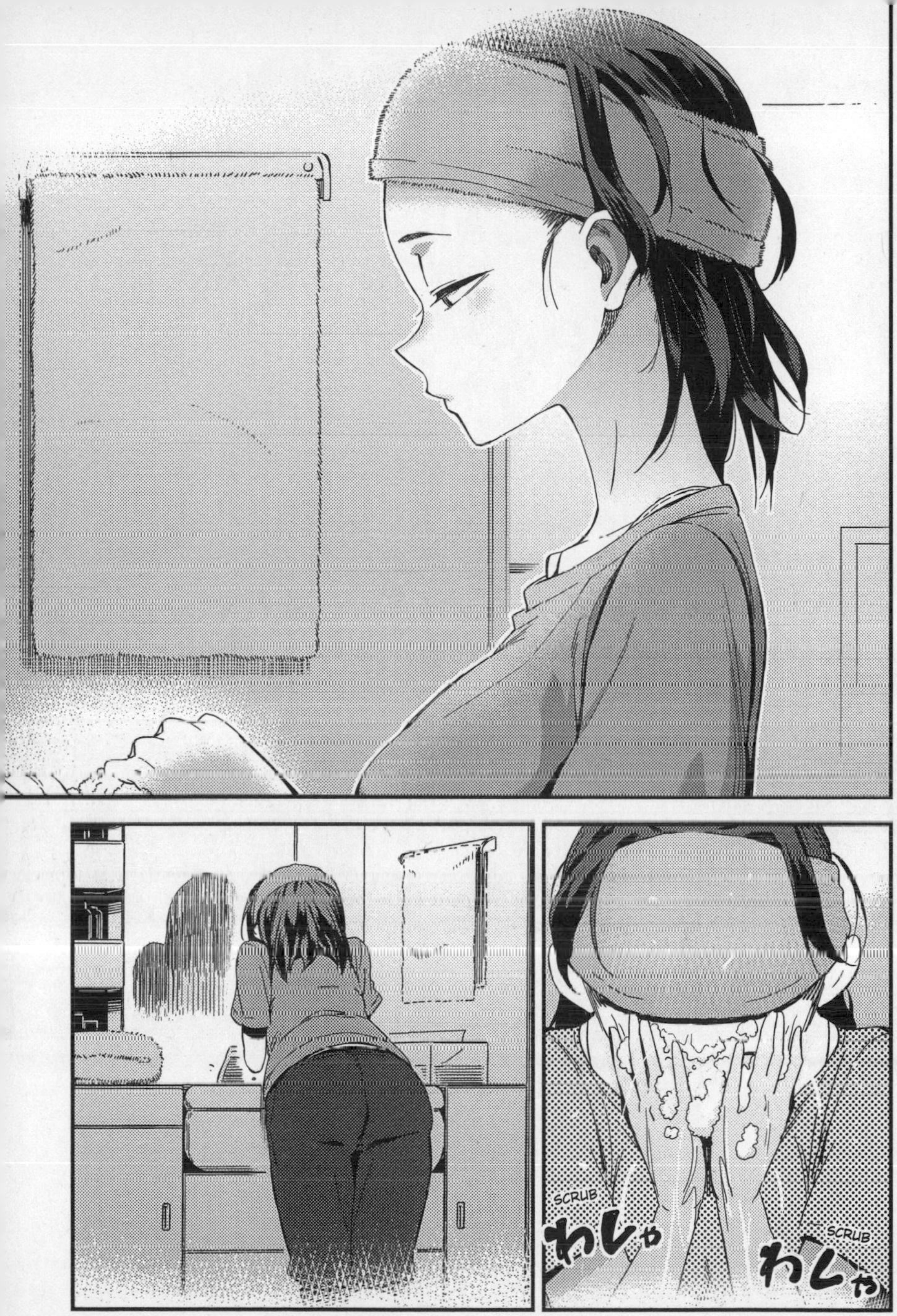
SCRUB
わしゃ
SCRUB
わしゃ

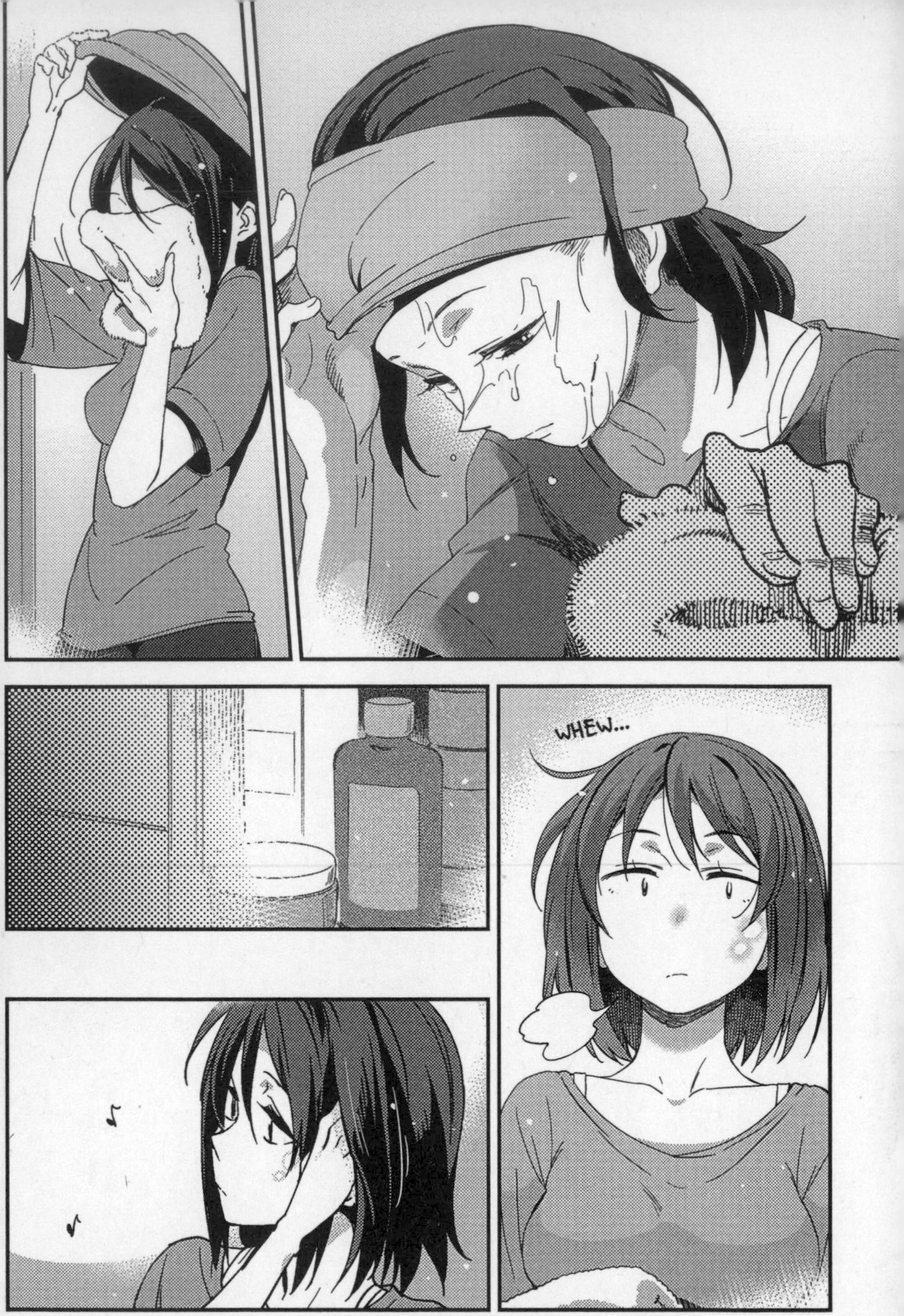
WHEW...

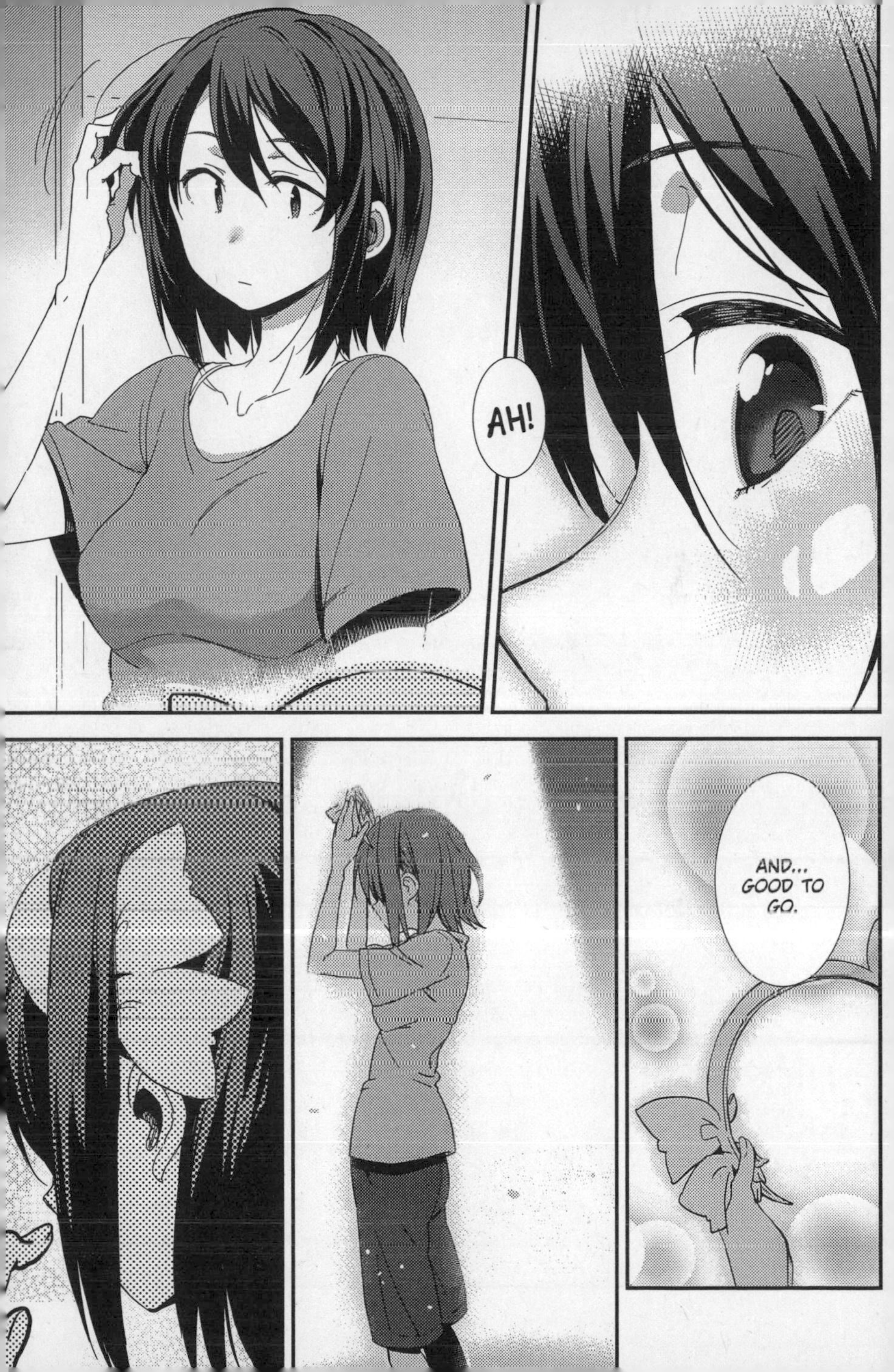
AH!
AND... GOOD TO GO.

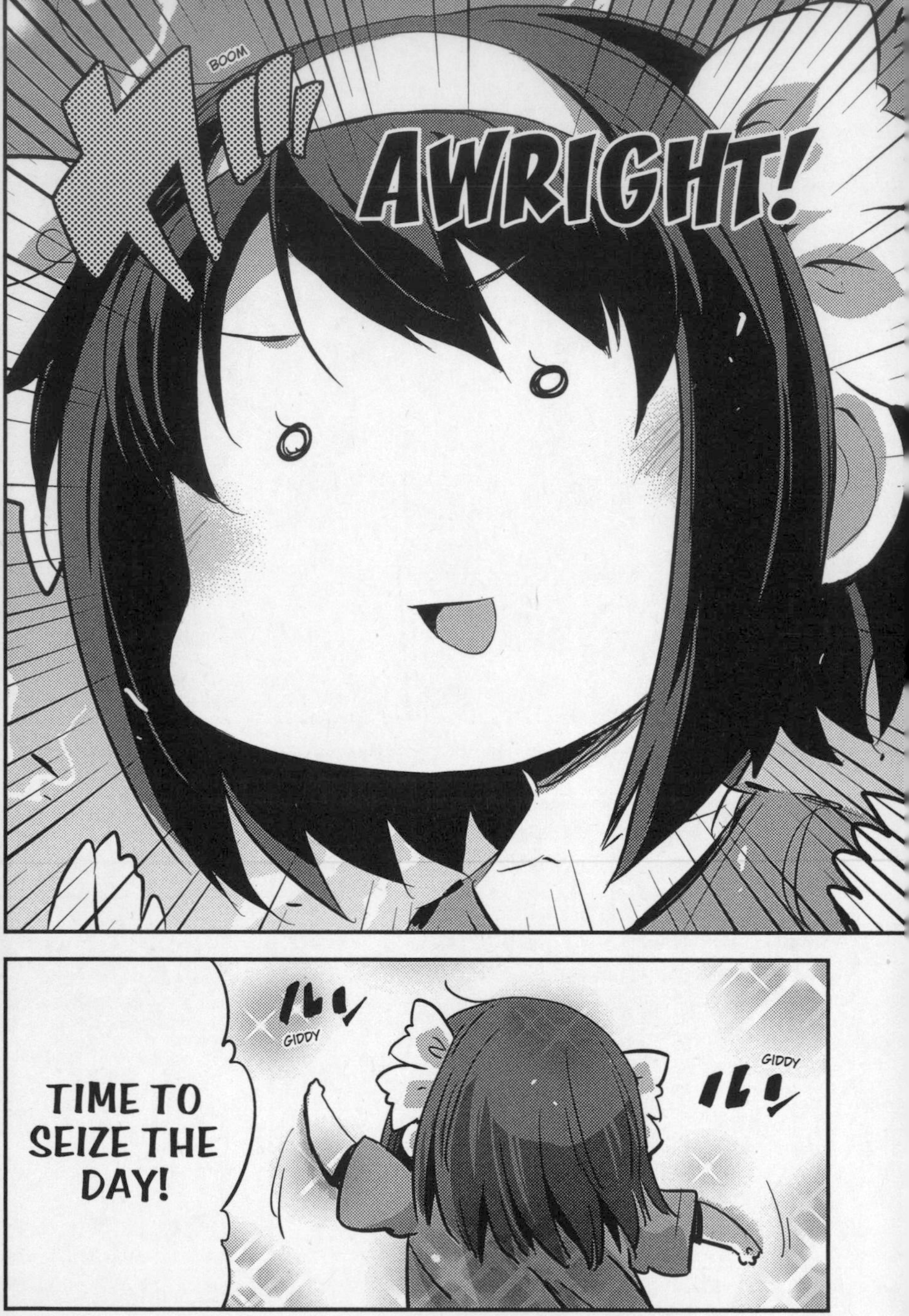
AWRIGHT!
BOOM
GIDDY
GIDDY
TIME TO SEIZE THE DAY!

KYON,
HURRY UP
AND EAT
BREAKFAST!

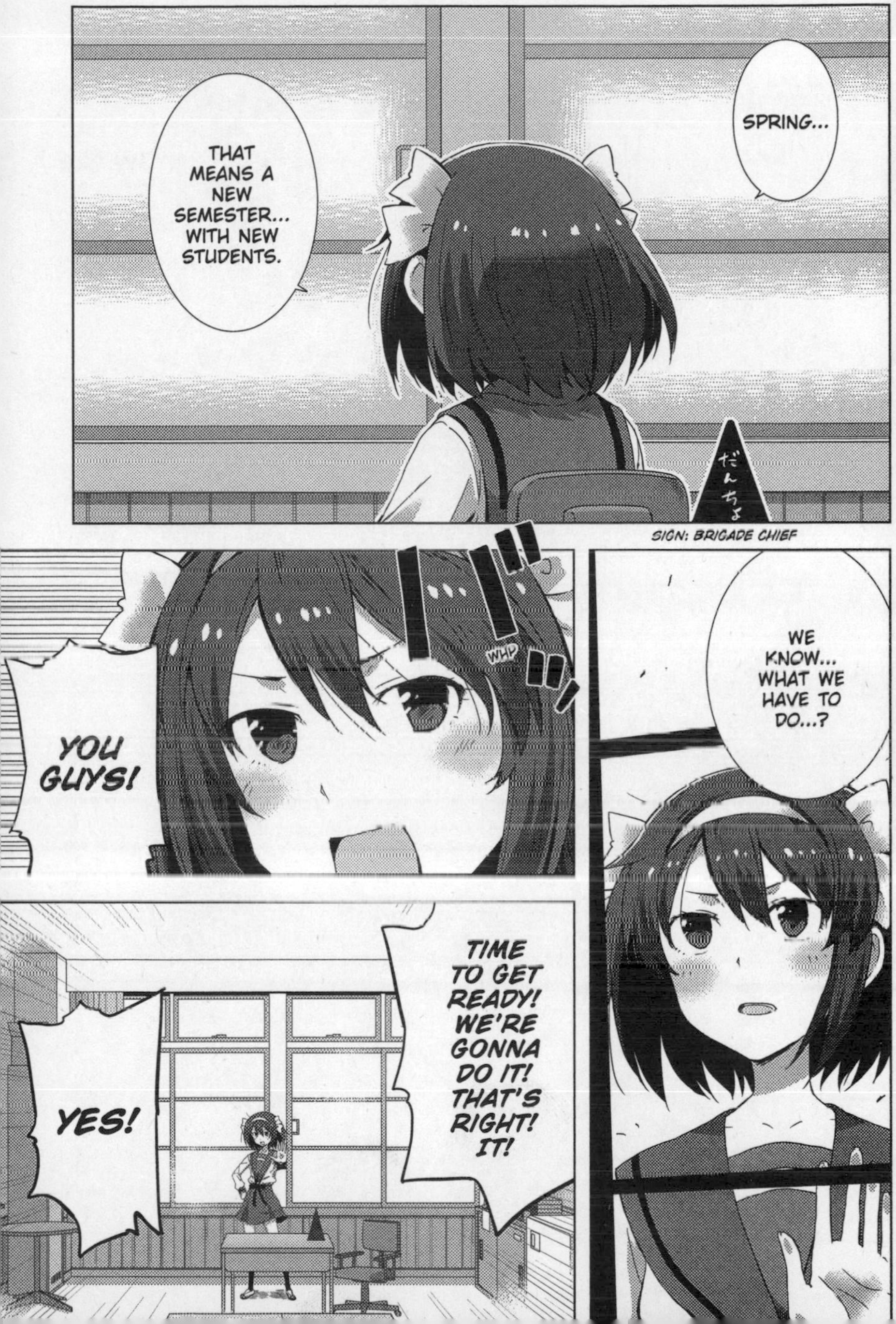
SPRING...
THAT MEANS A NEW SEMESTER... WITH NEW STUDENTS.
だんちょ
SIGN: BRIGADE CHIEF
WE KNOW... WHAT WE HAVE TO DO...?
WHP
YOU GUYS!
TIME TO GET READY! WE'RE GONNA DO IT! THAT'S RIGHT! IT!
YES!

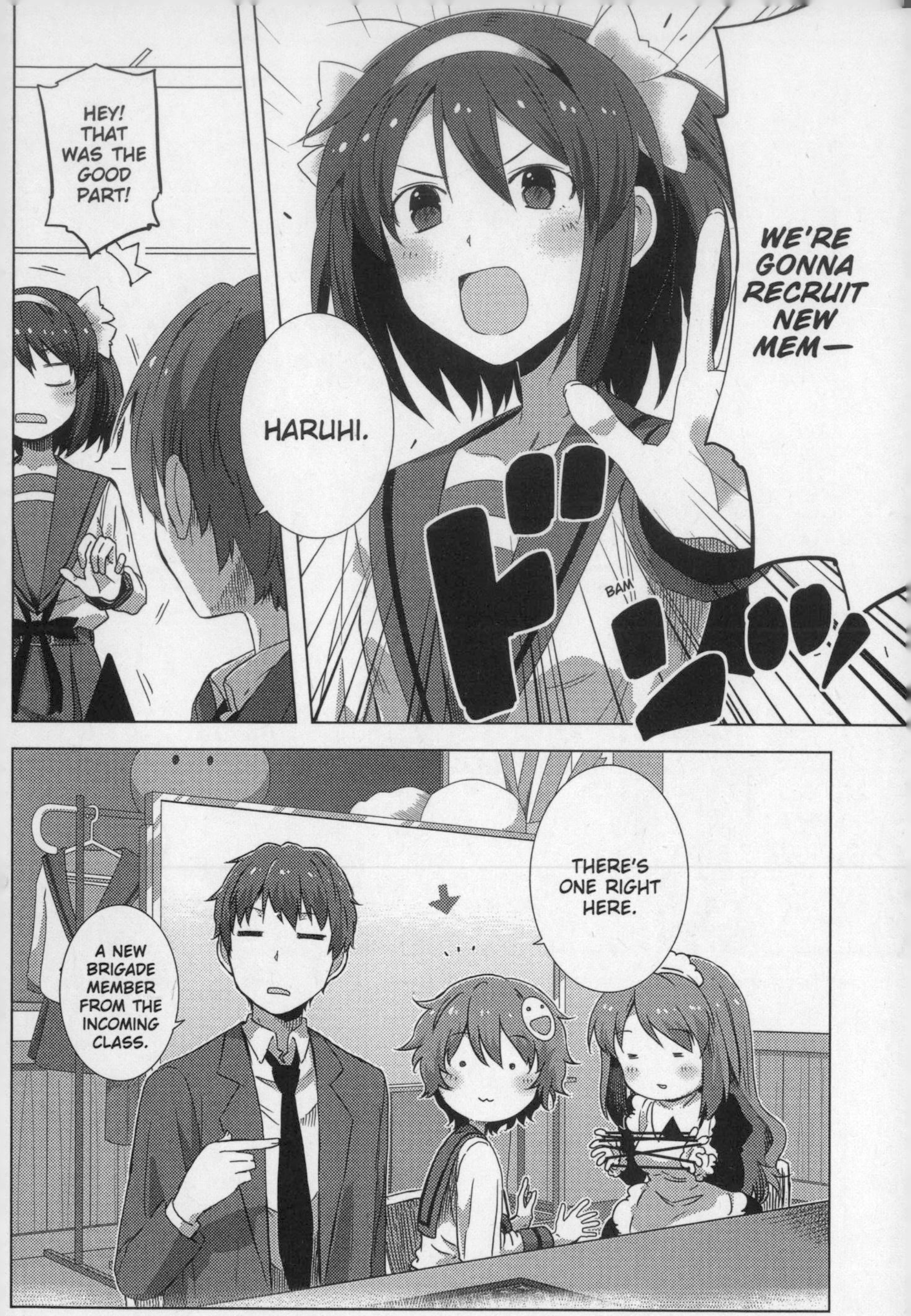
WE'RE GONNA RECRUIT NEW MEM—
BAM
HARUHI.
HEY! THAT WAS THE GOOD PART!
THERE'S ONE RIGHT HERE.
A NEW BRIGADE MEMBER FROM THE INCOMING CLASS.

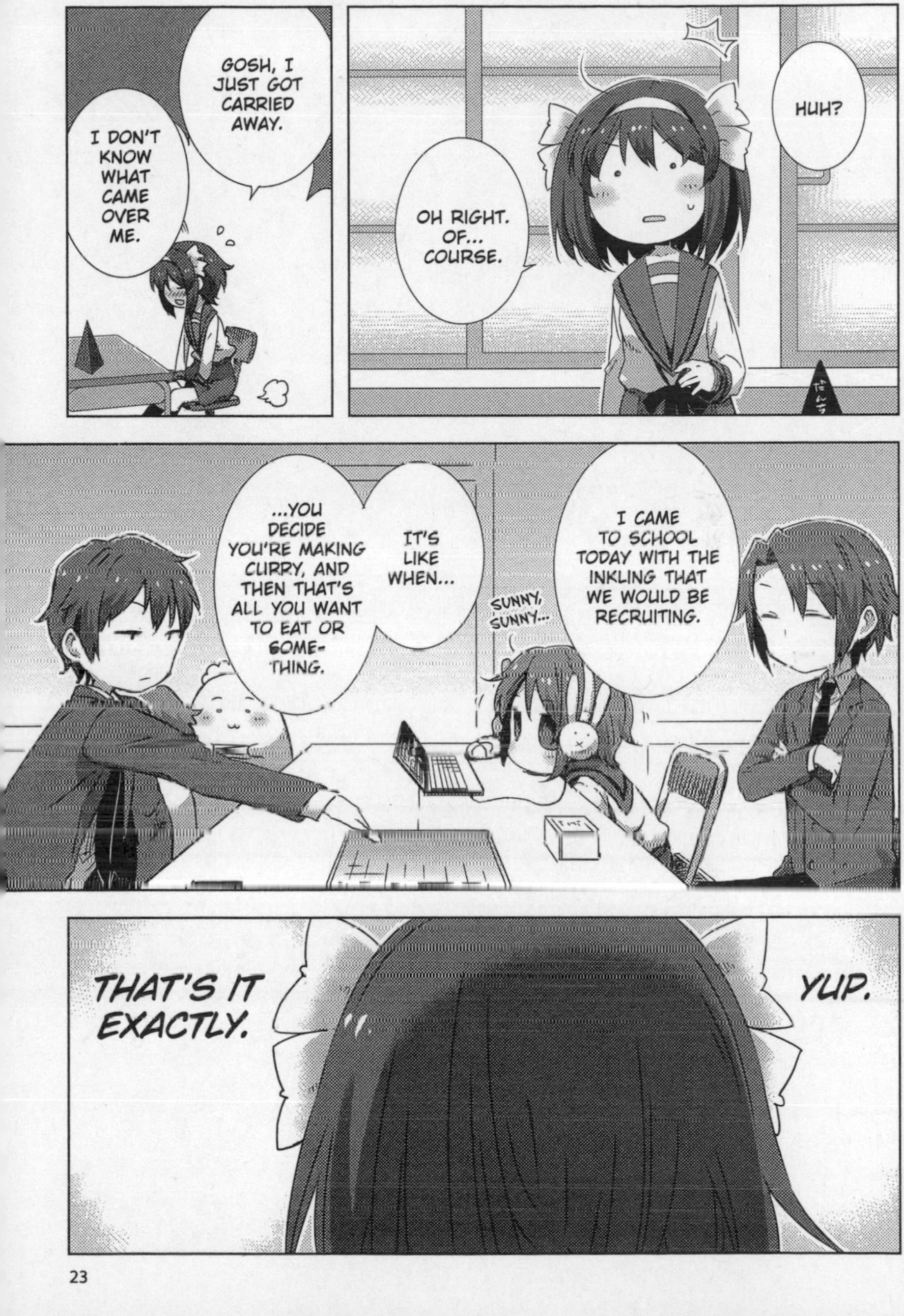
HUH?
OH RIGHT. OF... COURSE.
GOSH, I JUST GOT CARRIED AWAY.
I DON'T KNOW WHAT CAME OVER ME.
I CAME TO SCHOOL TODAY WITH THE INKLING THAT WE WOULD BE RECRUITING.
SUNNY, SUNNY...
IT'S LIKE WHEN...
...YOU DECIDE YOU'RE MAKING CURRY, AND THEN THAT'S ALL YOU WANT TO EAT OR SOME-THING.
YUP.
THAT'S IT EXACTLY.

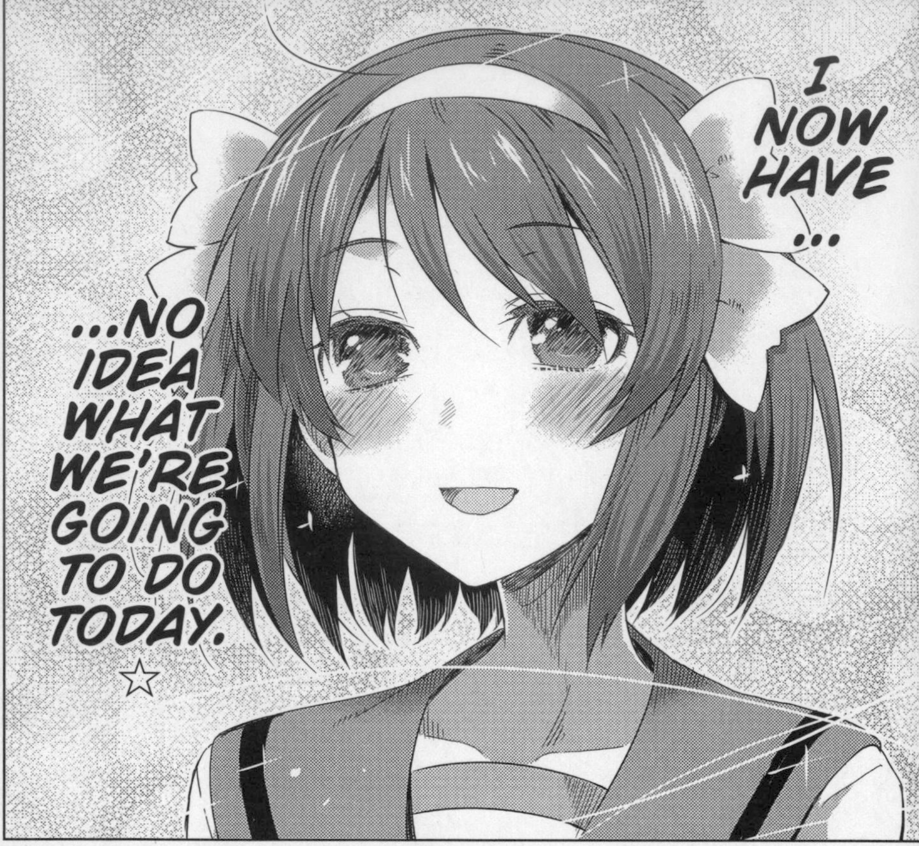
I NOW HAVE...
...NO IDEA WHAT WE'RE GOING TO DO TODAY. ☆

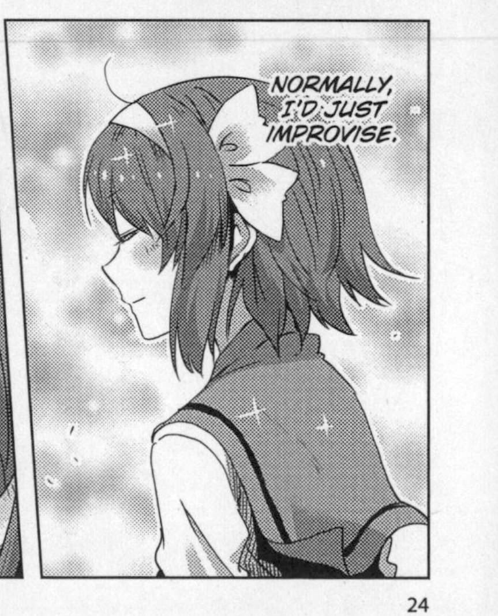
NORMALLY, I'D JUST IMPROVISE.

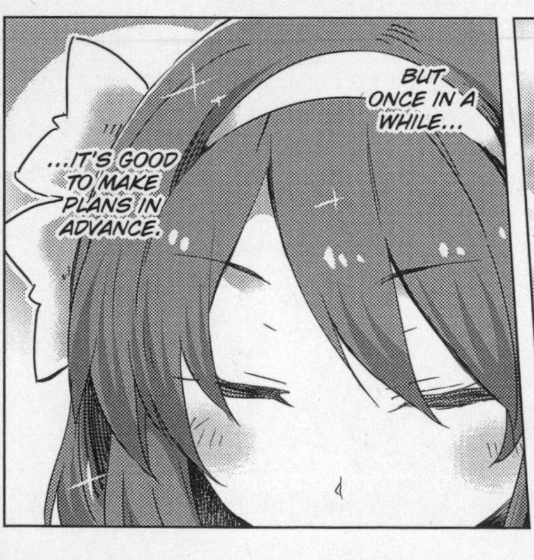
BUT ONCE IN A WHILE...
...IT'S GOOD TO MAKE PLANS IN ADVANCE.

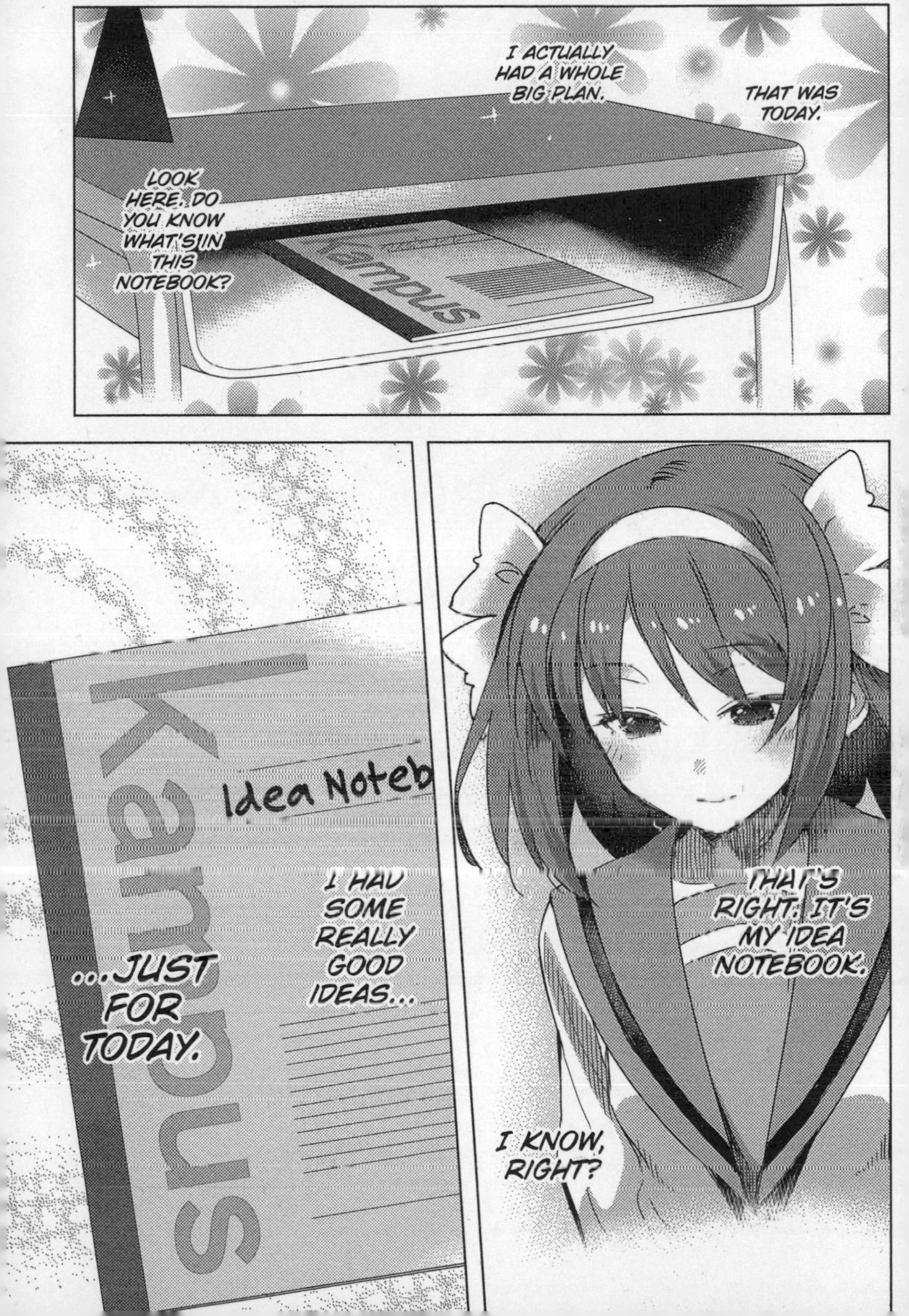
THAT WAS TODAY.
I ACTUALLY HAD A WHOLE BIG PLAN.
LOOK HERE. DO YOU KNOW WHAT'S IN THIS NOTEBOOK?
Kampus
THAT'S RIGHT. IT'S MY IDEA NOTEBOOK.
I KNOW, RIGHT?
Kampus
Idea Noteb
I HAD SOME REALLY GOOD IDEAS...
...JUST FOR TODAY.

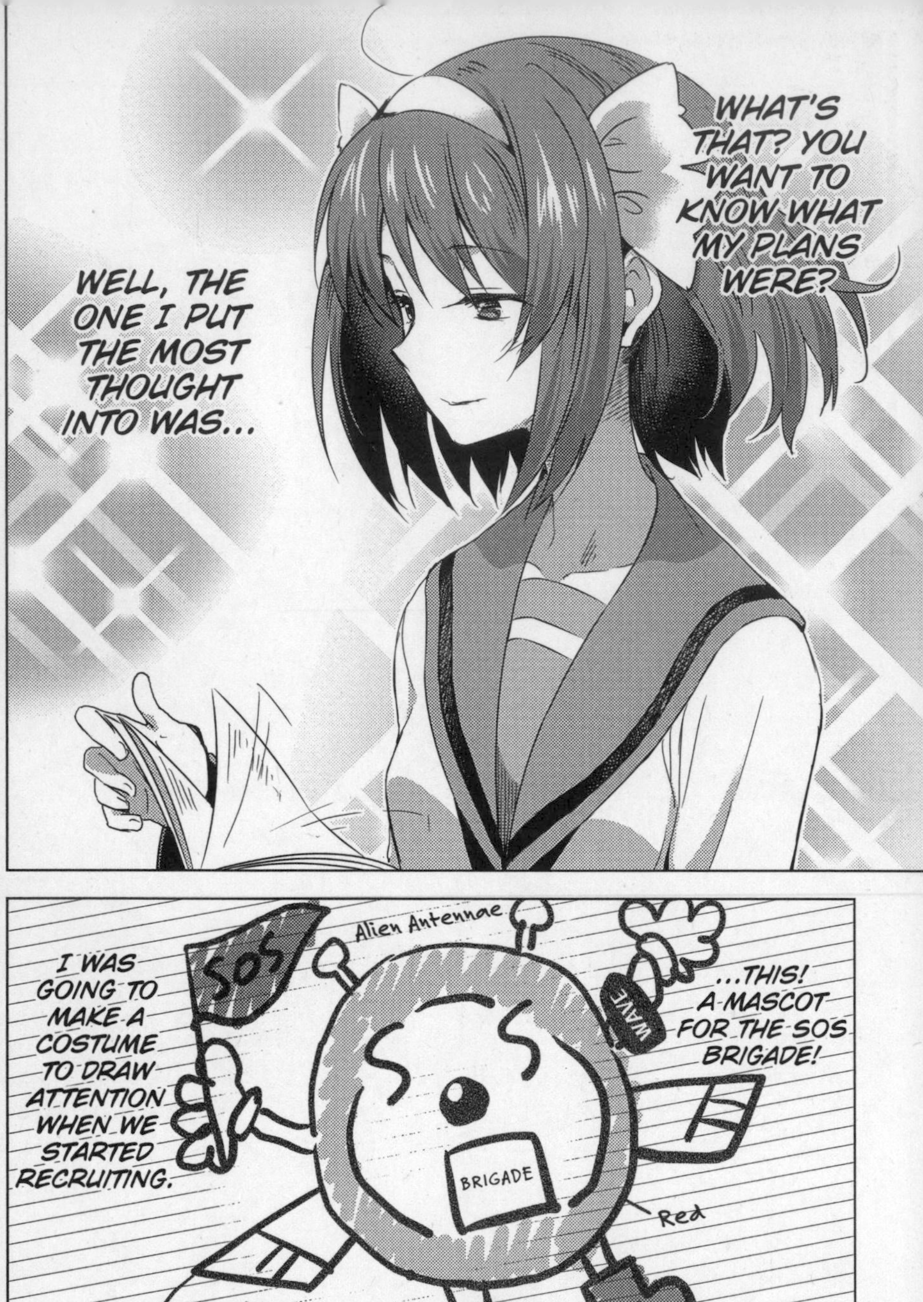
WHAT'S THAT? YOU WANT TO KNOW WHAT MY PLANS WERE?
WELL, THE ONE I PUT THE MOST THOUGHT INTO WAS...
...THIS! A MASCOT FOR THE SOS BRIGADE!
Alien Antennae
SOS
WAVE
BRIGADE
Red
Futuristic Parts
I WAS GOING TO MAKE A COSTUME TO DRAW ATTENTION WHEN WE STARTED RECRUITING.

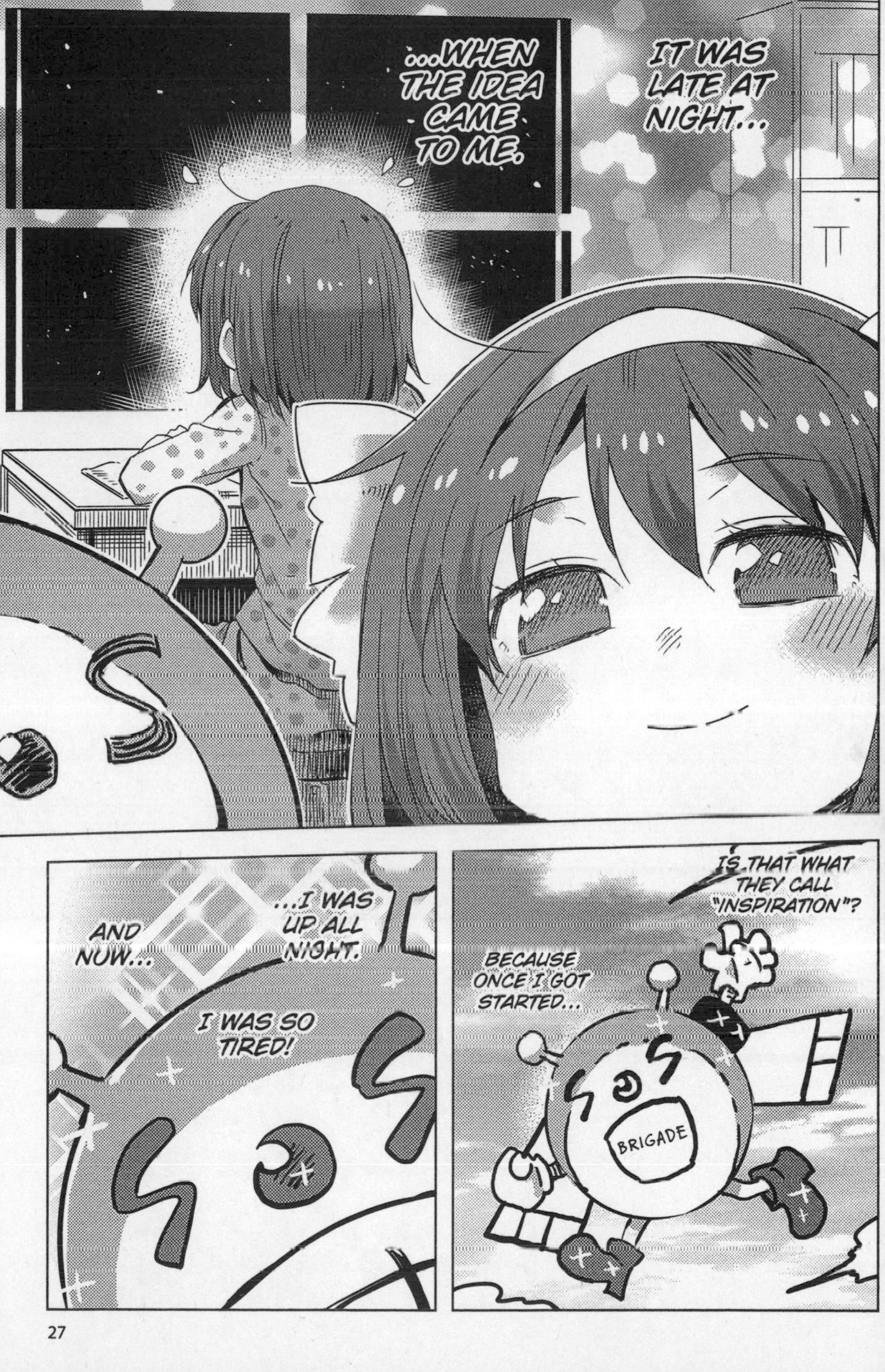
IT WAS LATE AT NIGHT...
...WHEN THE IDEA CAME TO ME.
IS THAT WHAT THEY CALL "INSPIRATION"?
BECAUSE ONCE I GOT STARTED...
SOS
BRIGADE
...I WAS UP ALL NIGHT.
AND NOW...
I WAS SO TIRED!

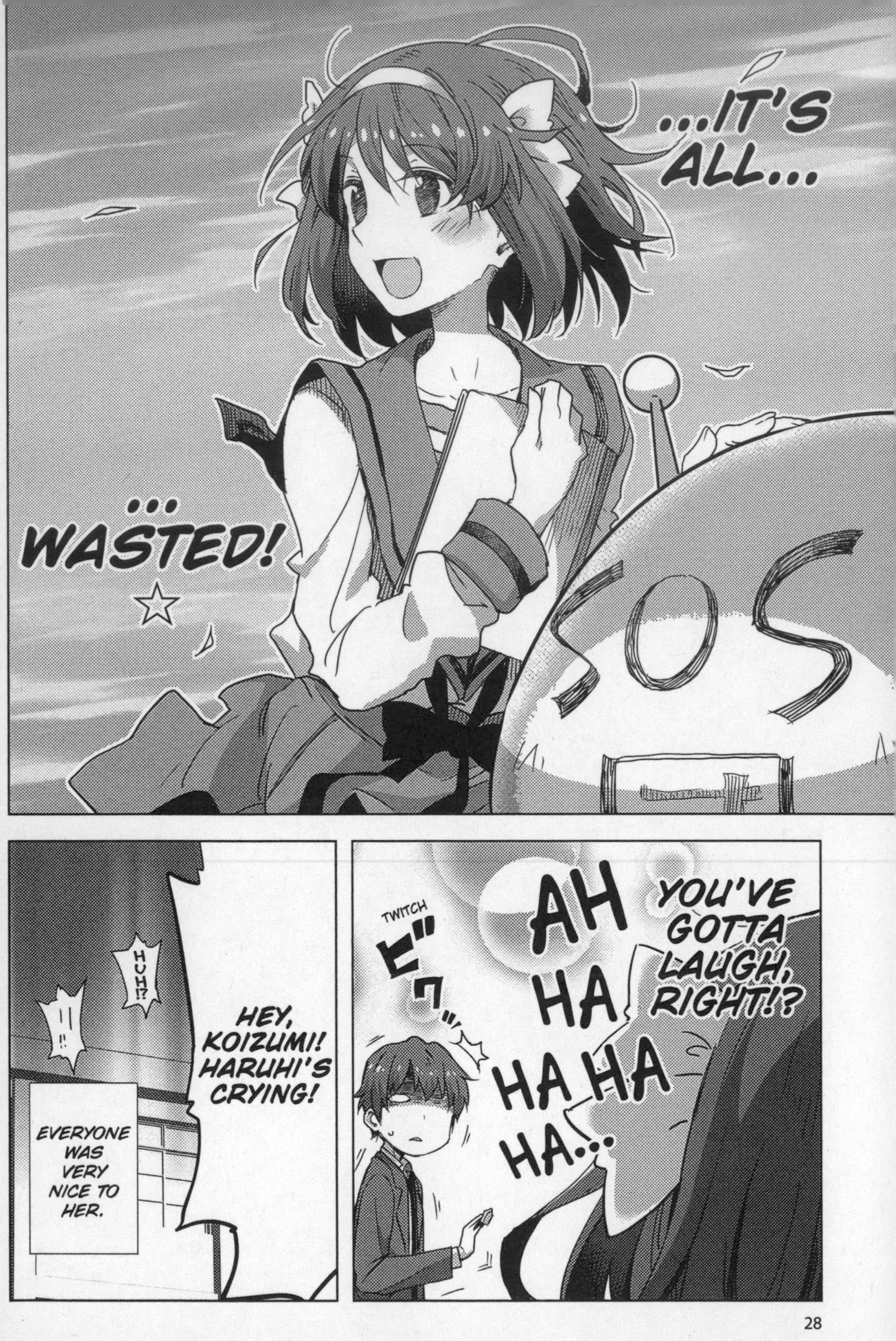
...IT'S ALL...
...WASTED!
TWITCH
AH HA HA HA HA HA...
YOU'VE GOTTA LAUGH, RIGHT!?
HUH!?
!!
HEY, KOIZUMI! HARUHI'S CRYING!
EVERYONE WAS VERY NICE TO HER.

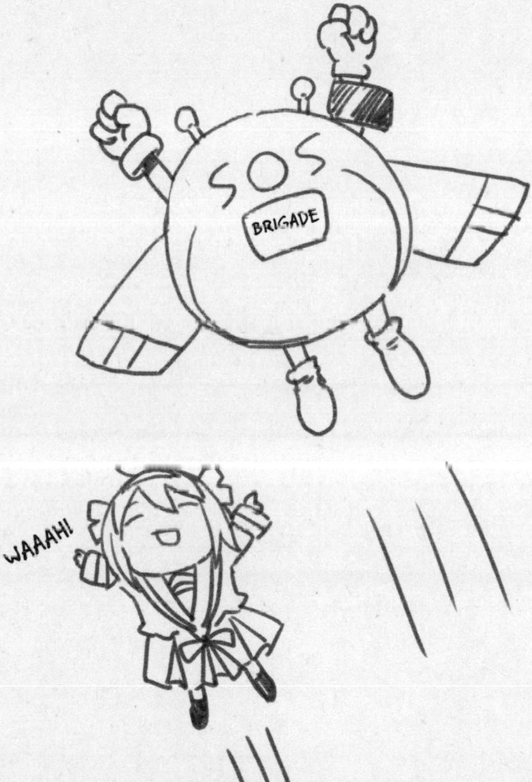
SOS
BRIGADE
WAAAH!

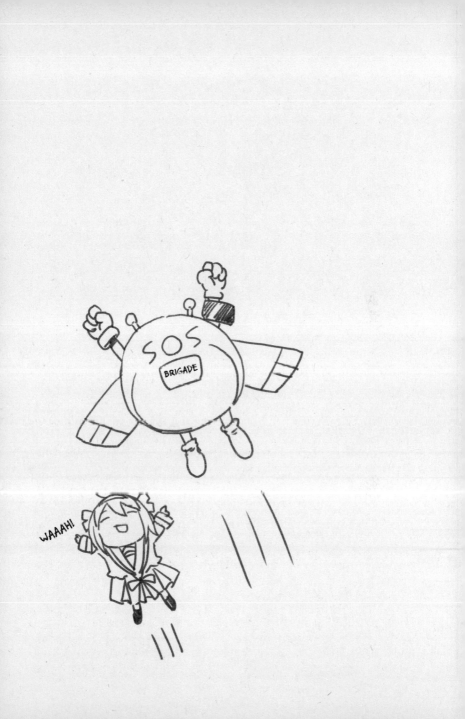

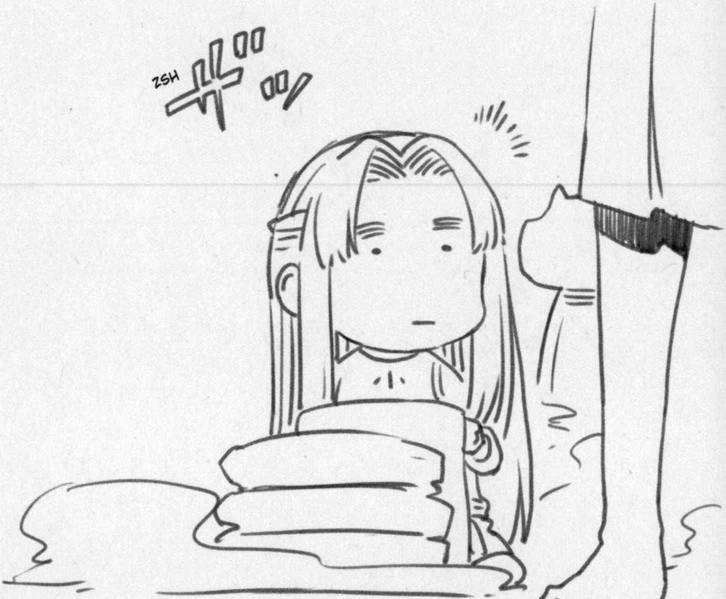
ZSH

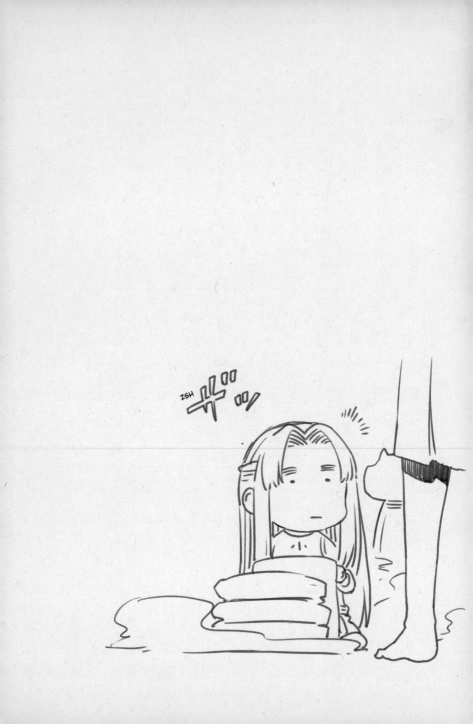

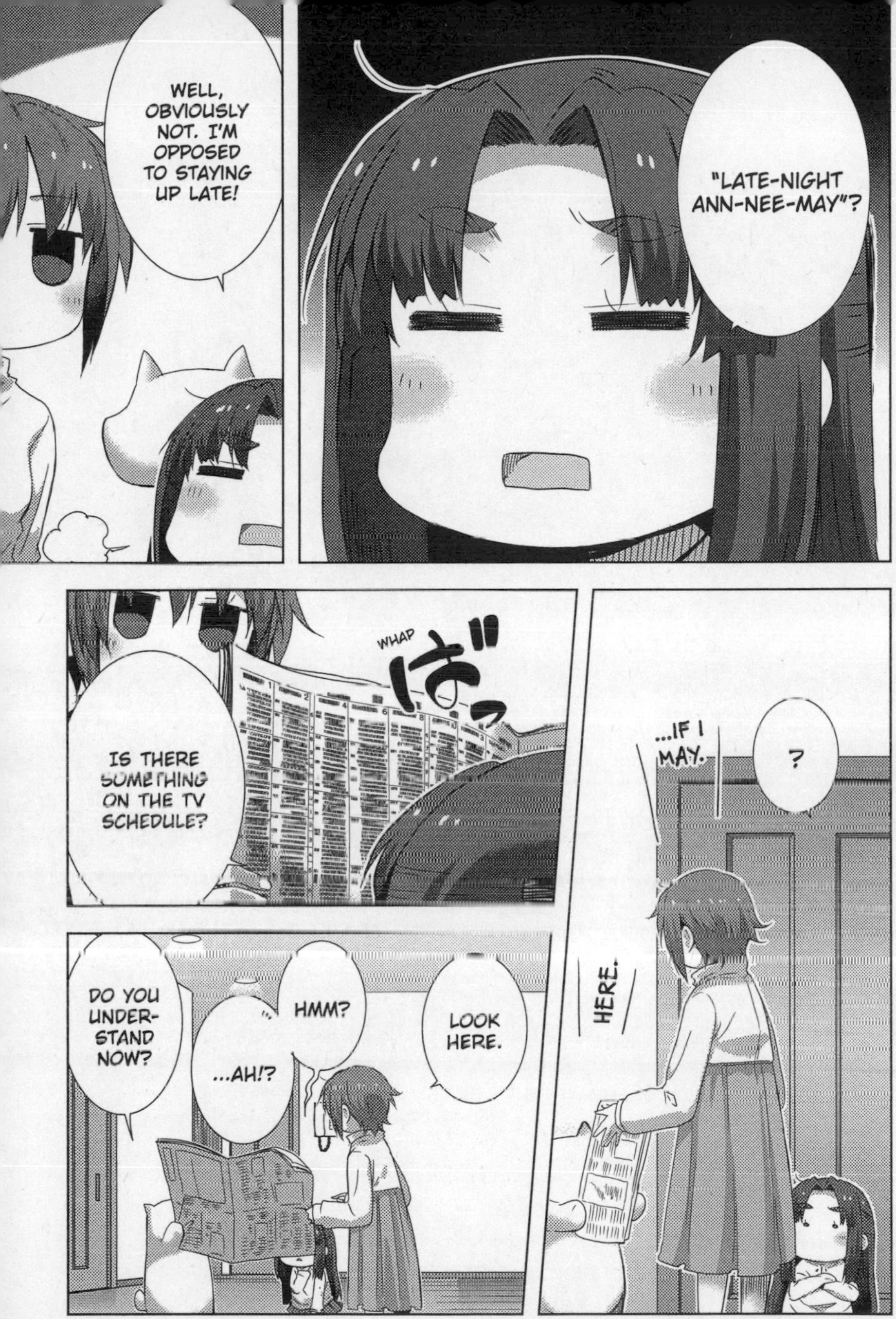
"LATE-NIGHT ANN-NEE-MAY"?
WELL, OBVIOUSLY NOT. I'M OPPOSED TO STAYING UP LATE!
?
...IF I MAY.
HERE.
WHAP
ばっ
IS THERE SOMETHING ON THE TV SCHEDULE?
LOOK HERE.
HMM?
...AH!?
DO YOU UNDER-STAND NOW?

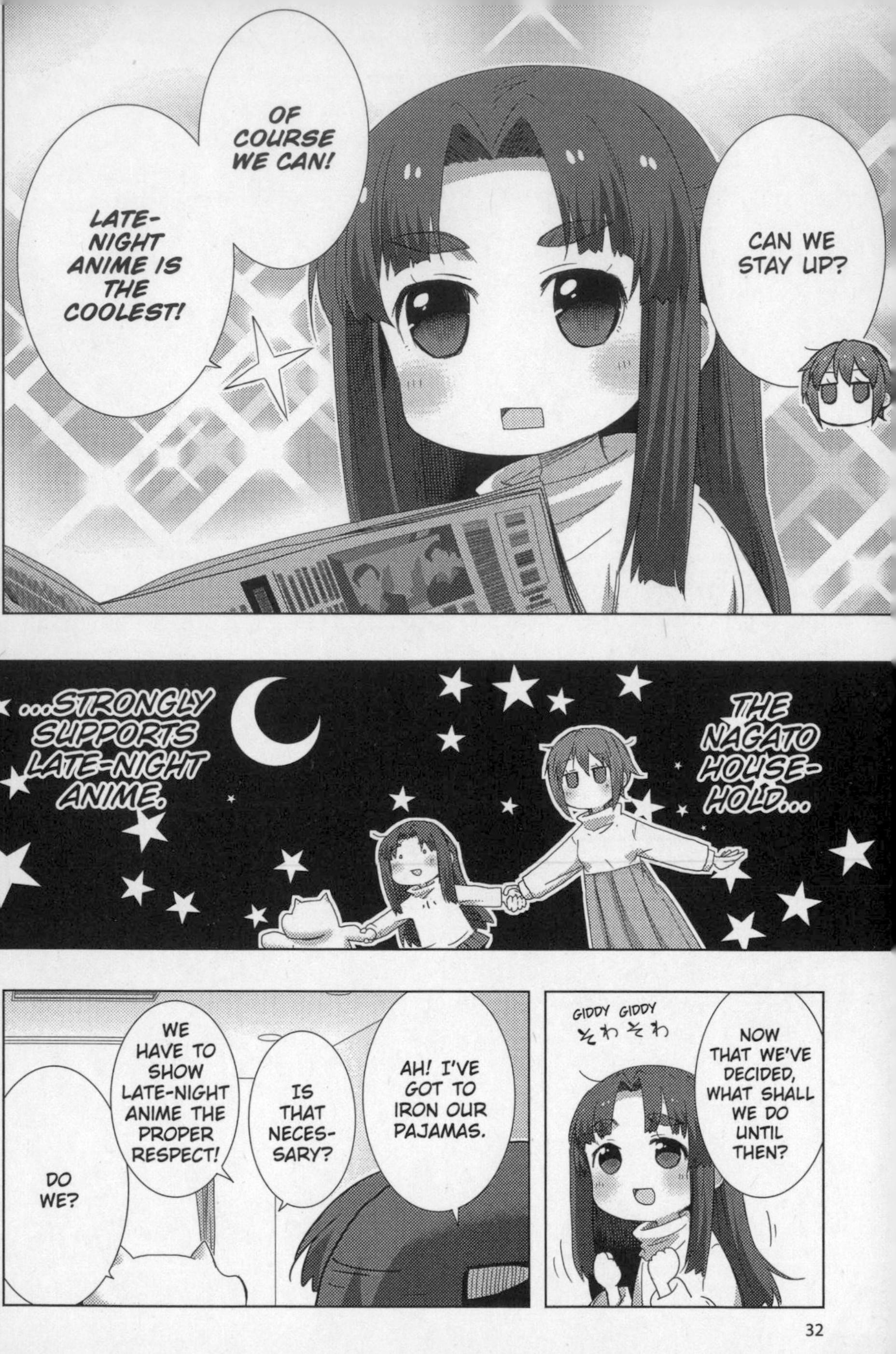
CAN WE STAY UP?
OF COURSE WE CAN!
LATE-NIGHT ANIME IS THE COOLEST!
THE NAGATO HOUSEHOLD...
...STRONGLY SUPPORTS LATE-NIGHT ANIME.
GIDDY GIDDY
そわそわ
NOW THAT WE'VE DECIDED, WHAT SHALL WE DO UNTIL THEN?
AH! I'VE GOT TO IRON OUR PAJAMAS.
IS THAT NECESSARY?
WE HAVE TO SHOW LATE-NIGHT ANIME THE PROPER RESPECT!
DO WE?

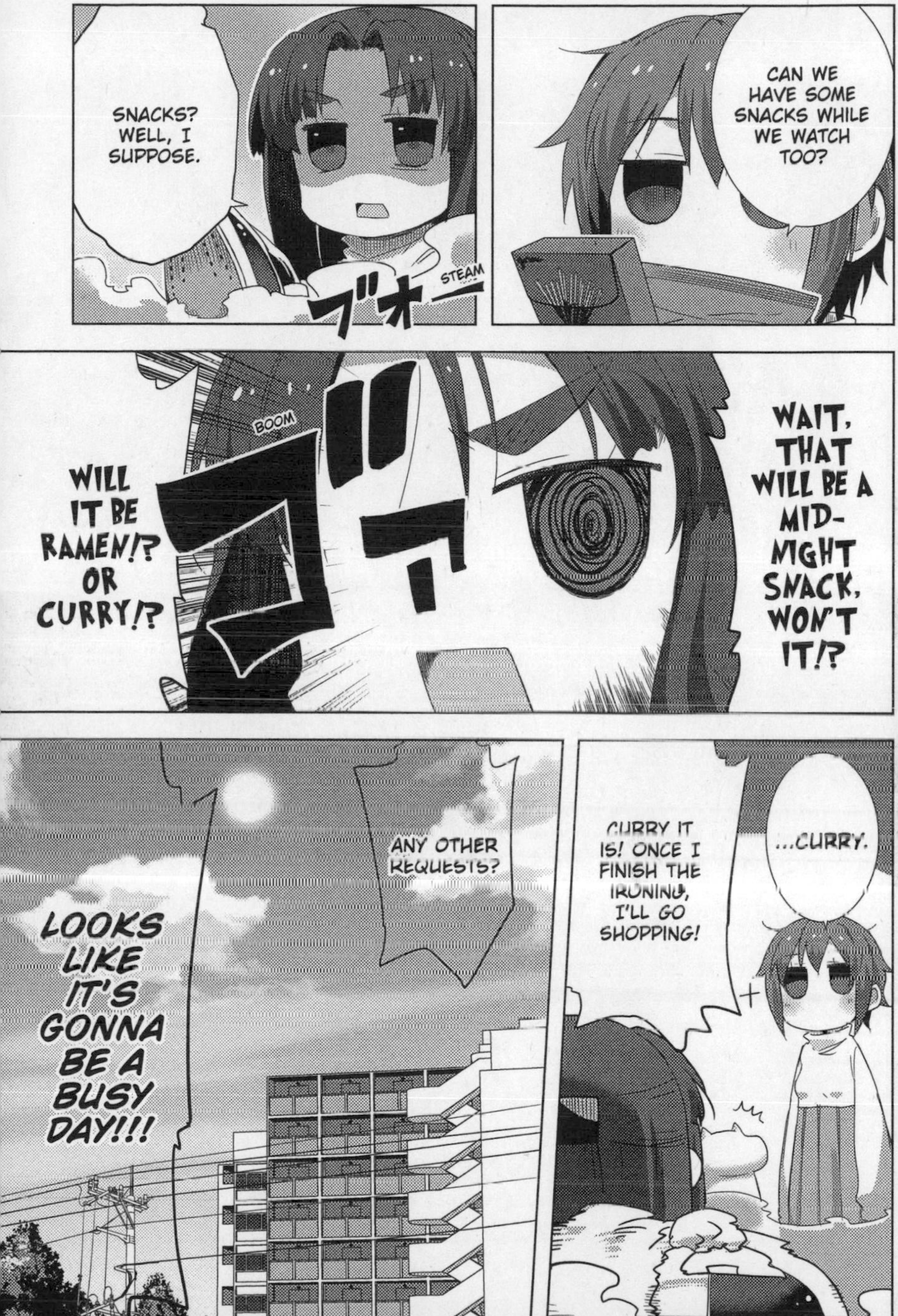
CAN WE HAVE SOME SNACKS WHILE WE WATCH TOO?
SNACKS? WELL, I SUPPOSE.
STEAM
ブオー
WAIT, THAT WILL BE A MID-NIGHT SNACK, WON'T IT!?
BOOM
WILL IT BE RAMEN!? OR CURRY!?
...CURRY.
CURRY IT IS! ONCE I FINISH THE IRONING, I'LL GO SHOPPING!
ANY OTHER REQUESTS?
LOOKS LIKE IT'S GONNA BE A BUSY DAY!!!

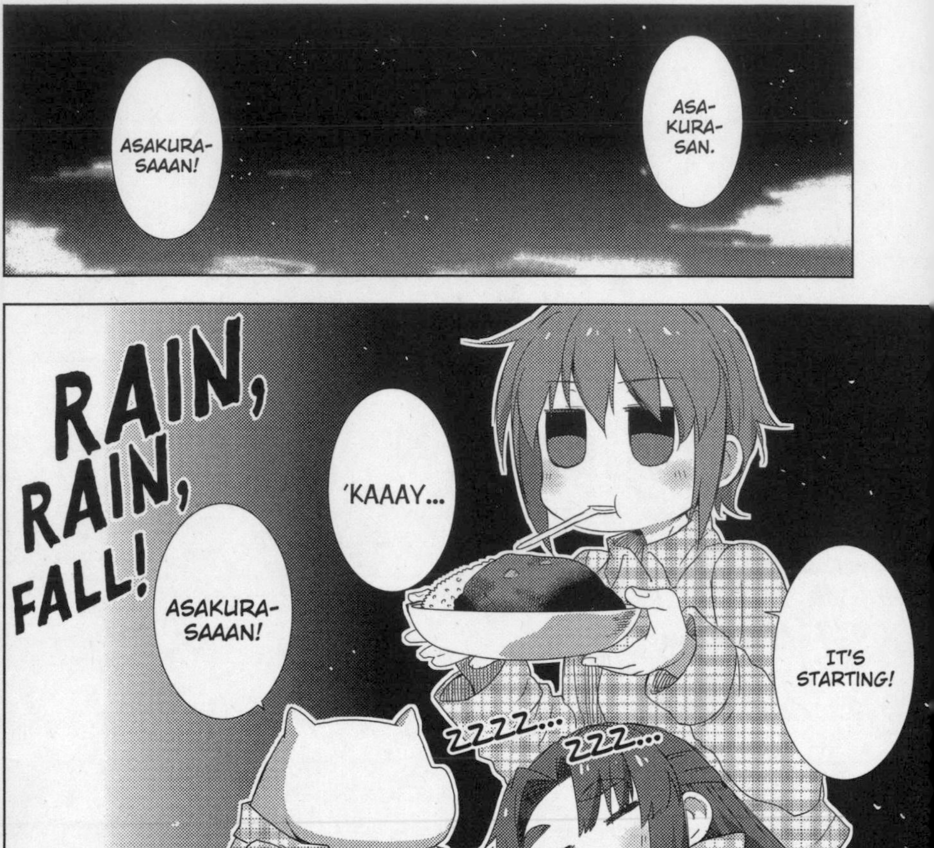
ASA-KURA-SAN.
ASAKURA-SAAAN!
IT'S STARTING!
'KAAAY...
ASAKURA-SAAAN!
RAIN, RAIN, FALL!
ZZZ...
ZZZZ...

NOTE: TRANSLATION OF THE LINE, "FURE, FURE, YO!" FROM THE NAGATO YUKI-CHAN ANIME OPENING THEME

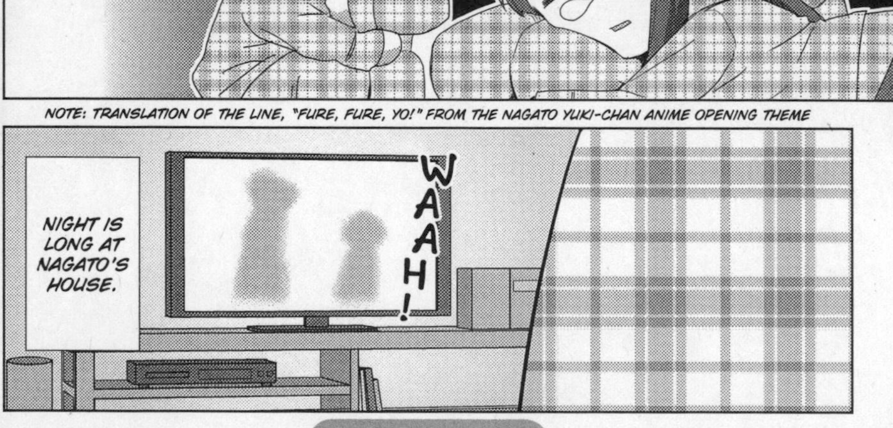
WAAAH!
NIGHT IS LONG AT NAGATO'S HOUSE.

END

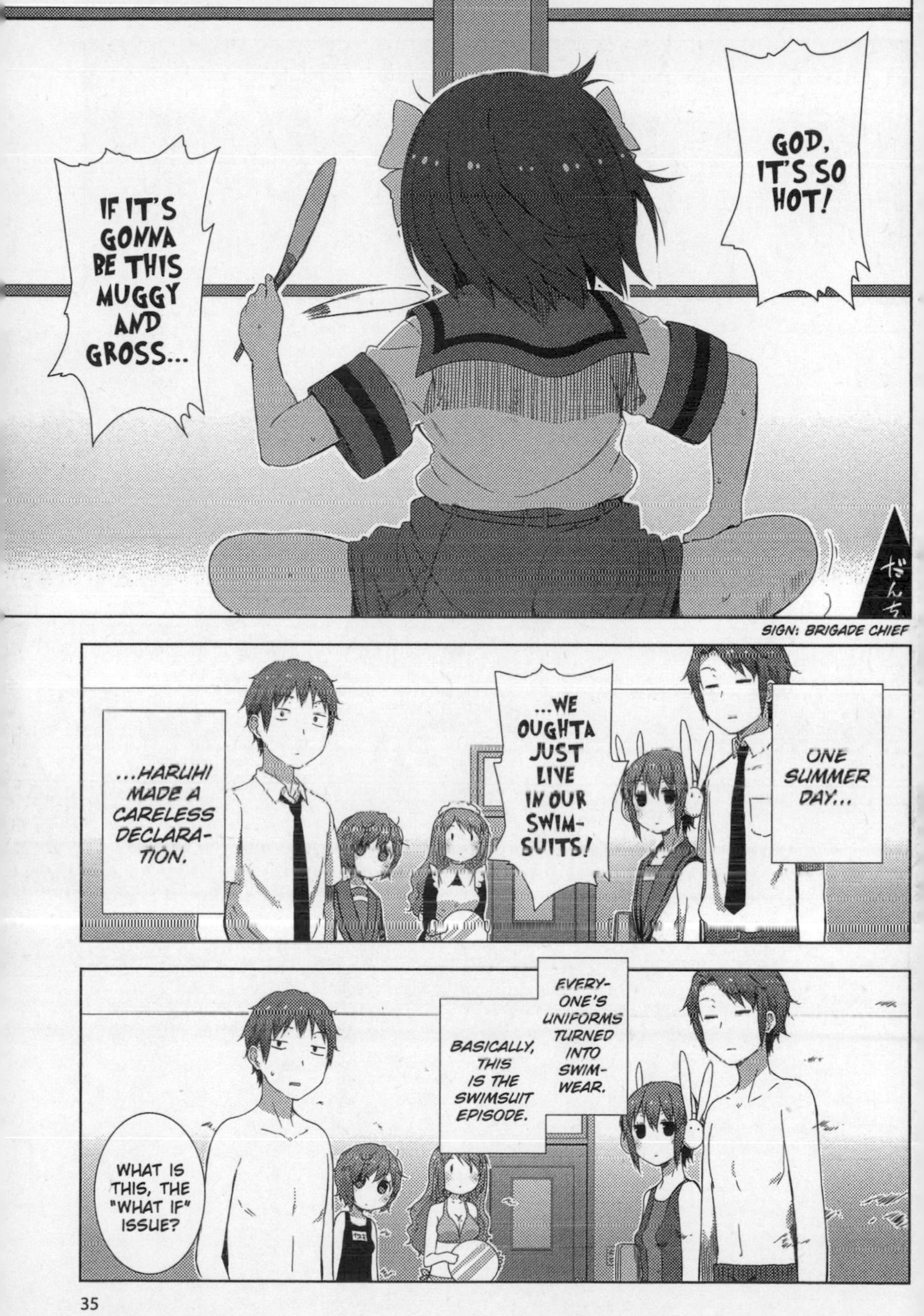
GOD, IT'S SO HOT!
IF IT'S GONNA BE THIS MUGGY AND GROSS...
だんち
SIGN: BRIGADE CHIEF
ONE SUMMER DAY...
...WE OUGHTA JUST LIVE IN OUR SWIM-SUITS!
...HARUHI MADE A CARELESS DECLARA-TION.
EVERY-ONE'S UNIFORMS TURNED INTO SWIM-WEAR.
BASICALLY, THIS IS THE SWIMSUIT EPISODE.
WHAT IS THIS, THE "WHAT IF" ISSUE?

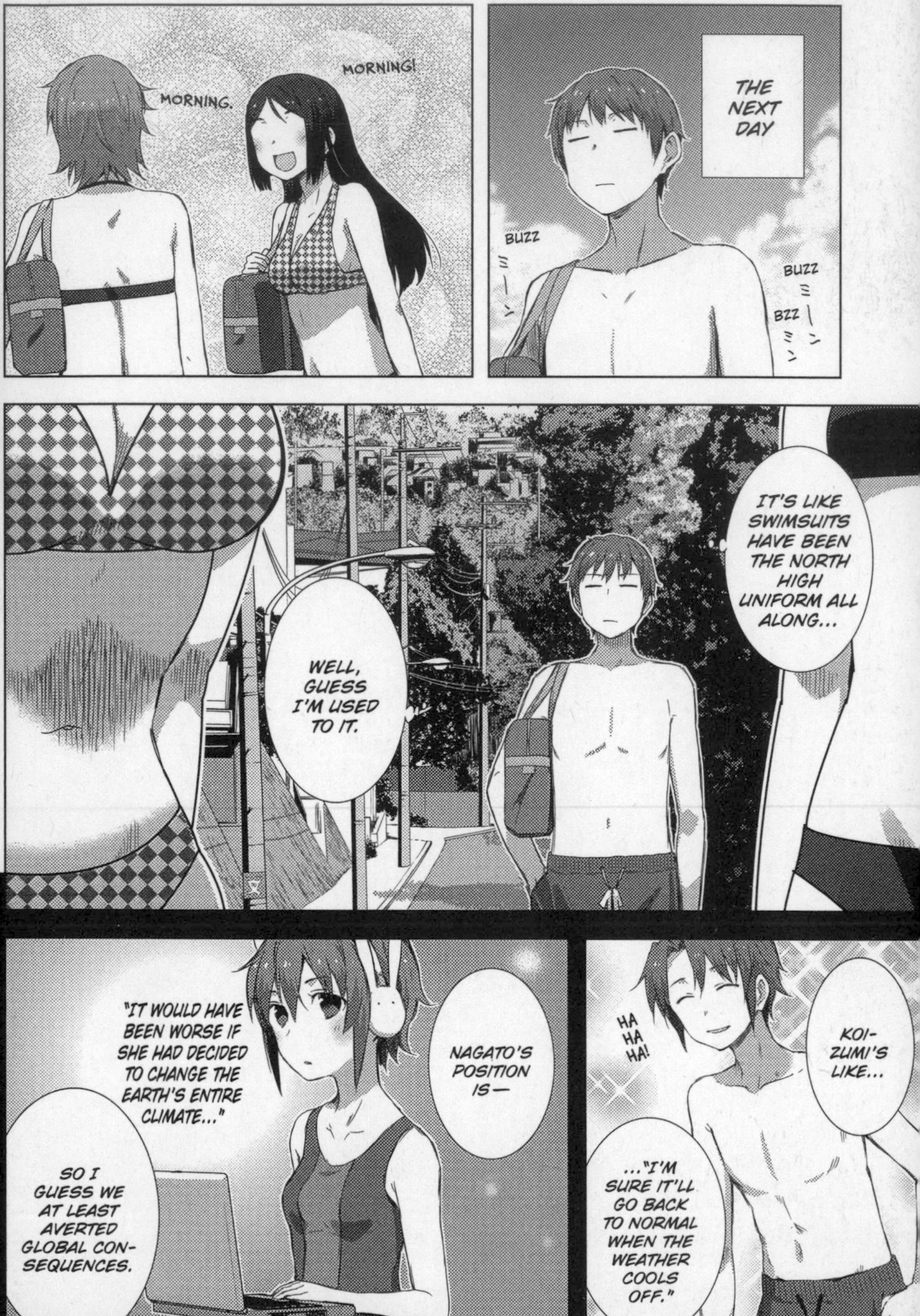
THE NEXT DAY
BUZZ
BUZZ
BZZ
MORNING!
MORNING.
IT'S LIKE SWIMSUITS HAVE BEEN THE NORTH HIGH UNIFORM ALL ALONG...
WELL, GUESS I'M USED TO IT.
KOI-ZUMI'S LIKE...
HA HA HA!
..."I'M SURE IT'LL GO BACK TO NORMAL WHEN THE WEATHER COOLS OFF."
NAGATO'S POSITION IS—
"IT WOULD HAVE BEEN WORSE IF SHE HAD DECIDED TO CHANGE THE EARTH'S ENTIRE CLIMATE..."
SO I GUESS WE AT LEAST AVERTED GLOBAL CON-SEQUENCES.

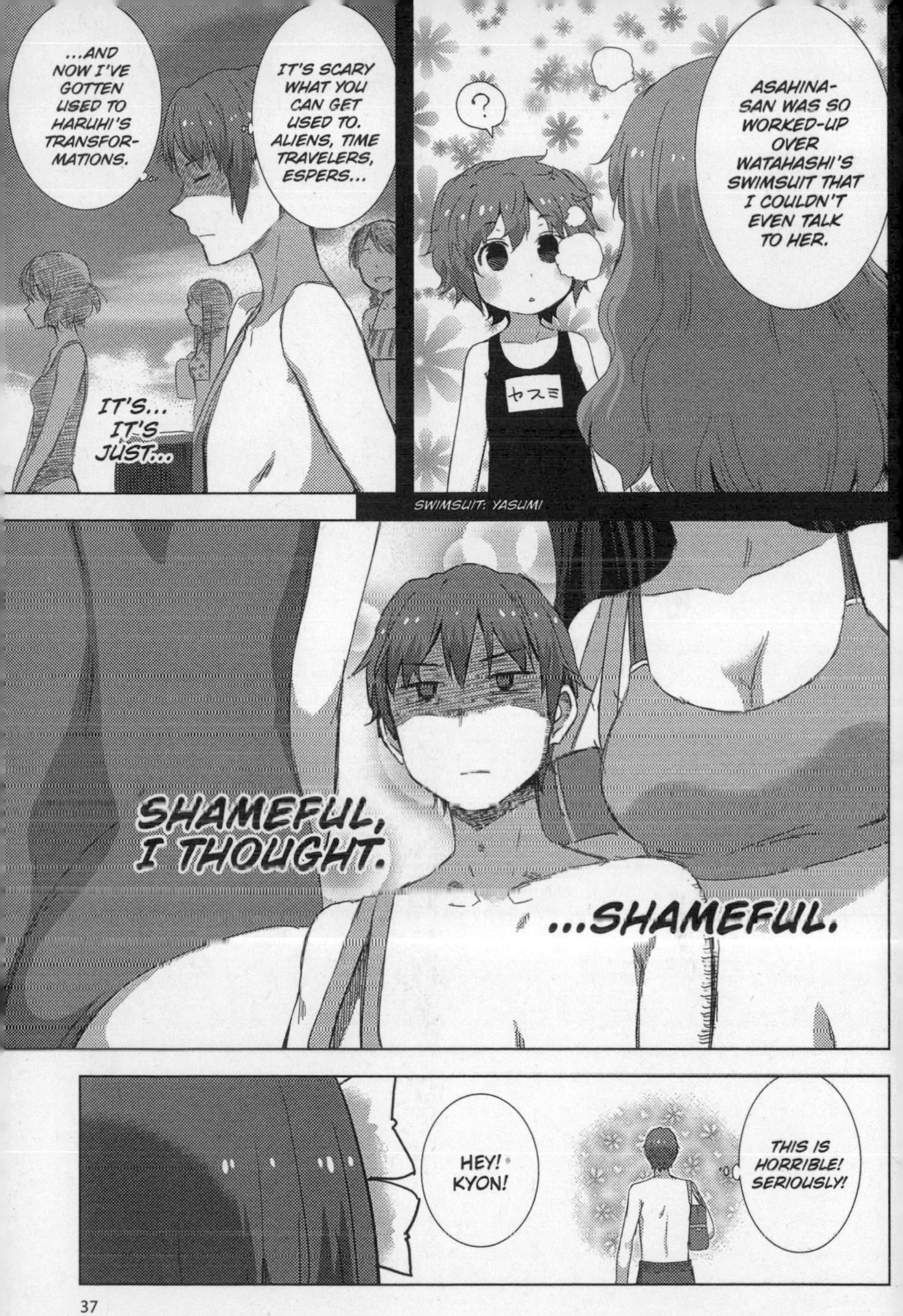
?
ASAHINA-SAN WAS SO WORKED-UP OVER WATAHASHI'S SWIMSUIT THAT I COULDN'T EVEN TALK TO HER.
ヤスミ
SWIMSUIT: YASUMI
IT'S SCARY WHAT YOU CAN GET USED TO. ALIENS, TIME TRAVELERS, ESPERS...
...AND NOW I'VE GOTTEN USED TO HARUHI'S TRANSFORMATIONS.
IT'S... IT'S JUST...
SHAMEFUL, I THOUGHT.
...SHAMEFUL.
THIS IS HORRIBLE! SERIOUSLY!
HEY! KYON!

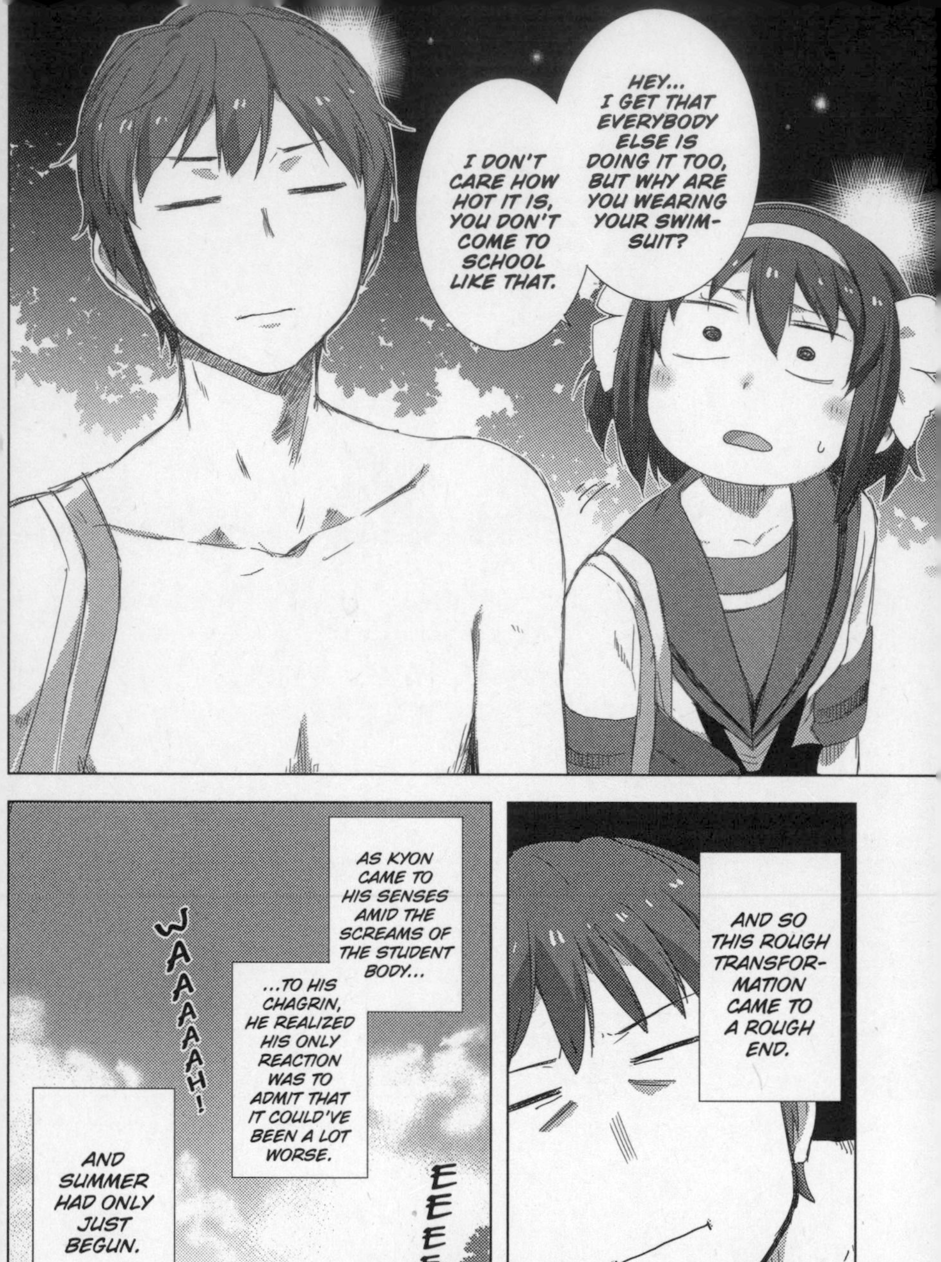
HEY... I GET THAT EVERYBODY ELSE IS DOING IT TOO, BUT WHY ARE YOU WEARING YOUR SWIM-SUIT?
I DON'T CARE HOW HOT IT IS, YOU DON'T COME TO SCHOOL LIKE THAT.
AND SO THIS ROUGH TRANSFOR-MATION CAME TO A ROUGH END.
AS KYON CAME TO HIS SENSES AMID THE SCREAMS OF THE STUDENT BODY...
...TO HIS CHAGRIN, HE REALIZED HIS ONLY REACTION WAS TO ADMIT THAT IT COULD'VE BEEN A LOT WORSE.
EEEEEEEK!
WAAAAAH!
AND SUMMER HAD ONLY JUST BEGUN.

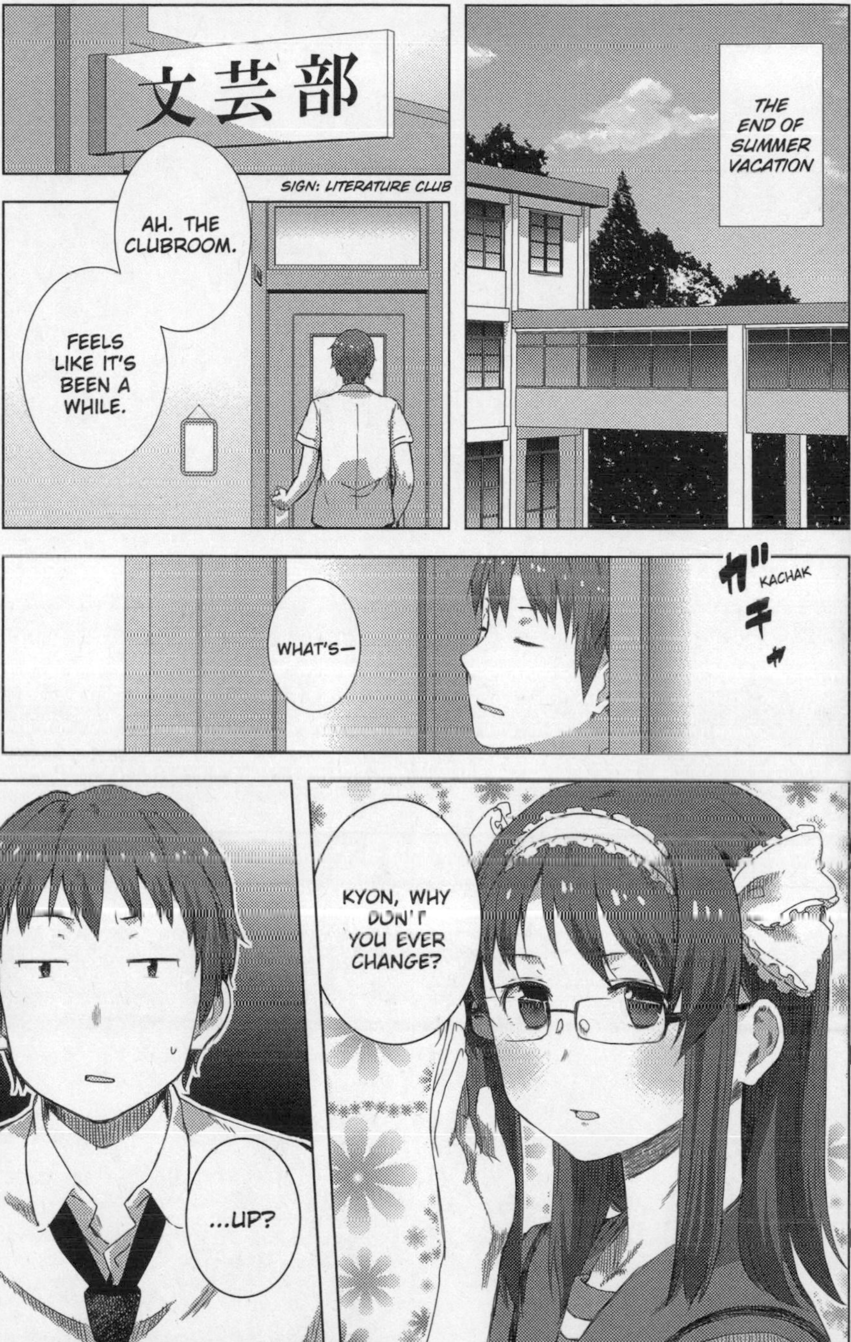
THE END OF SUMMER VACATION
文芸部
SIGN: LITERATURE CLUB
AH. THE CLUBROOM.
FEELS LIKE IT'S BEEN A WHILE.
ガチャ
KACHAK
WHAT'S—
KYON, WHY DON'T YOU EVER CHANGE?
...UP?

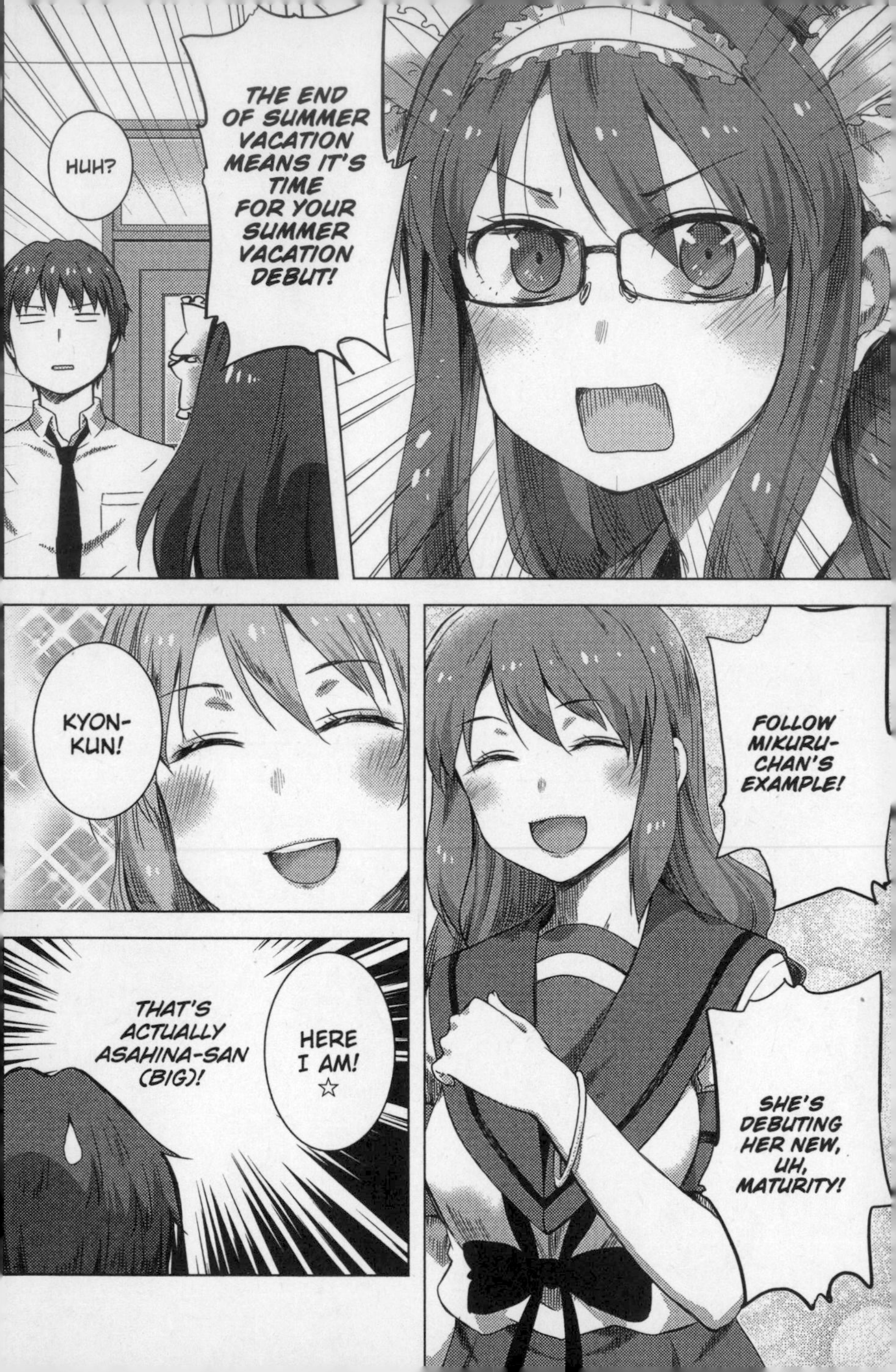
THE END OF SUMMER VACATION MEANS IT'S TIME FOR YOUR SUMMER VACATION DEBUT!
HUH?
FOLLOW MIKURU-CHAN'S EXAMPLE!
SHE'S DEBUTING HER NEW, UH, MATURITY!
KYON-KUN!
HERE I AM! ☆
THAT'S ACTUALLY ASAHINA-SAN (BIG)!

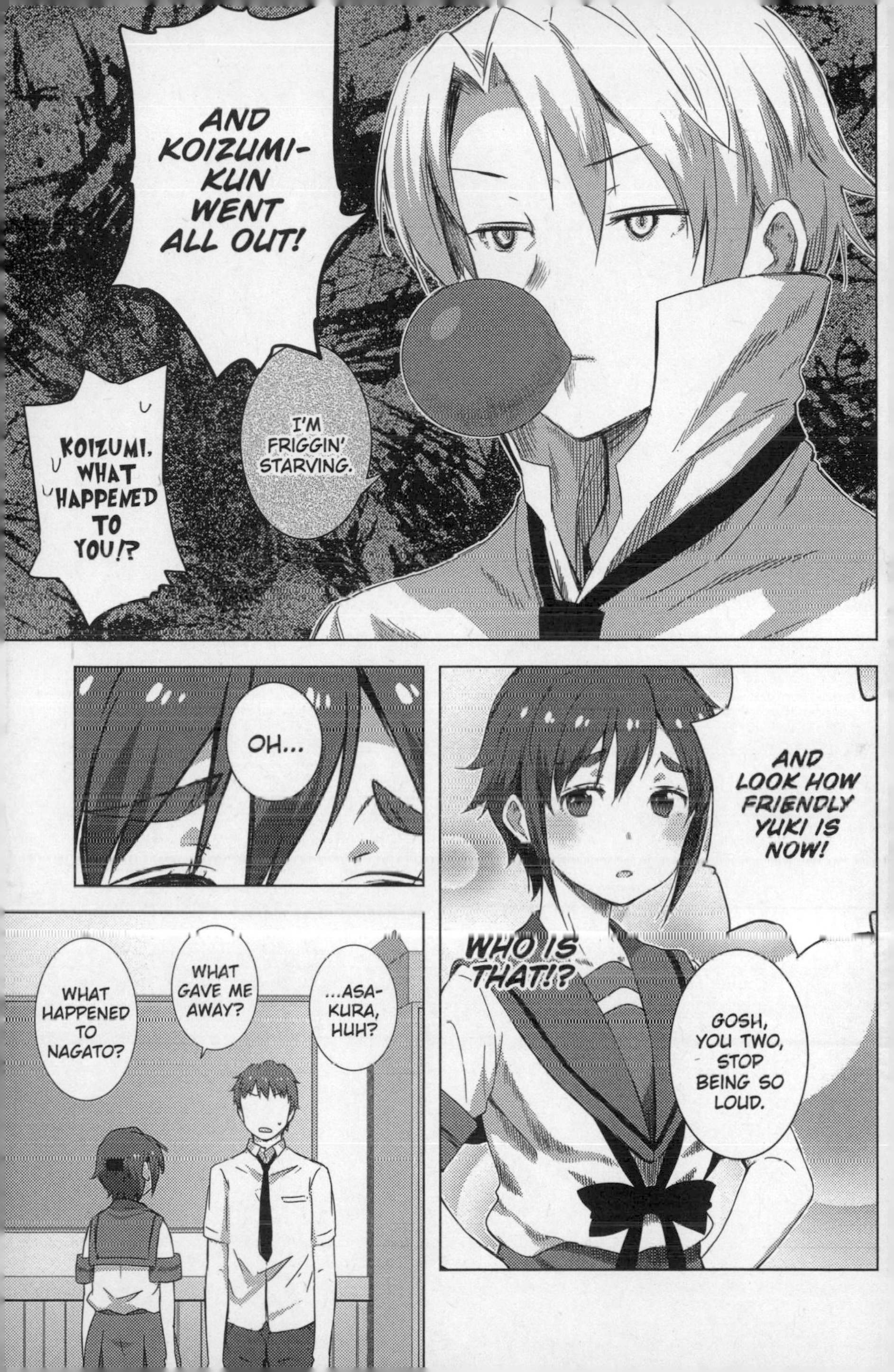
AND KOIZUMI-KUN WENT ALL OUT!
I'M FRIGGIN' STARVING.
KOIZUMI, WHAT HAPPENED TO YOU!?
AND LOOK HOW FRIENDLY YUKI IS NOW!
WHO IS THAT!?
GOSH, YOU TWO, STOP BEING SO LOUD.
OH...
...ASA-KURA, HUH?
WHAT GAVE ME AWAY?
WHAT HAPPENED TO NAGATO?

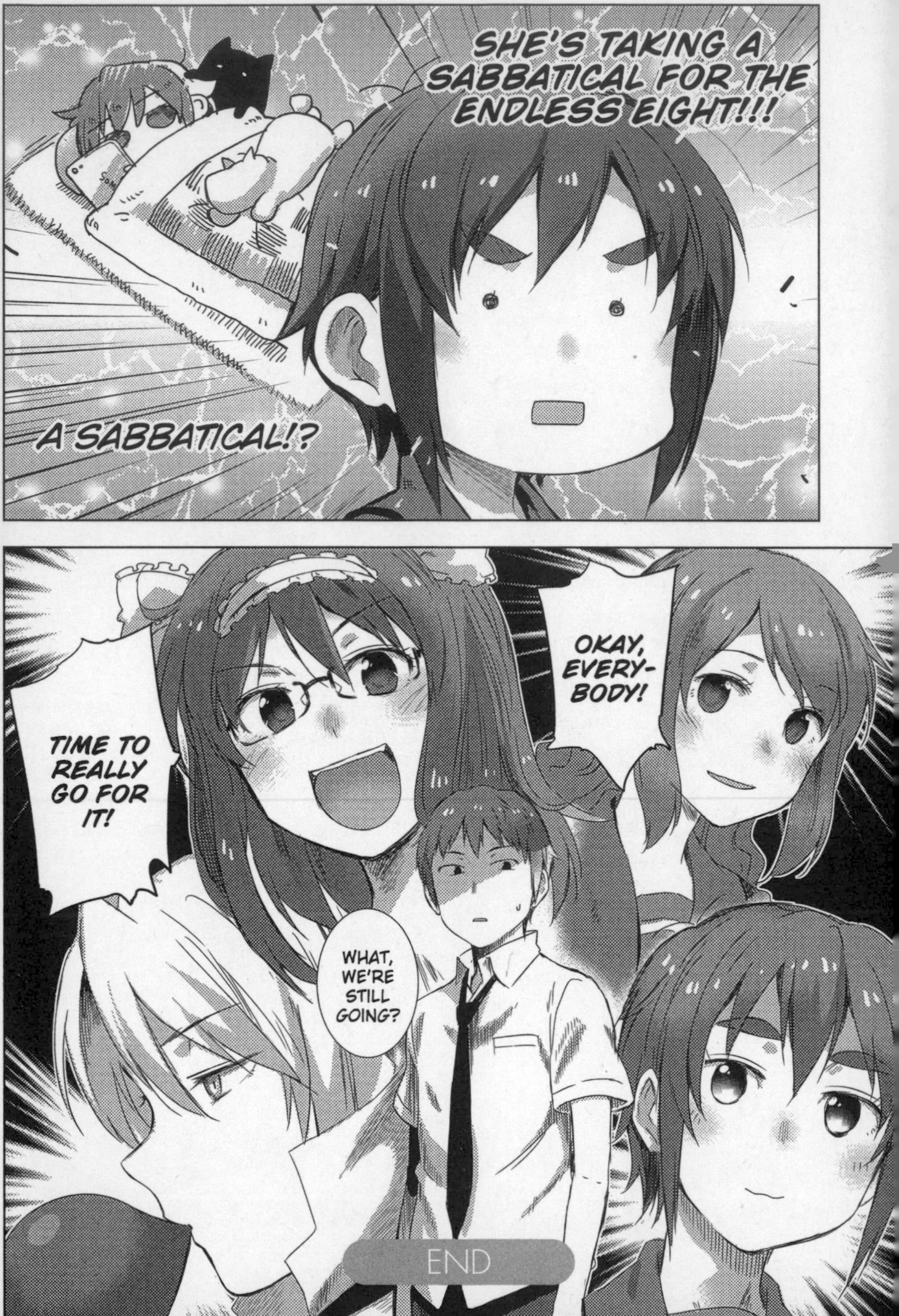
SHE'S TAKING A SABBATICAL FOR THE ENDLESS EIGHT!!!
A SABBATICAL!?
OKAY, EVERYBODY!
TIME TO REALLY GO FOR IT!
WHAT, WE'RE STILL GOING?
END

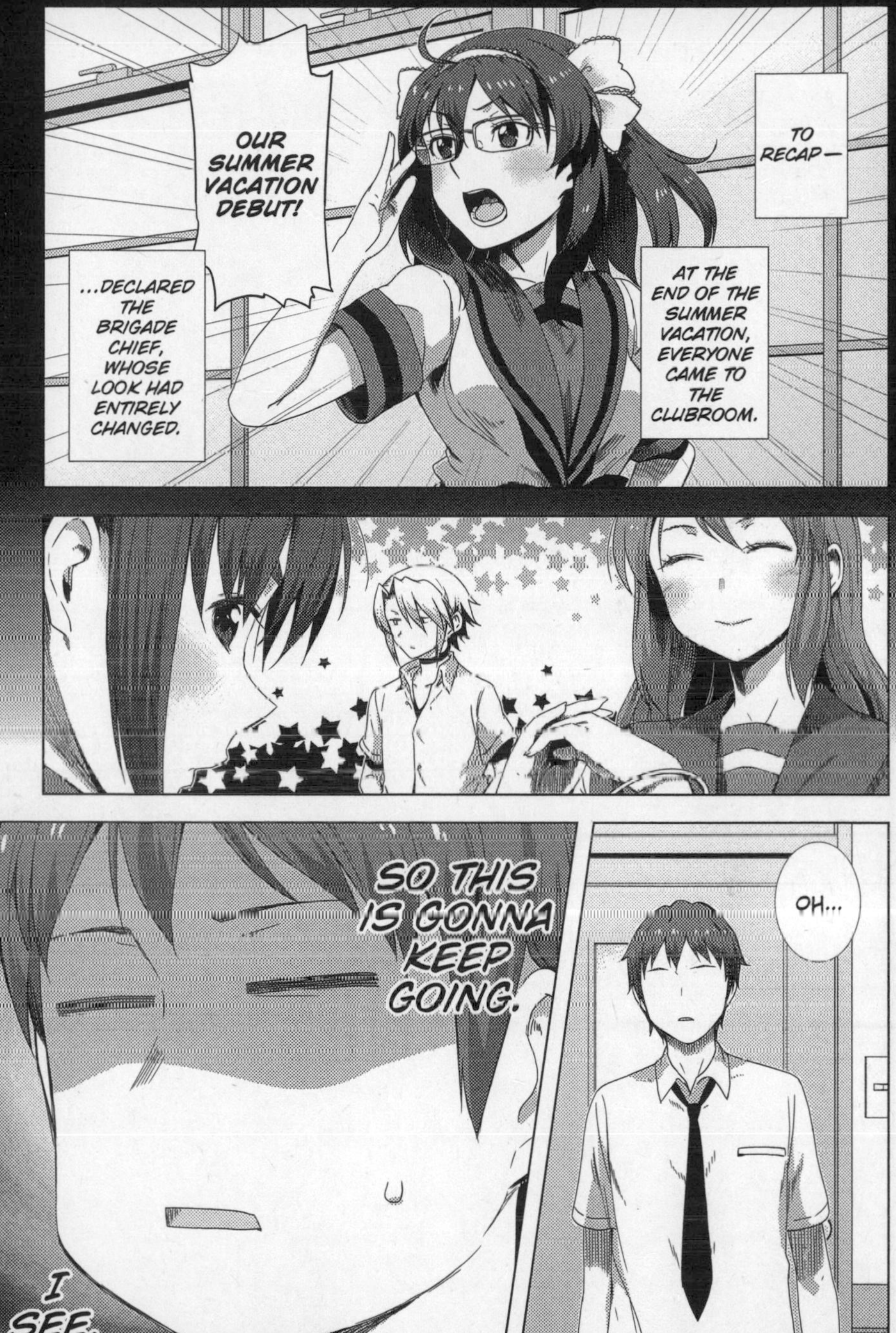
TO RECAP—
AT THE END OF THE SUMMER VACATION, EVERYONE CAME TO THE CLUBROOM.
OUR SUMMER VACATION DEBUT!
...DECLARED THE BRIGADE CHIEF, WHOSE LOOK HAD ENTIRELY CHANGED.
OH...
SO THIS IS GONNA KEEP GOING.
I SEE.

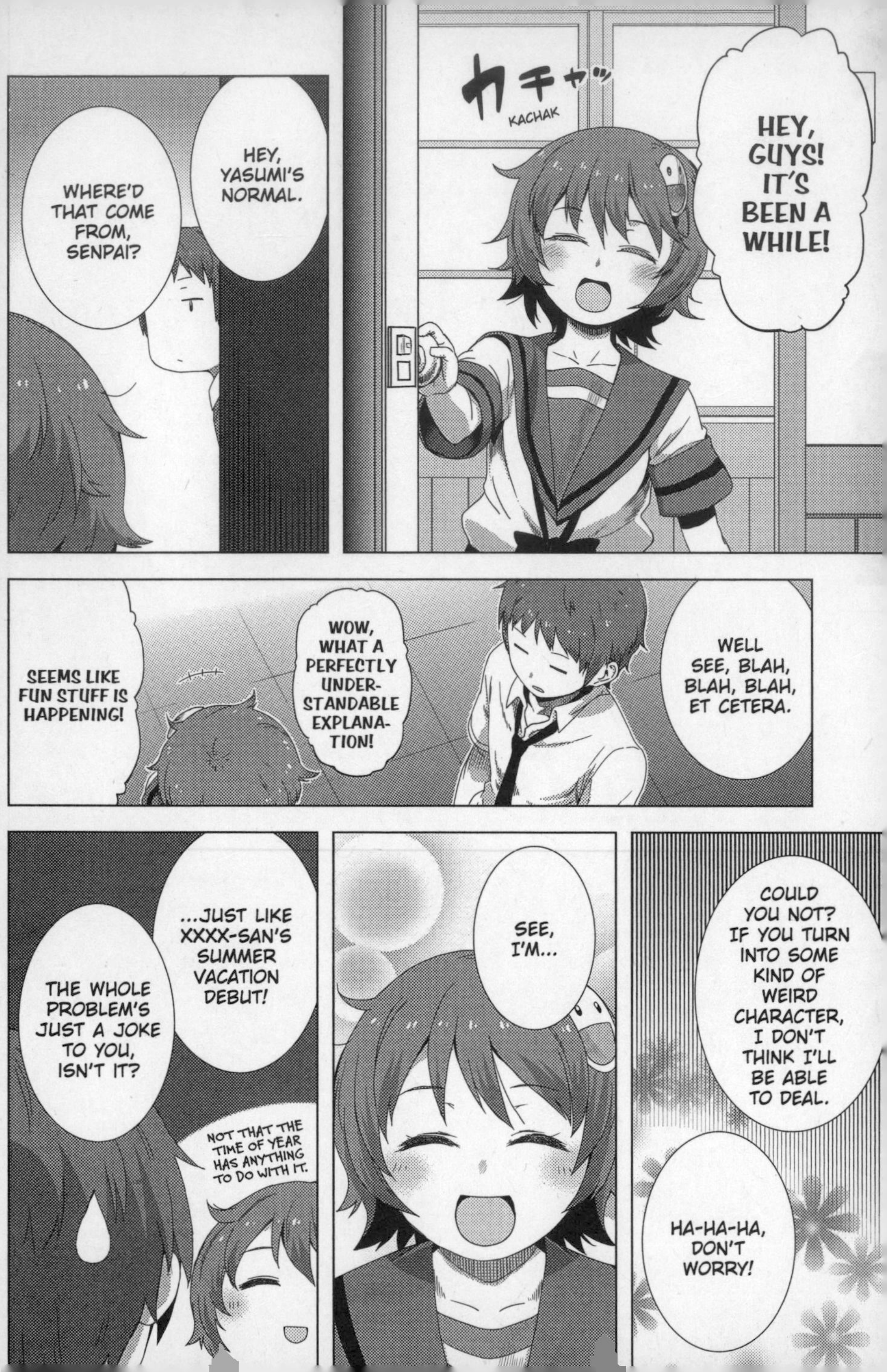
カチャッ
KACHAK
HEY, GUYS! IT'S BEEN A WHILE!
HEY, YASUMI'S NORMAL.
WHERE'D THAT COME FROM, SENPAI?
WELL SEE, BLAH, BLAH, BLAH, ET CETERA.
WOW, WHAT A PERFECTLY UNDER-STANDABLE EXPLANA-TION!
SEEMS LIKE FUN STUFF IS HAPPENING!
COULD YOU NOT? IF YOU TURN INTO SOME KIND OF WEIRD CHARACTER, I DON'T THINK I'LL BE ABLE TO DEAL.
HA-HA-HA, DON'T WORRY!
SEE, I'M...
...JUST LIKE XXXX-SAN'S SUMMER VACATION DEBUT!
THE WHOLE PROBLEM'S JUST A JOKE TO YOU, ISN'T IT?
NOT THAT THE TIME OF YEAR HAS ANYTHING TO DO WITH IT.

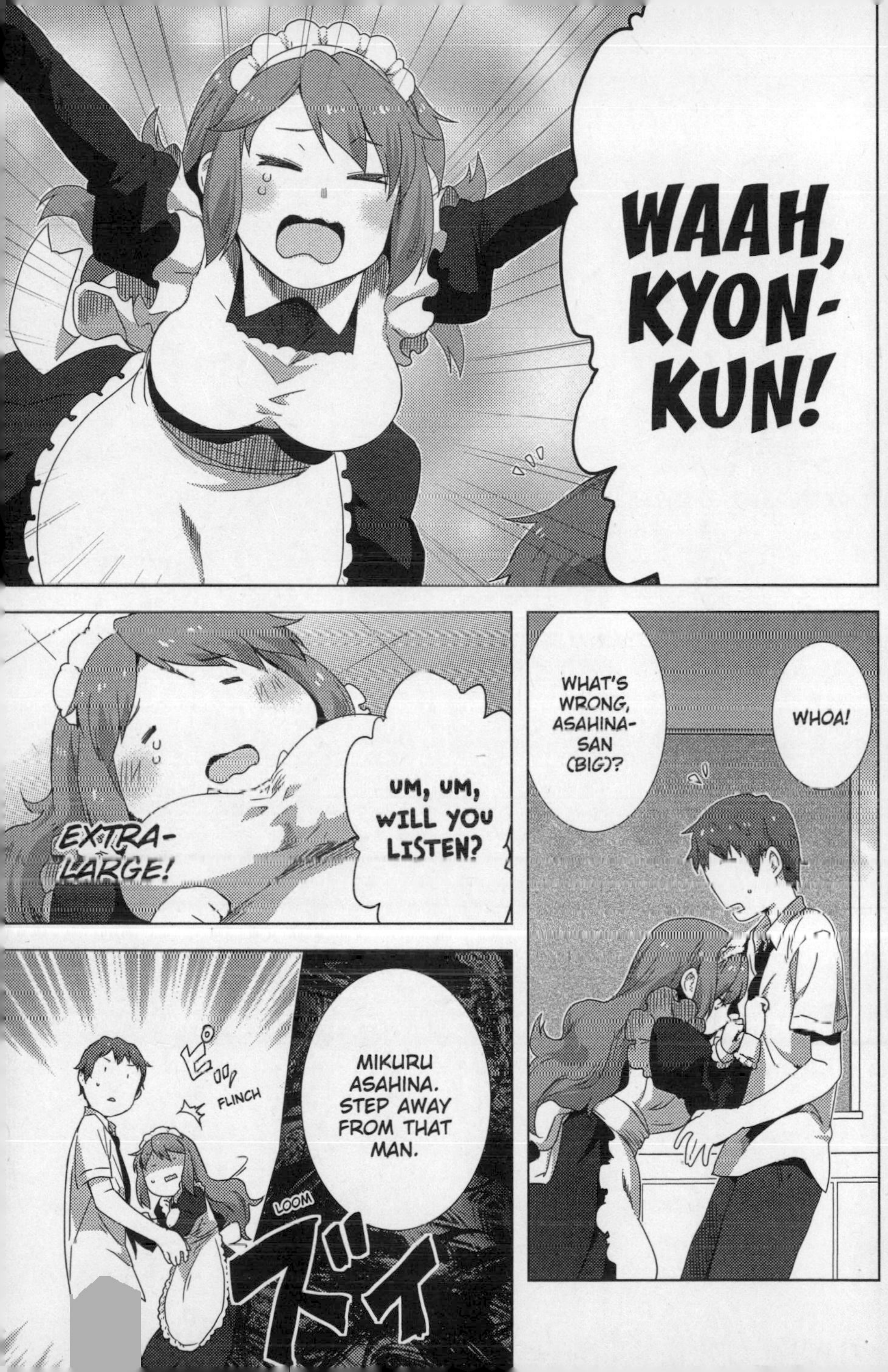
WAAH, KYON-KUN!
WHOA!
WHAT'S WRONG, ASAHINA-SAN (BIG)?
UM, UM, WILL YOU LISTEN?
EXTRA-LARGE!
MIKURU ASAHINA. STEP AWAY FROM THAT MAN.
FLINCH
LOOM

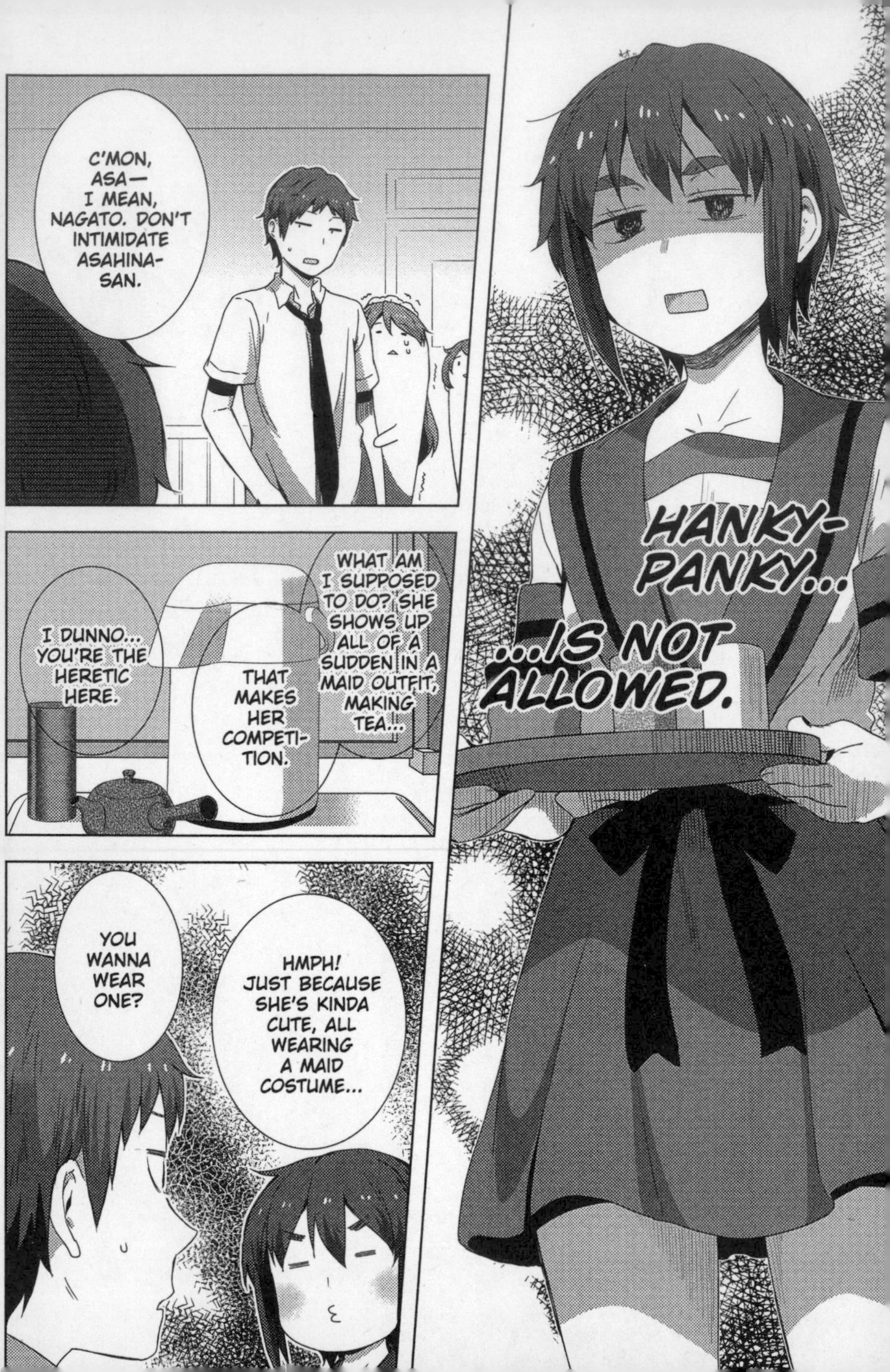
HANKY-PANKY...
...IS NOT ALLOWED.
C'MON, ASA— I MEAN, NAGATO. DON'T INTIMIDATE ASAHINA-SAN.
WHAT AM I SUPPOSED TO DO? SHE SHOWS UP ALL OF A SUDDEN IN A MAID OUTFIT, MAKING TEA...
THAT MAKES HER COMPETITION.
I DUNNO... YOU'RE THE HERETIC HERE.
HMPH! JUST BECAUSE SHE'S KINDA CUTE, ALL WEARING A MAID COSTUME...
YOU WANNA WEAR ONE?

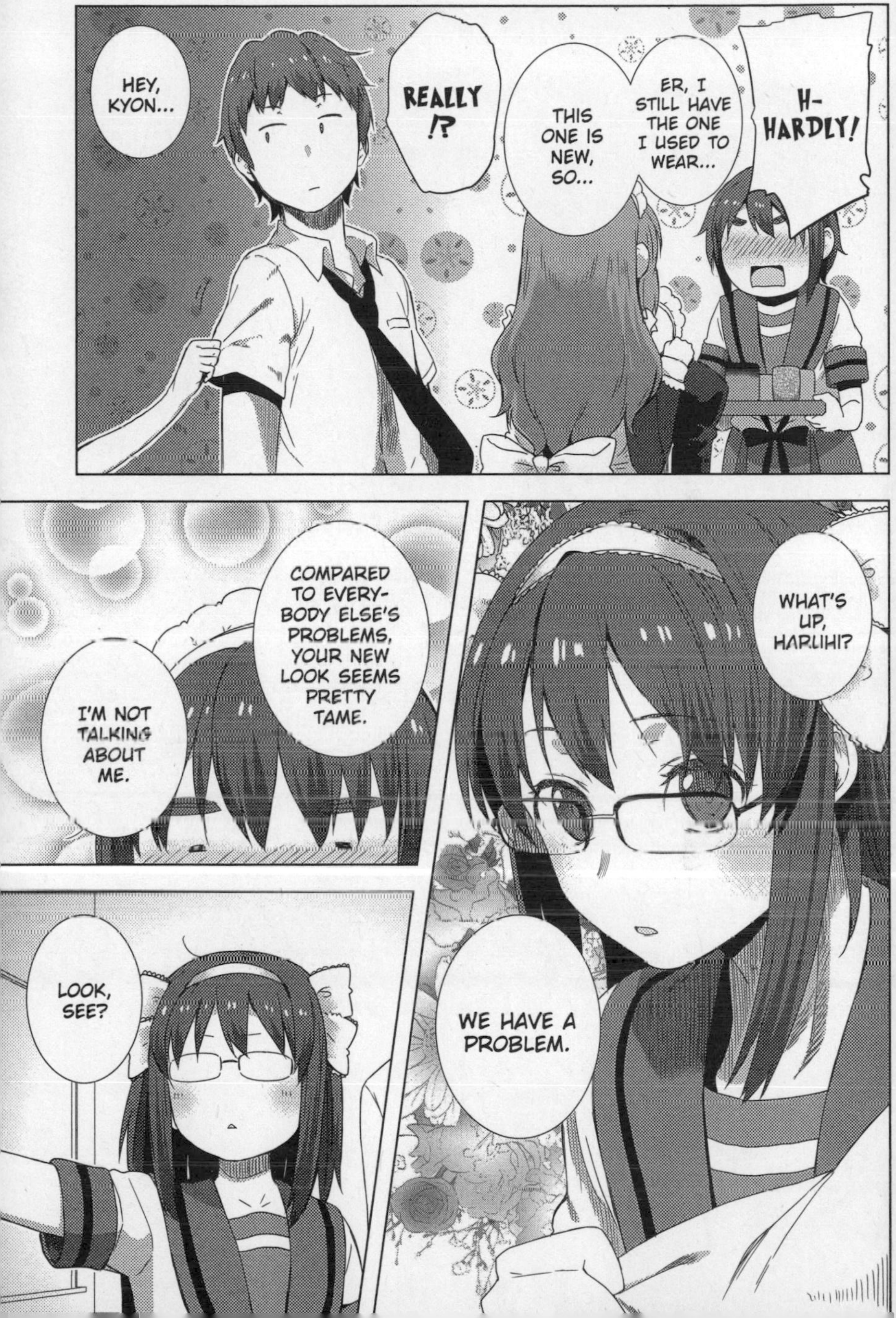
H-HARDLY!
ER, I STILL HAVE THE ONE I USED TO WEAR...
THIS ONE IS NEW, SO...
REALLY !?
HEY, KYON...
WHAT'S UP, HARUHI?
WE HAVE A PROBLEM.
COMPARED TO EVERY-BODY ELSE'S PROBLEMS, YOUR NEW LOOK SEEMS PRETTY TAME.
I'M NOT TALKING ABOUT ME.
LOOK, SEE?

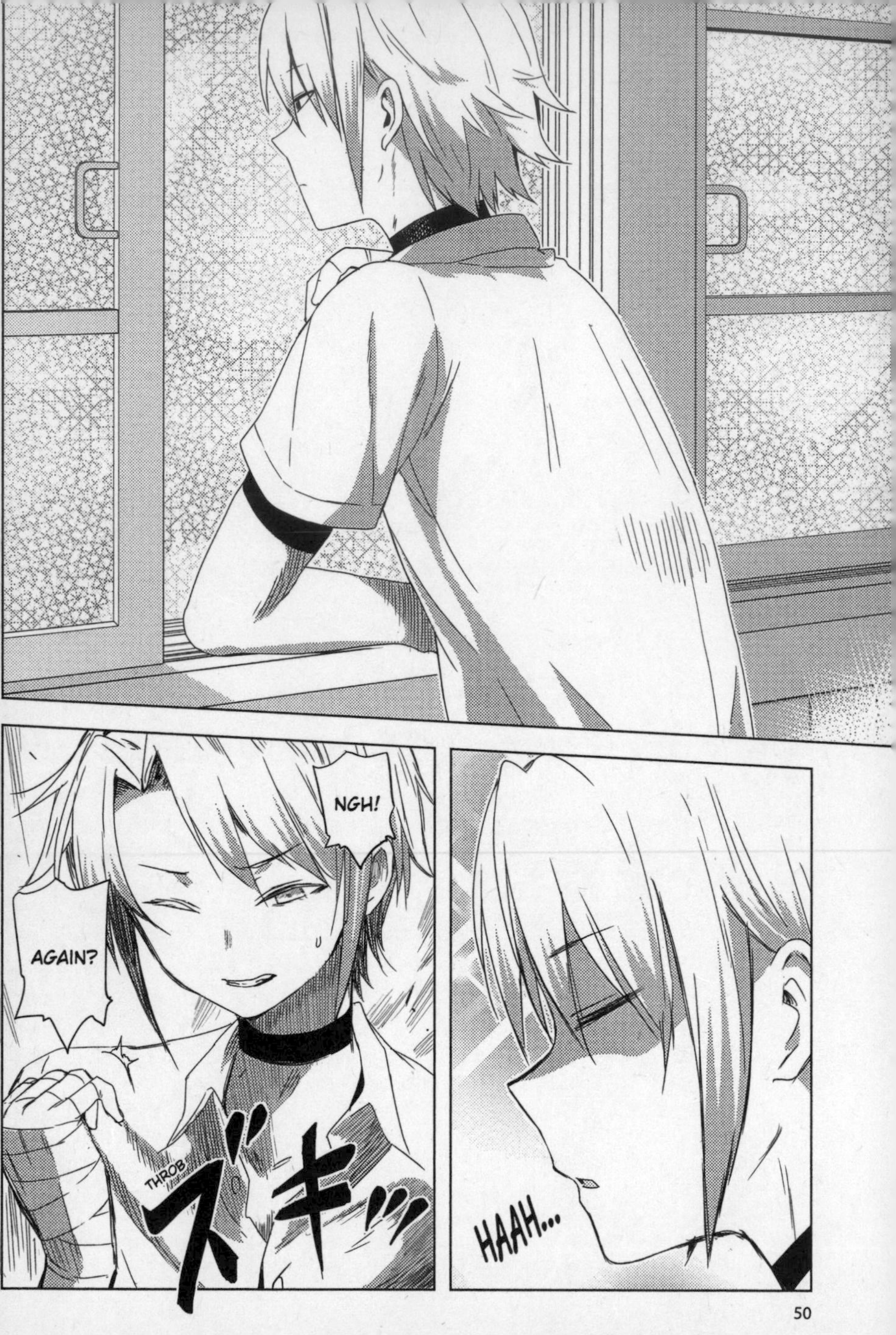
HAAH...
NGH!
AGAIN?
THROB

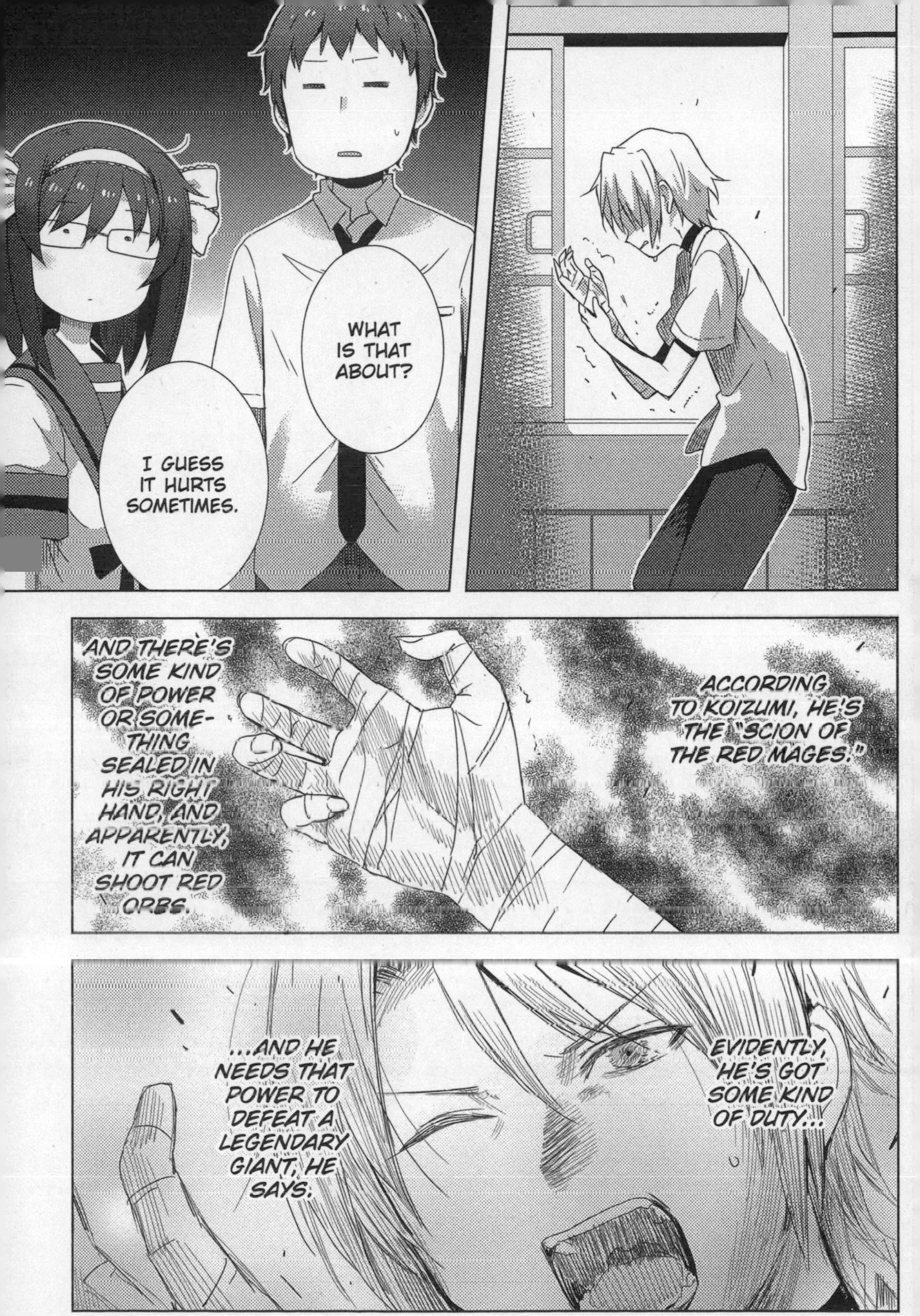
WHAT IS THAT ABOUT?
I GUESS IT HURTS SOMETIMES.
ACCORDING TO KOIZUMI, HE'S THE "SCION OF THE RED MAGES."
AND THERE'S SOME KIND OF POWER OR SOME-THING SEALED IN HIS RIGHT HAND, AND APPARENTLY, IT CAN SHOOT RED ORBS.
EVIDENTLY, HE'S GOT SOME KIND OF DUTY...
...AND HE NEEDS THAT POWER TO DEFEAT A LEGENDARY GIANT, HE SAYS.

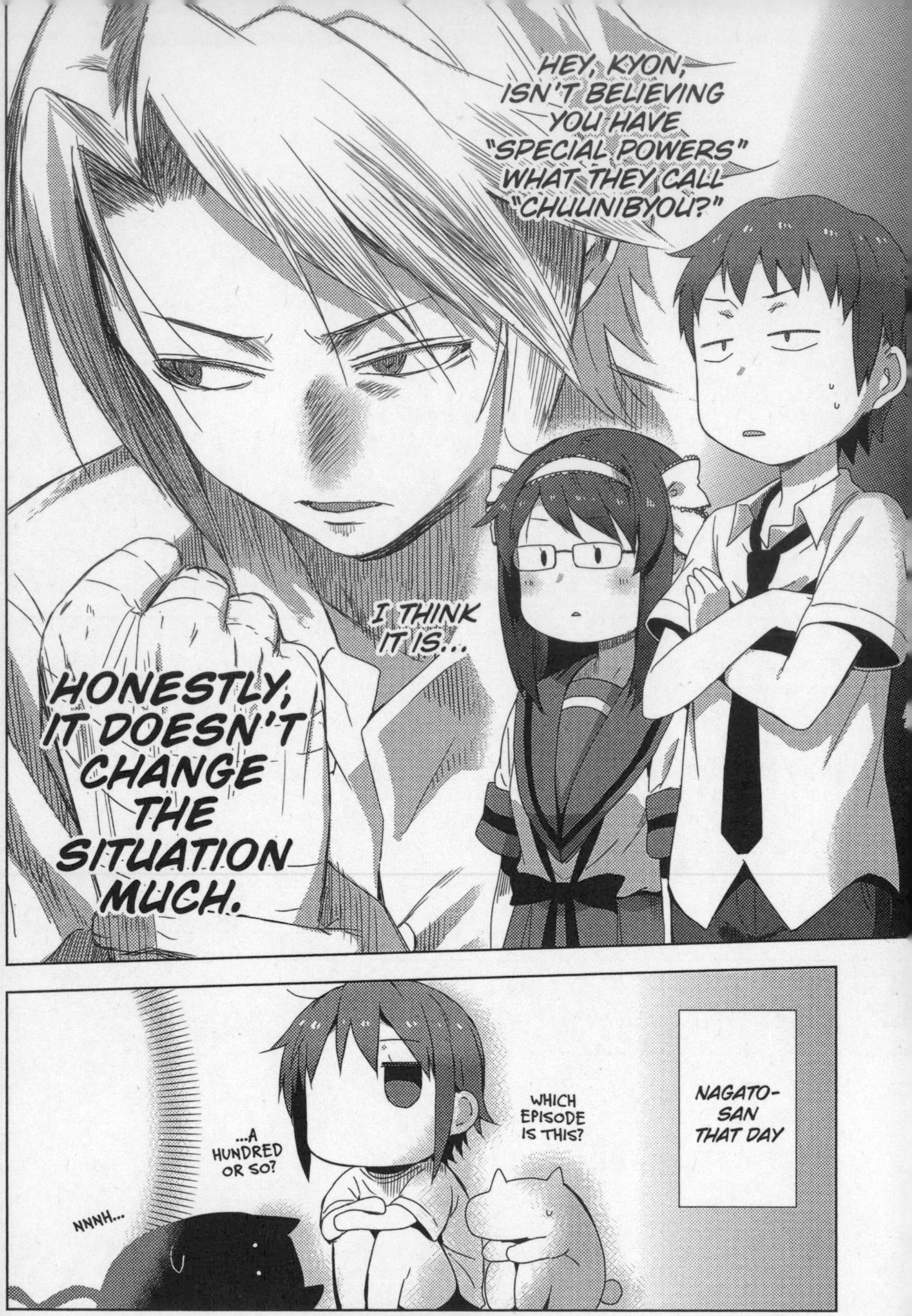
HEY, KYON, ISN'T BELIEVING YOU HAVE "SPECIAL POWERS" WHAT THEY CALL "CHUUNIBYOU?"
I THINK IT IS...
HONESTLY, IT DOESN'T CHANGE THE SITUATION MUCH.
NAGATO-SAN THAT DAY
WHICH EPISODE IS THIS?
...A HUNDRED OR SO?
NNNH...

END

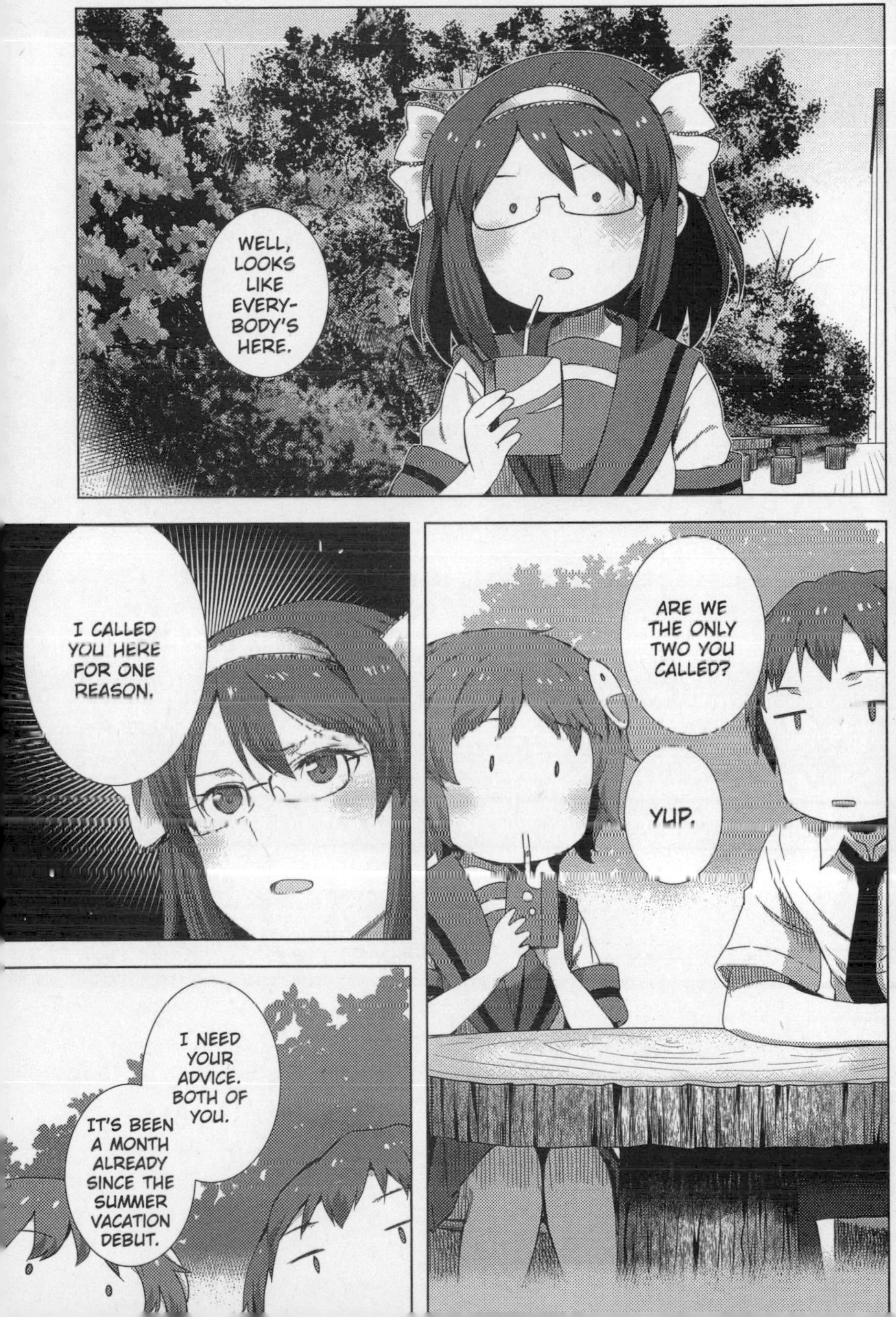
WELL, LOOKS LIKE EVERY-BODY'S HERE.
ARE WE THE ONLY TWO YOU CALLED?
YUP.
I CALLED YOU HERE FOR ONE REASON.
I NEED YOUR ADVICE. BOTH OF YOU.
IT'S BEEN A MONTH ALREADY SINCE THE SUMMER VACATION DEBUT.

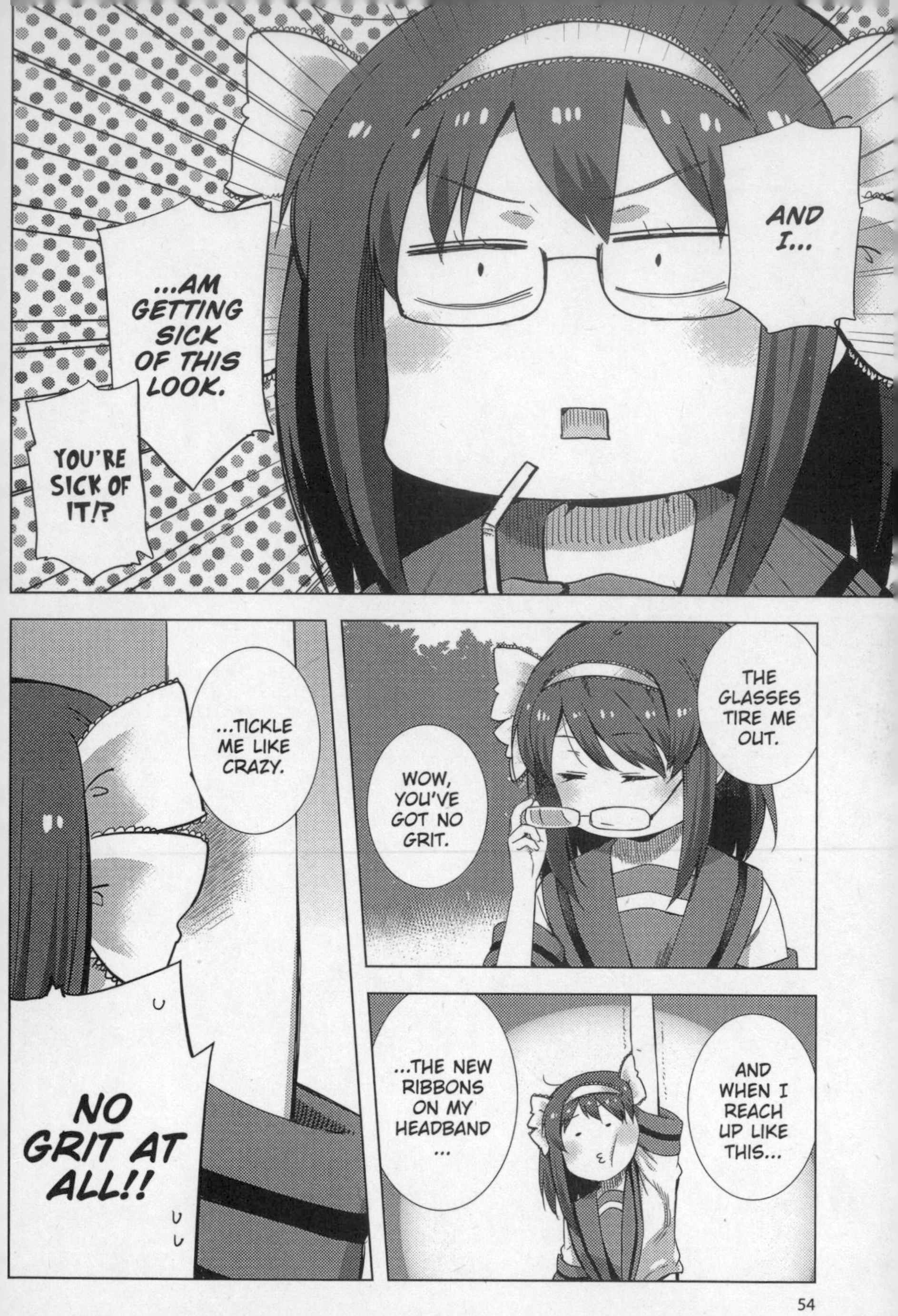
AND I...
...AM GETTING SICK OF THIS LOOK.
YOU'RE SICK OF IT!?
THE GLASSES TIRE ME OUT.
WOW, YOU'VE GOT NO GRIT.
AND WHEN I REACH UP LIKE THIS...
...THE NEW RIBBONS ON MY HEADBAND ...
...TICKLE ME LIKE CRAZY.
NO GRIT AT ALL!!

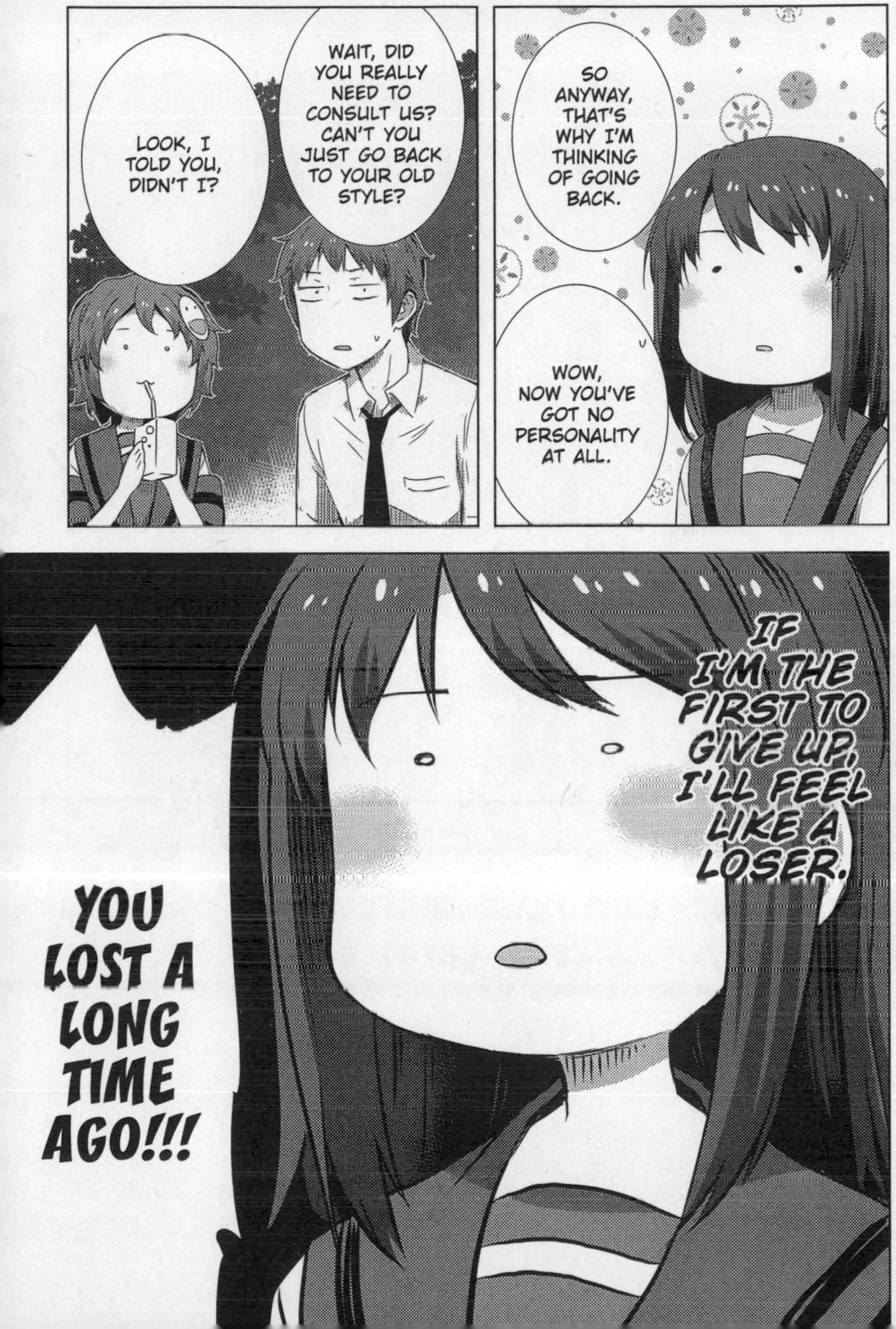
SO ANYWAY, THAT'S WHY I'M THINKING OF GOING BACK.
WOW, NOW YOU'VE GOT NO PERSONALITY AT ALL.
WAIT, DID YOU REALLY NEED TO CONSULT US? CAN'T YOU JUST GO BACK TO YOUR OLD STYLE?
LOOK, I TOLD YOU, DIDN'T I?
IF I'M THE FIRST TO GIVE UP, I'LL FEEL LIKE A LOSER.
YOU LOST A LONG TIME AGO!!!

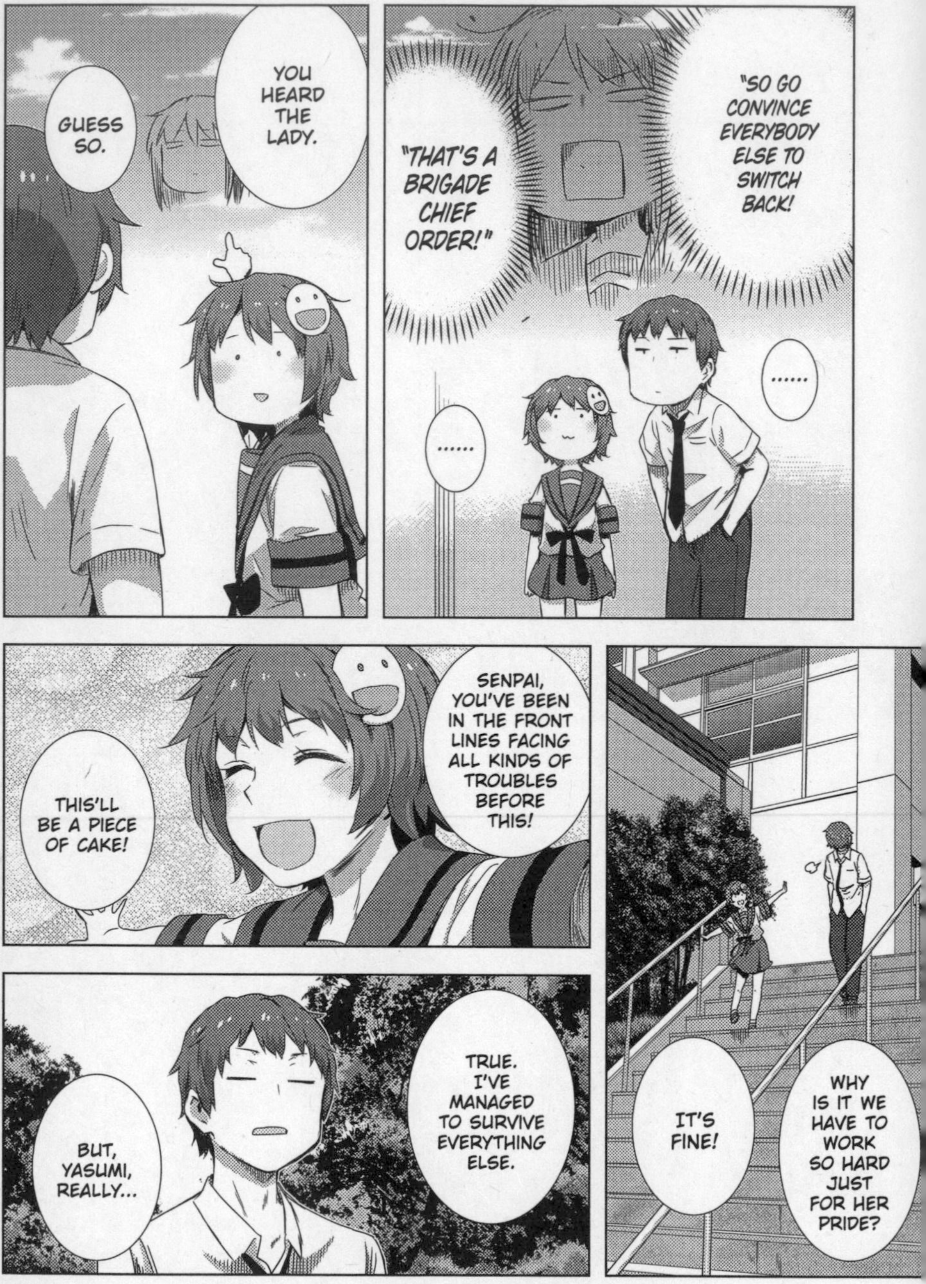
"SO GO CONVINCE EVERYBODY ELSE TO SWITCH BACK!
"THAT'S A BRIGADE CHIEF ORDER!"
......
......
YOU HEARD THE LADY.
GUESS SO.
WHY IS IT WE HAVE TO WORK SO HARD JUST FOR HER PRIDE?
IT'S FINE!
SENPAI, YOU'VE BEEN IN THE FRONT LINES FACING ALL KINDS OF TROUBLES BEFORE THIS!
THIS'LL BE A PIECE OF CAKE!
TRUE. I'VE MANAGED TO SURVIVE EVERYTHING ELSE.
BUT, YASUMI, REALLY...

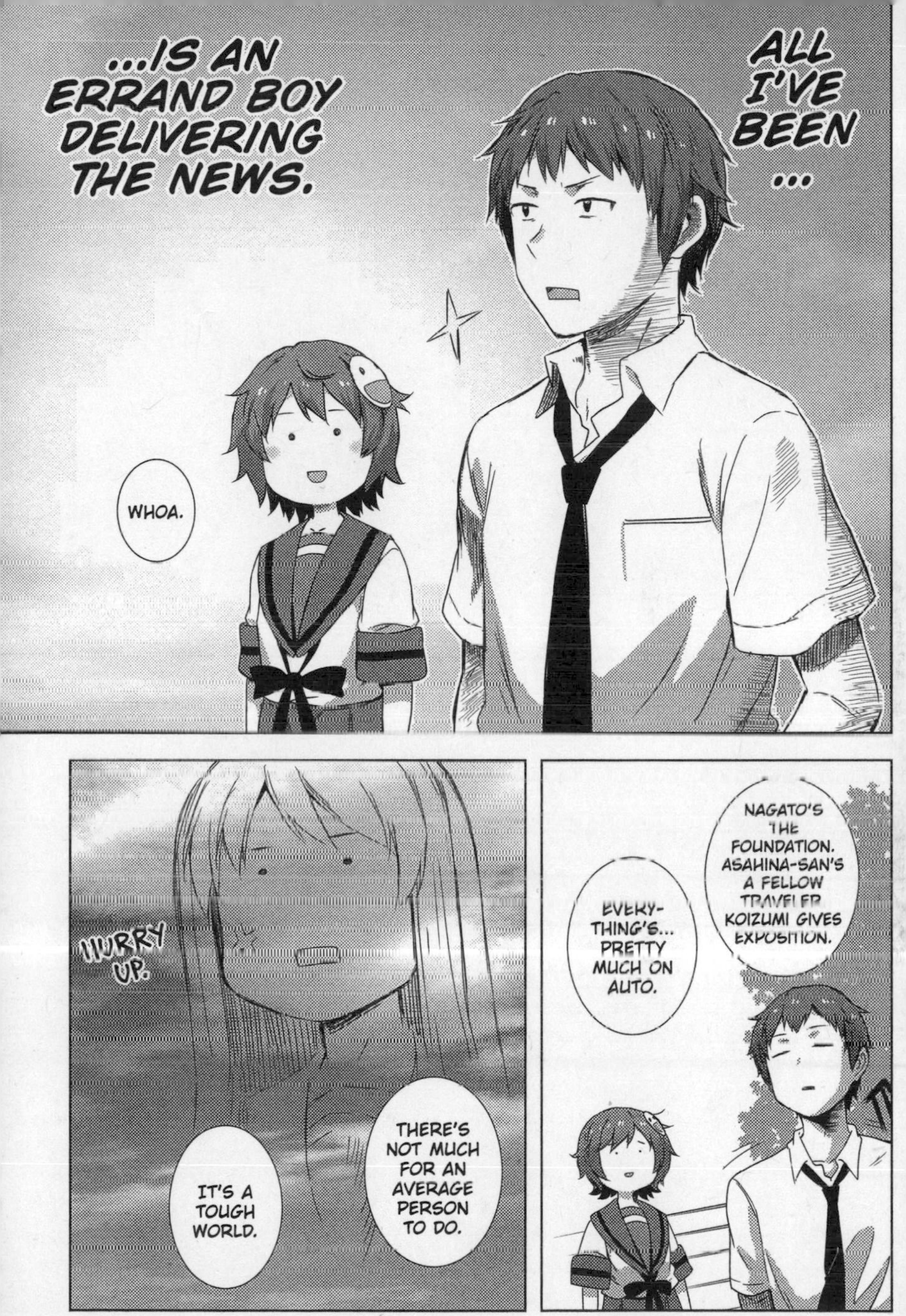
ALL I'VE BEEN...
...IS AN ERRAND BOY DELIVERING THE NEWS.
WHOA.
NAGATO'S THE FOUNDATION. ASAHINA-SAN'S A FELLOW TRAVELER KOIZUMI GIVES EXPOSITION.
EVERYTHING'S... PRETTY MUCH ON AUTO.
HURRY UP.
THERE'S NOT MUCH FOR AN AVERAGE PERSON TO DO.
IT'S A TOUGH WORLD.

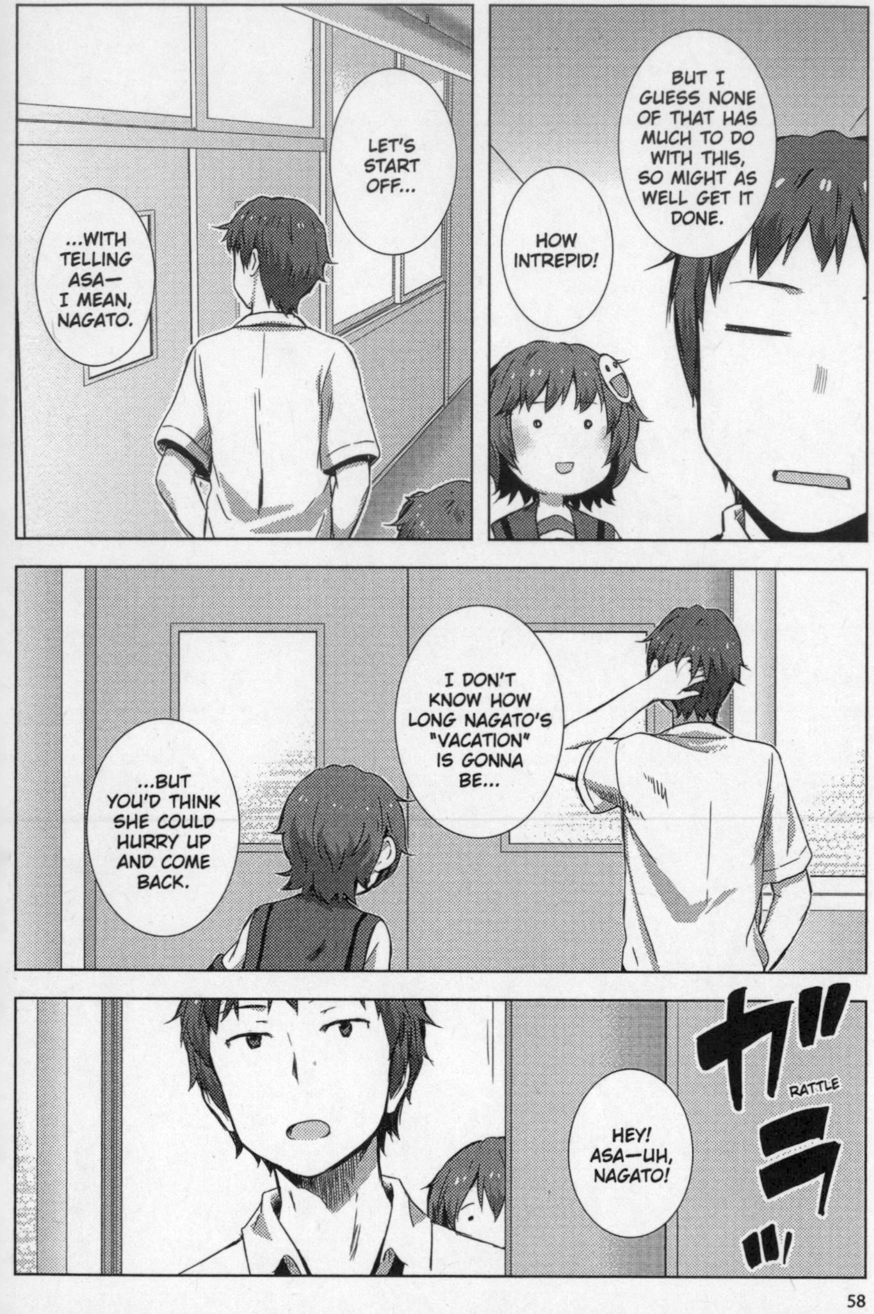
BUT I GUESS NONE OF THAT HAS MUCH TO DO WITH THIS, SO MIGHT AS WELL GET IT DONE.
HOW INTREPID!
LET'S START OFF...
...WITH TELLING ASA— I MEAN, NAGATO.
I DON'T KNOW HOW LONG NAGATO'S "VACATION" IS GONNA BE...
...BUT YOU'D THINK SHE COULD HURRY UP AND COME BACK.
ガラッ
RATTLE
HEY! ASA—UH, NAGATO!

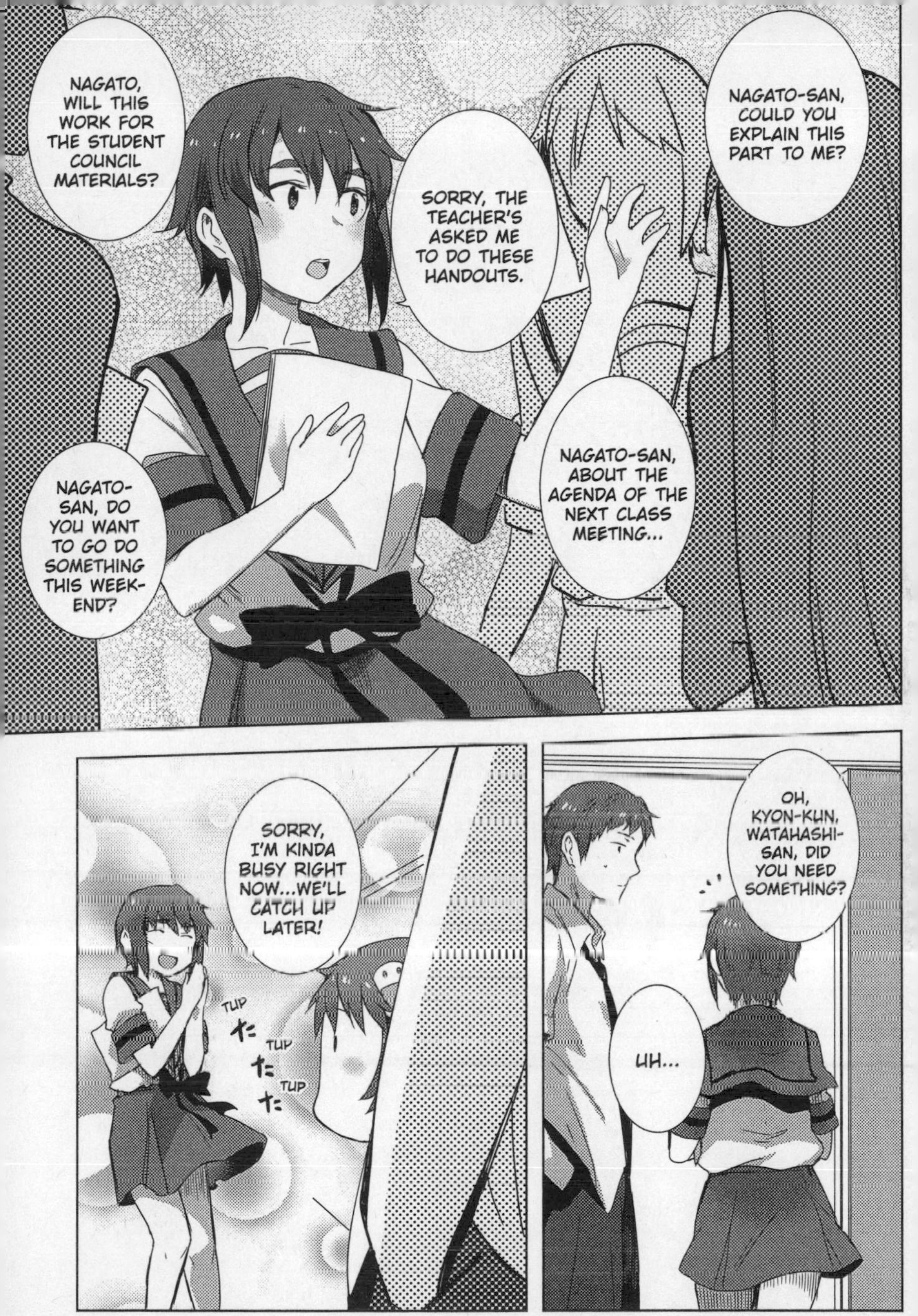
NAGATO-SAN, COULD YOU EXPLAIN THIS PART TO ME?
NAGATO, WILL THIS WORK FOR THE STUDENT COUNCIL MATERIALS?
SORRY, THE TEACHER'S ASKED ME TO DO THESE HANDOUTS.
NAGATO-SAN, ABOUT THE AGENDA OF THE NEXT CLASS MEETING...
NAGATO-SAN, DO YOU WANT TO GO DO SOMETHING THIS WEEK-END?
OH, KYON-KUN, WATAHASHI-SAN, DID YOU NEED SOMETHING?
UH...
SORRY, I'M KINDA BUSY RIGHT NOW...WE'LL CATCH UP LATER!
TUP た
TUP た
TUP た

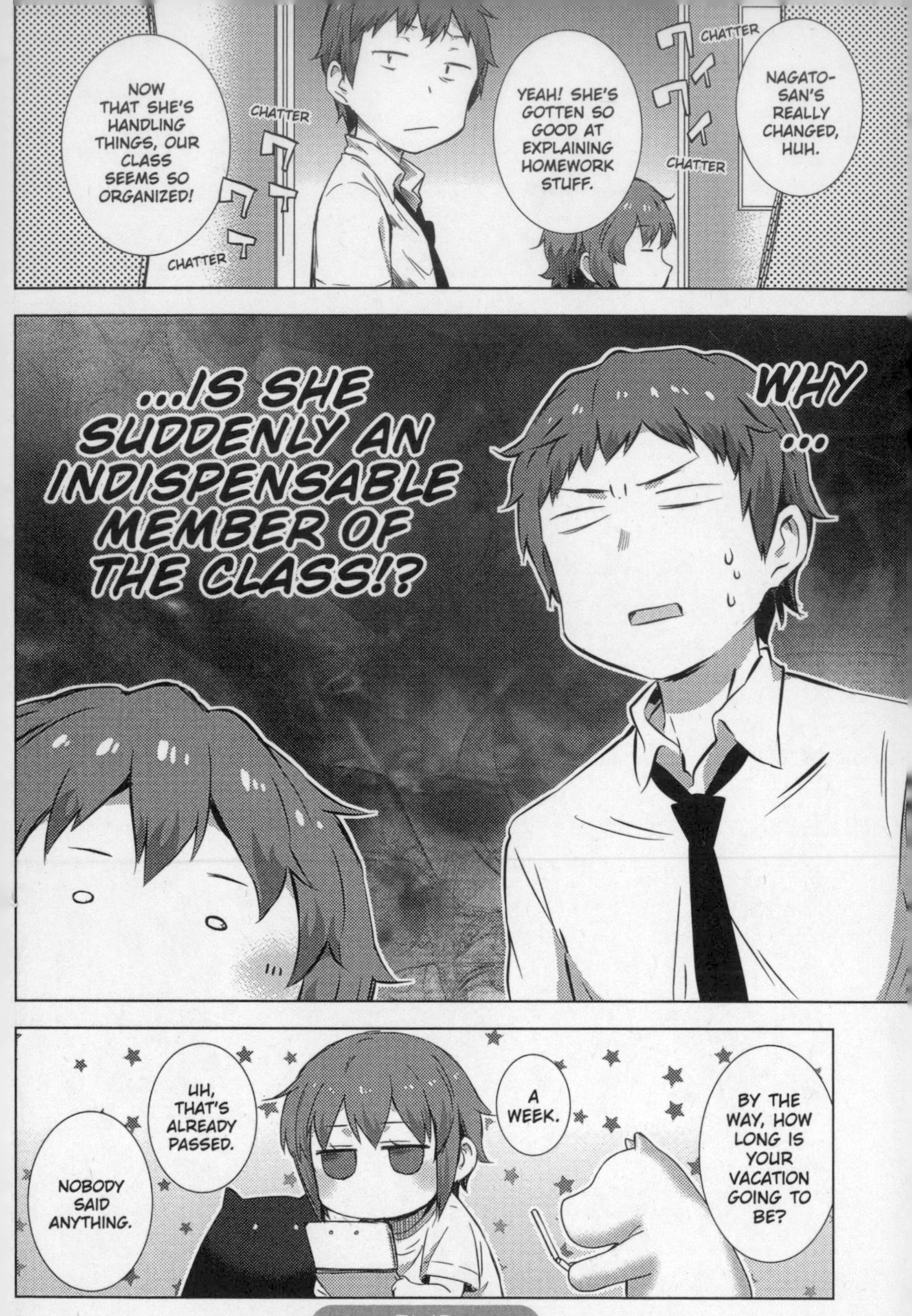
CHATTER
NAGATO-SAN'S REALLY CHANGED, HUH.
CHATTER
YEAH! SHE'S GOTTEN SO GOOD AT EXPLAINING HOMEWORK STUFF.
CHATTER
NOW THAT SHE'S HANDLING THINGS, OUR CLASS SEEMS SO ORGANIZED!
CHATTER
WHY...
...IS SHE SUDDENLY AN INDISPENSABLE MEMBER OF THE CLASS!?
BY THE WAY, HOW LONG IS YOUR VACATION GOING TO BE?
A WEEK.
UH, THAT'S ALREADY PASSED.
NOBODY SAID ANYTHING.

END

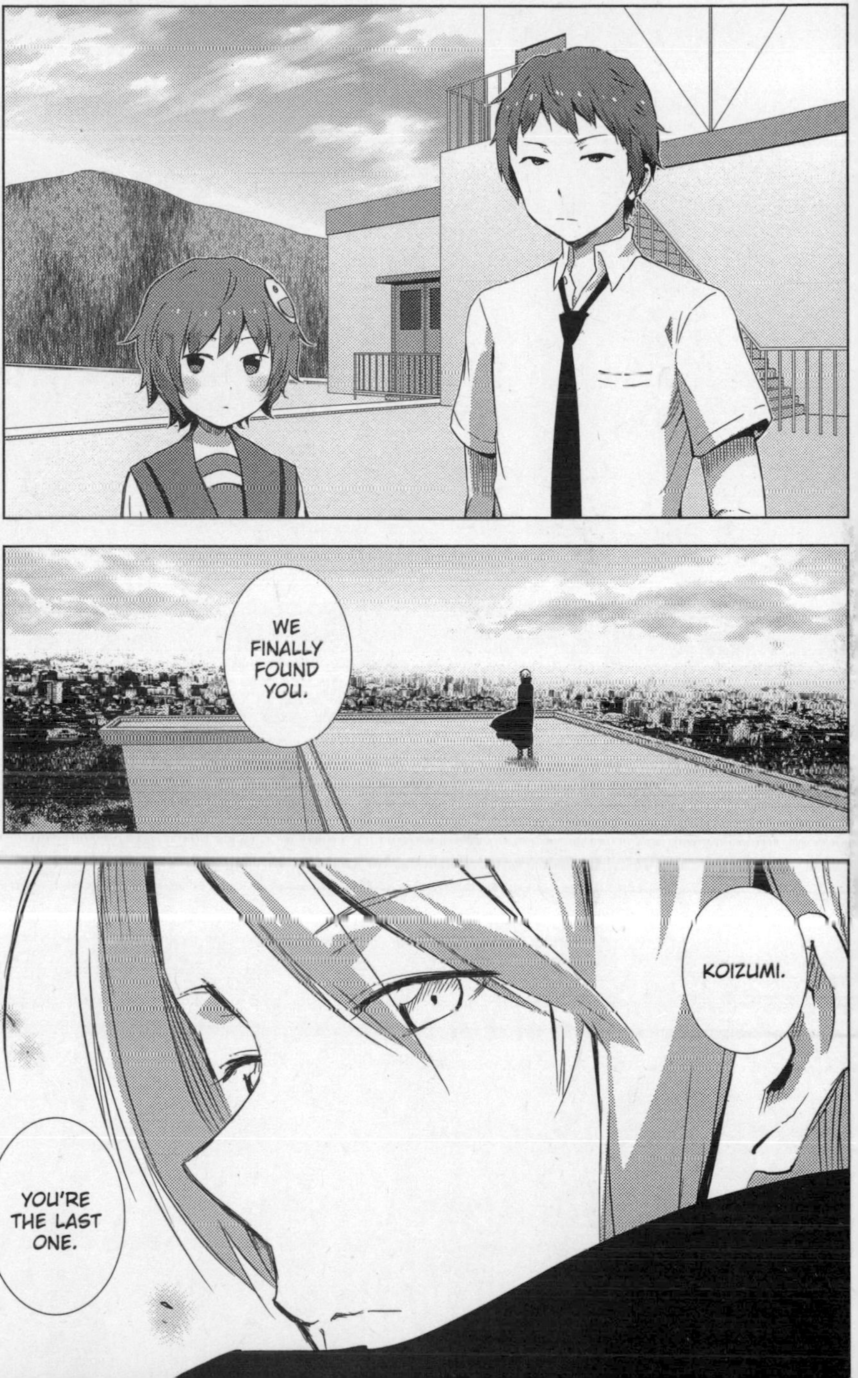
WE FINALLY FOUND YOU.
KOIZUMI.
YOU'RE THE LAST ONE.

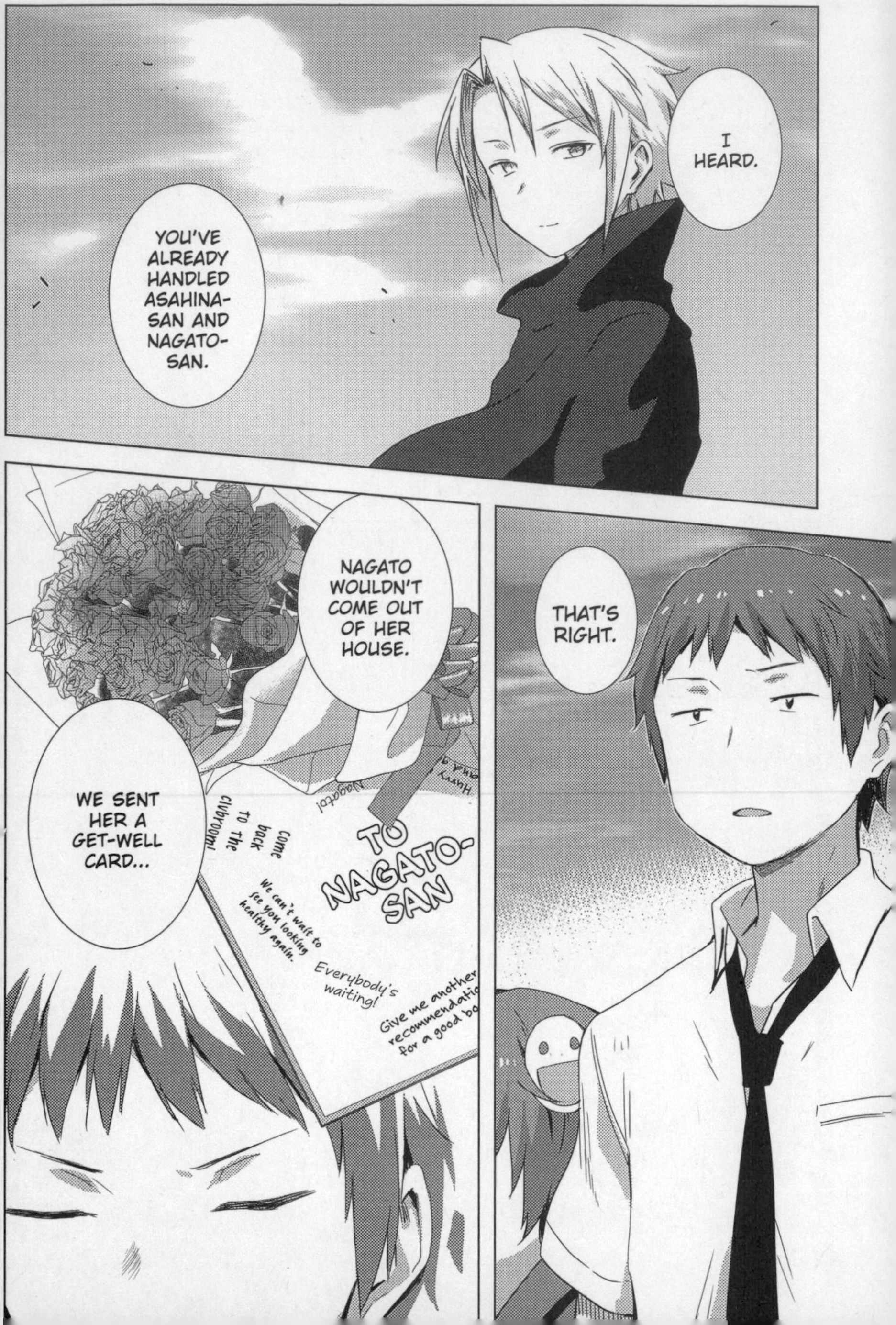
I HEARD.
YOU'VE ALREADY HANDLED ASAHINA-SAN AND NAGATO-SAN.
THAT'S RIGHT.
NAGATO WOULDN'T COME OUT OF HER HOUSE.
WE SENT HER A GET-WELL CARD...
TO NAGATO-SAN
Come back to the clubroom!
We can't wait to see you looking healthy again.
Everybody's waiting!

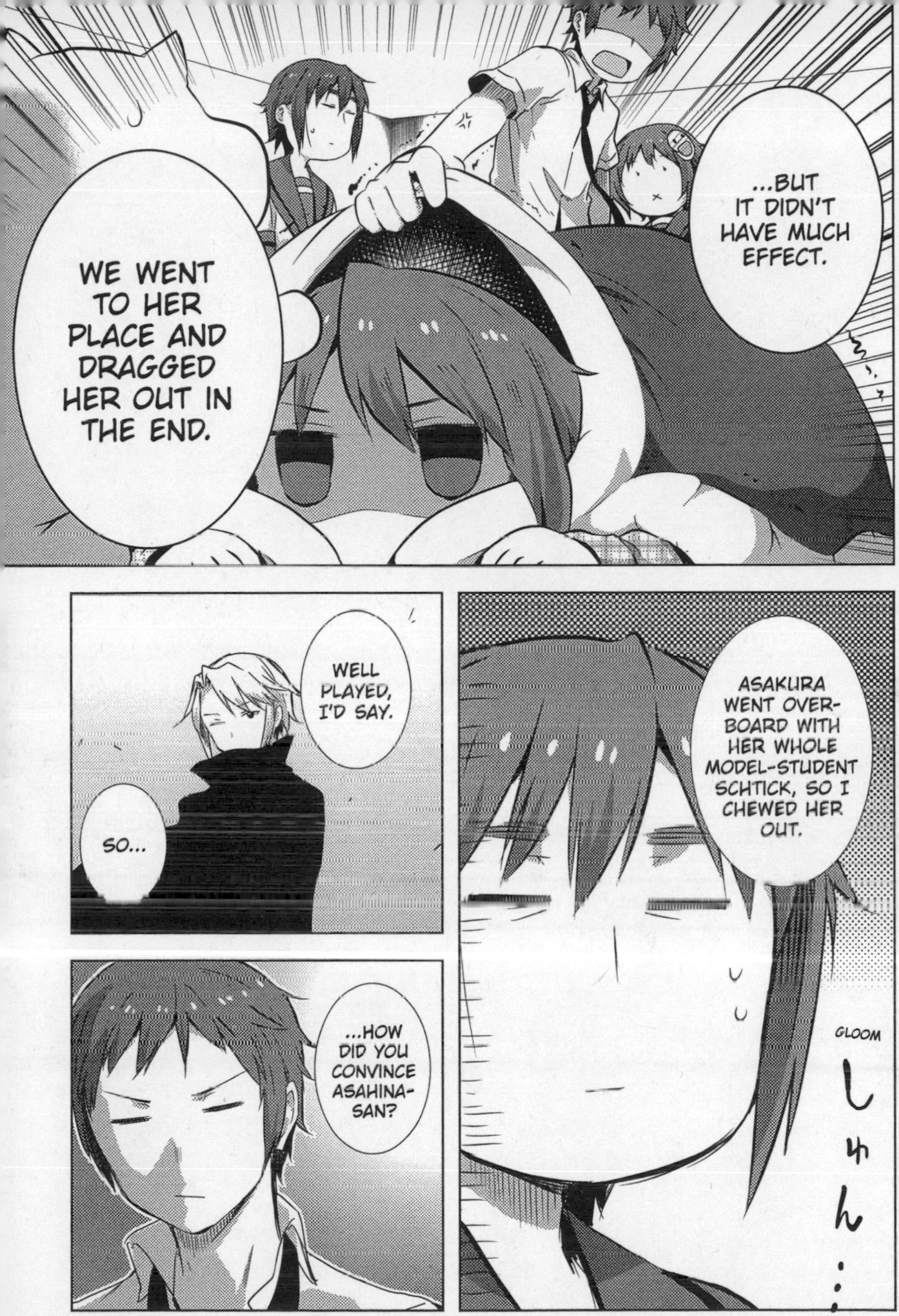
...BUT IT DIDN'T HAVE MUCH EFFECT.
WE WENT TO HER PLACE AND DRAGGED HER OUT IN THE END.
ASAKURA WENT OVER-BOARD WITH HER WHOLE MODEL-STUDENT SCHTICK, SO I CHEWED HER OUT.
GLOOM
しゅん…
WELL PLAYED, I'D SAY.
SO...
...HOW DID YOU CONVINCE ASAHINA-SAN?

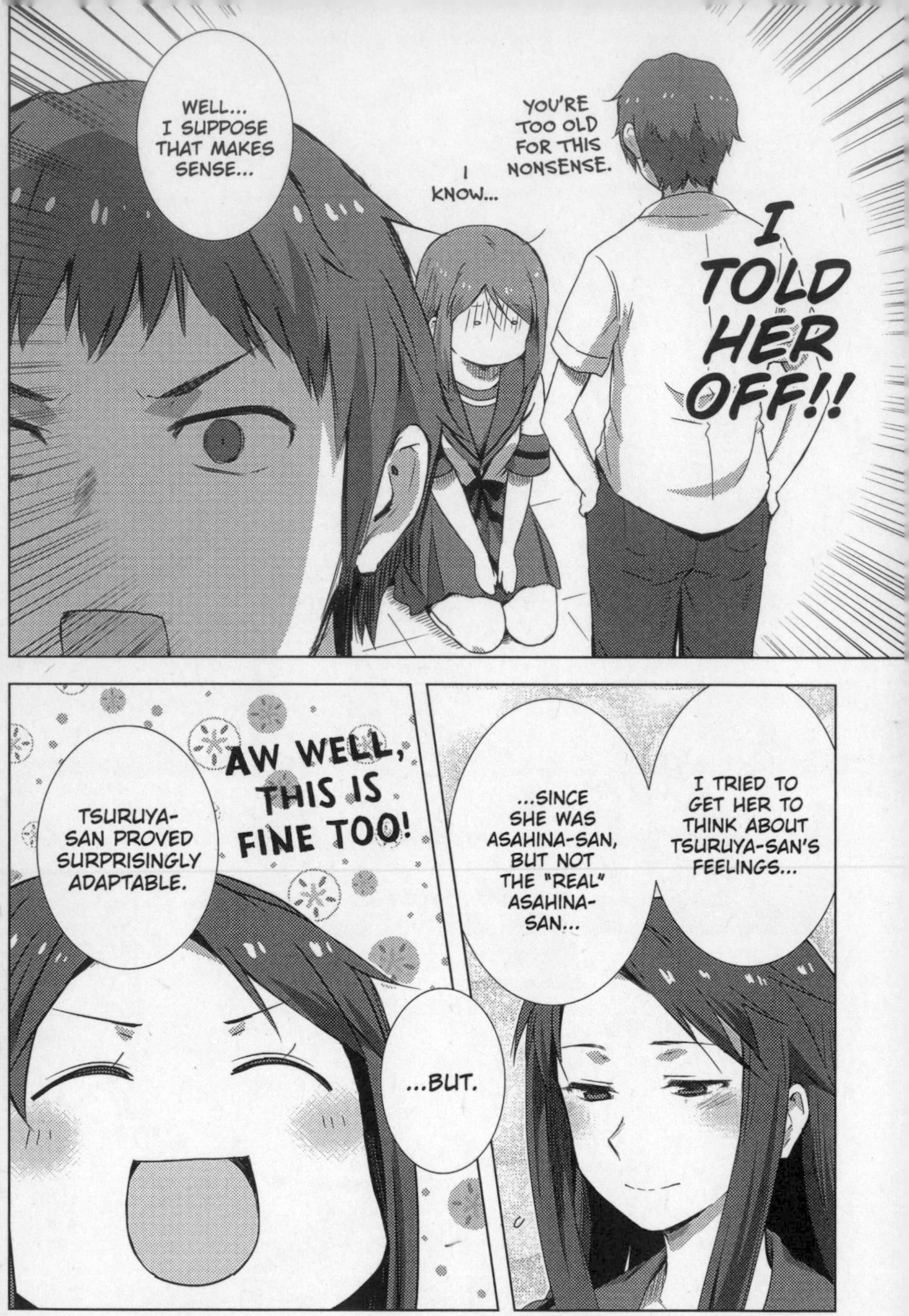
YOU'RE TOO OLD FOR THIS NONSENSE.
I KNOW...
I TOLD HER OFF!!
WELL... I SUPPOSE THAT MAKES SENSE...
I TRIED TO GET HER TO THINK ABOUT TSURUYA-SAN'S FEELINGS...
...SINCE SHE WAS ASAHINA-SAN, BUT NOT THE "REAL" ASAHINA-SAN...
AW WELL, THIS IS FINE TOO!
TSURUYA-SAN PROVED SURPRISINGLY ADAPTABLE.
...BUT.

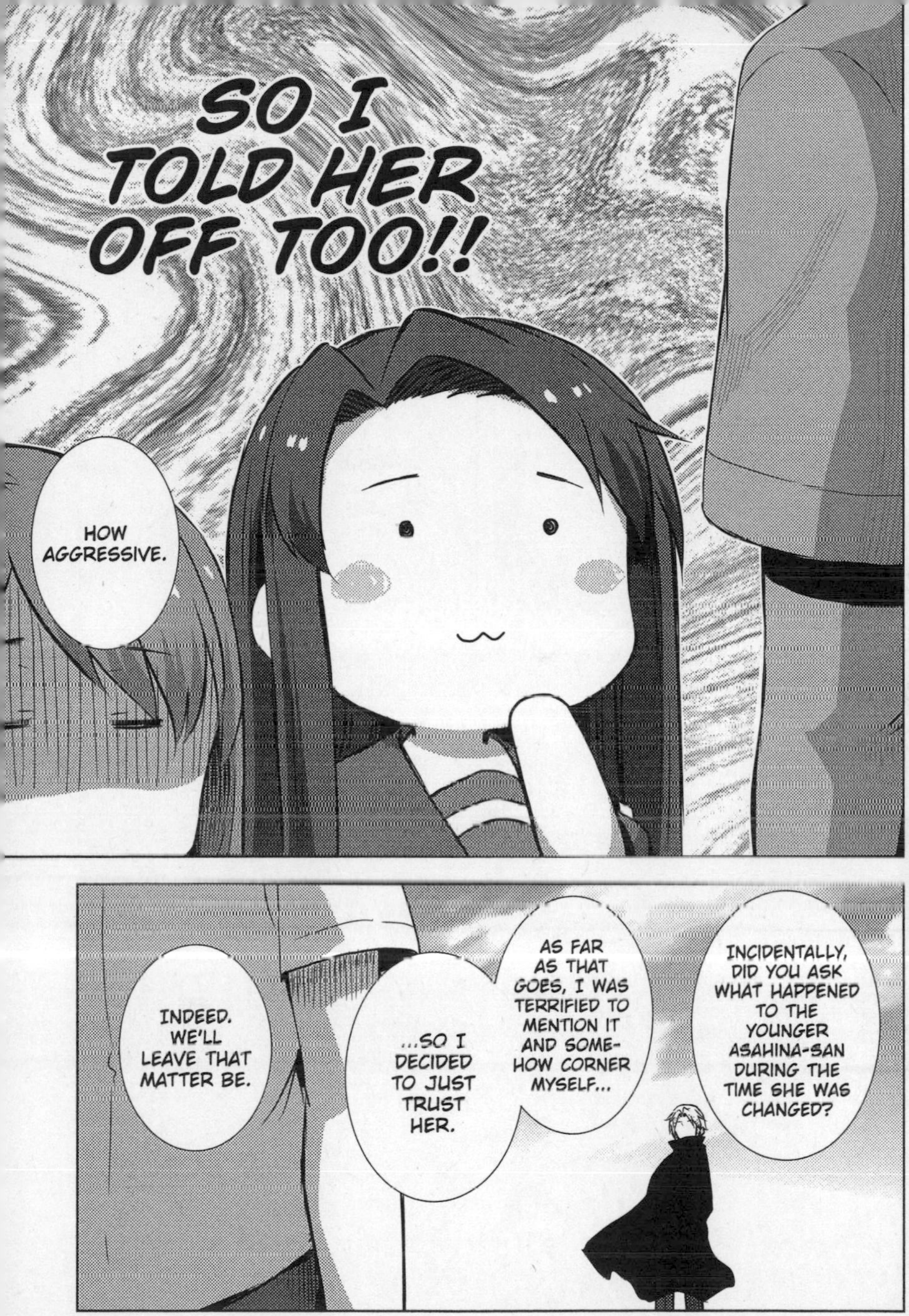
SO I TOLD HER OFF TOO!!
HOW AGGRESSIVE.
INCIDENTALLY, DID YOU ASK WHAT HAPPENED TO THE YOUNGER ASAHINA-SAN DURING THE TIME SHE WAS CHANGED?
AS FAR AS THAT GOES, I WAS TERRIFIED TO MENTION IT AND SOMEHOW CORNER MYSELF...
...SO I DECIDED TO JUST TRUST HER.
INDEED. WE'LL LEAVE THAT MATTER BE.

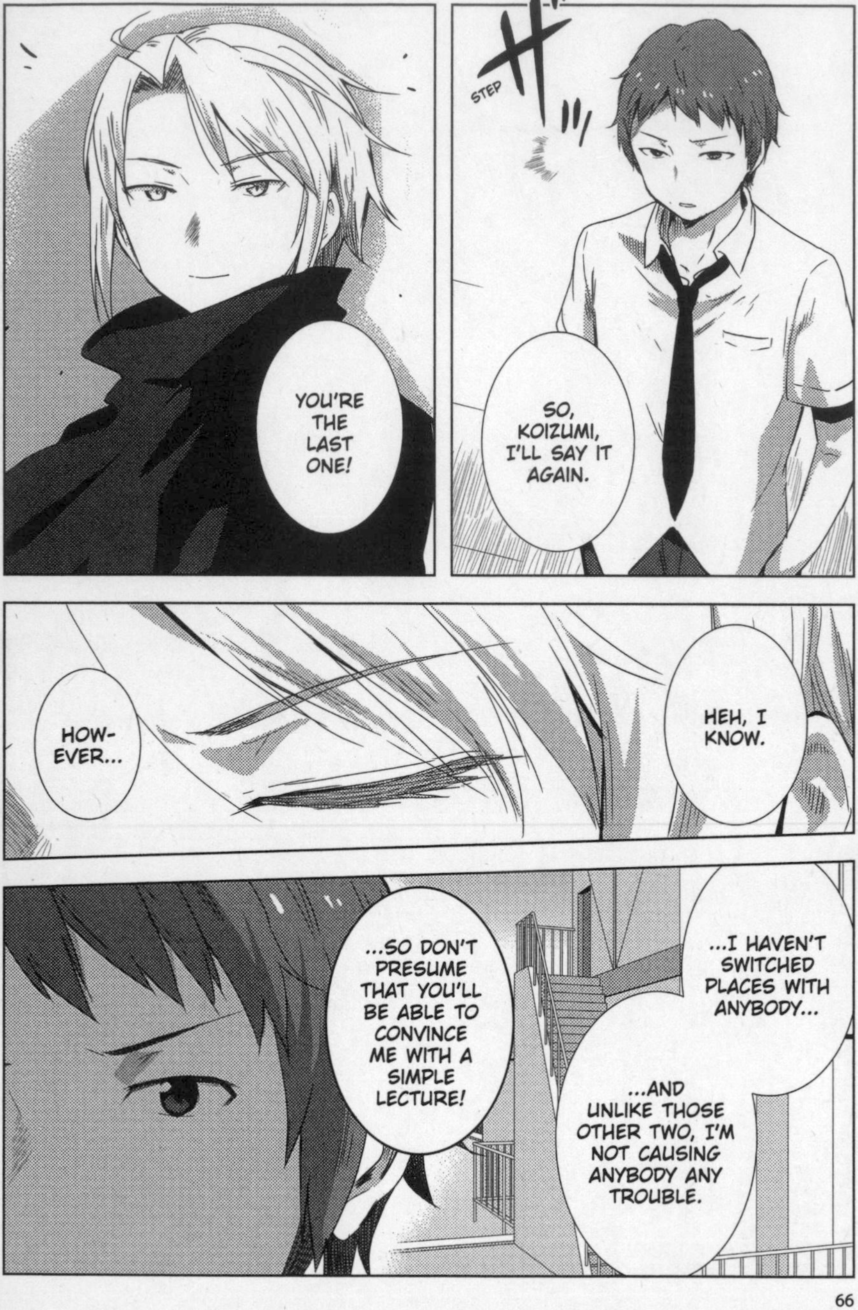
STEP
SO, KOIZUMI, I'LL SAY IT AGAIN.
YOU'RE THE LAST ONE!
HEH, I KNOW.
HOW-EVER...
...I HAVEN'T SWITCHED PLACES WITH ANYBODY...
...AND UNLIKE THOSE OTHER TWO, I'M NOT CAUSING ANYBODY ANY TROUBLE.
...SO DON'T PRESUME THAT YOU'LL BE ABLE TO CONVINCE ME WITH A SIMPLE LECTURE!

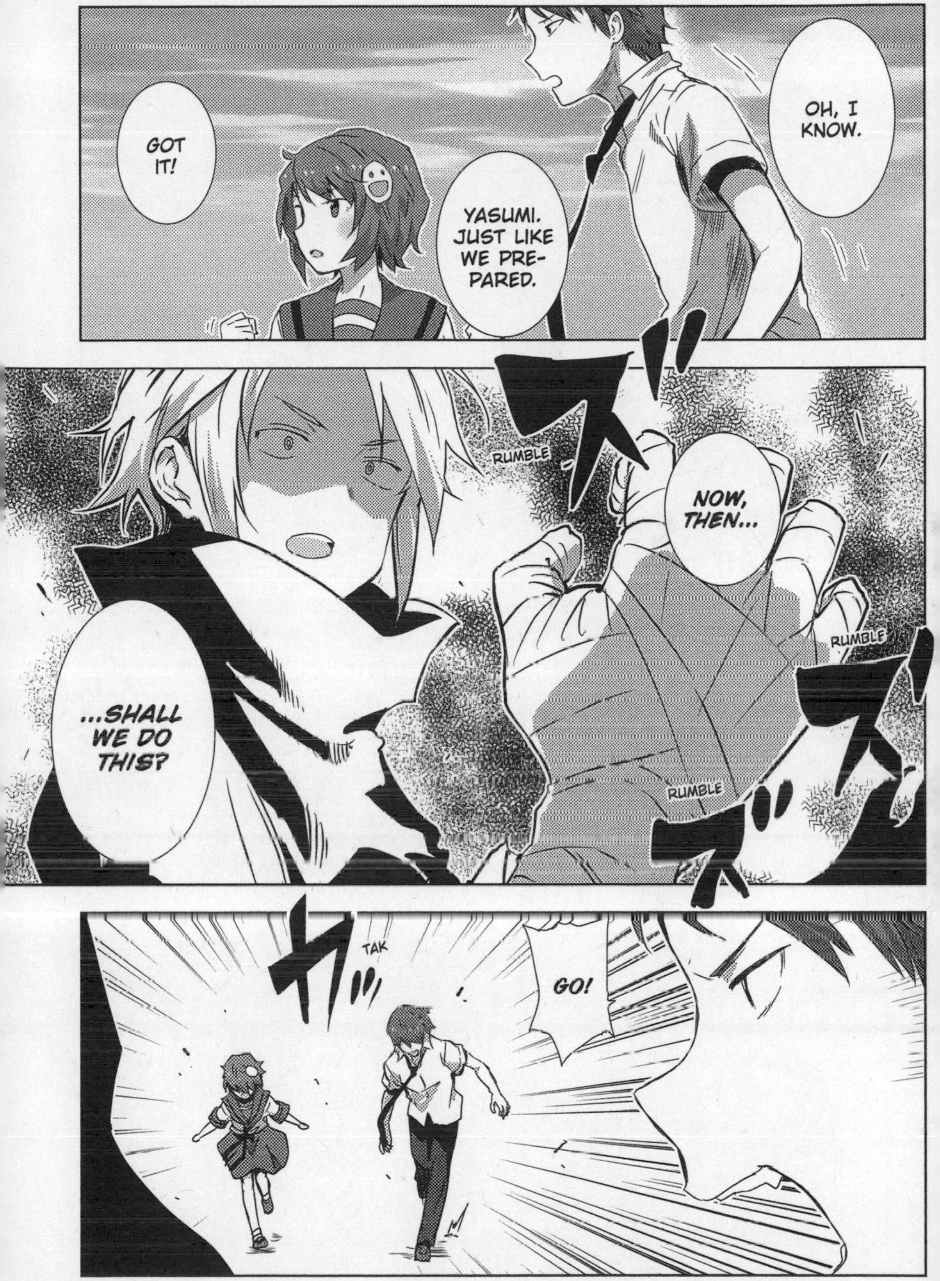
OH, I KNOW.
YASUMI. JUST LIKE WE PRE-PARED.
GOT IT!
RUMBLE
NOW, THEN...
RUMBLE
RUMBLE
...SHALL WE DO THIS?
GO!
TAK

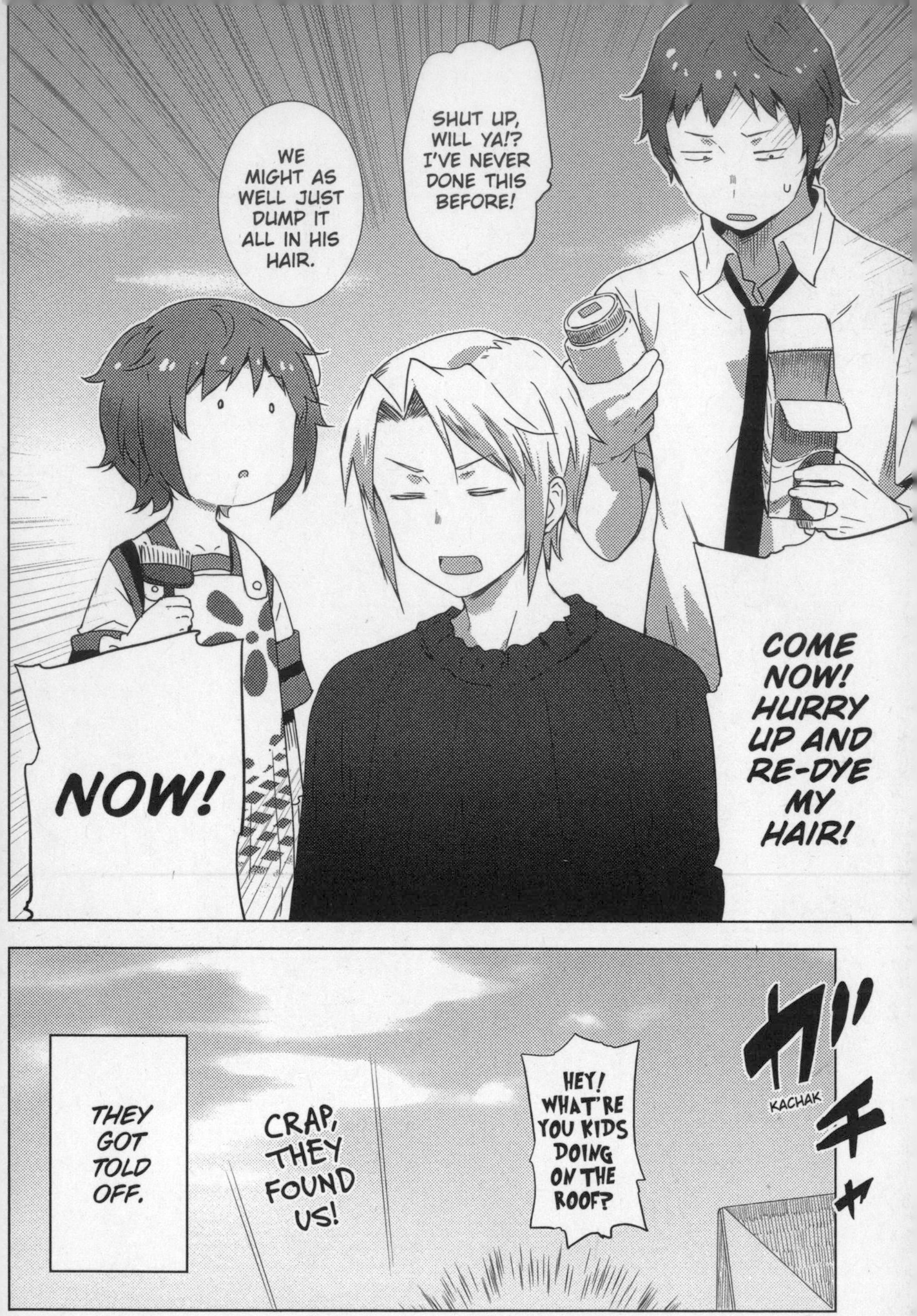

SHUT UP, WILL YA!? I'VE NEVER DONE THIS BEFORE!
WE MIGHT AS WELL JUST DUMP IT ALL IN HIS HAIR.
COME NOW! HURRY UP AND RE-DYE MY HAIR!
NOW!
ガチャ
KACHAK
HEY! WHAT'RE YOU KIDS DOING ON THE ROOF?
CRAP, THEY FOUND US!
THEY GOT TOLD OFF.

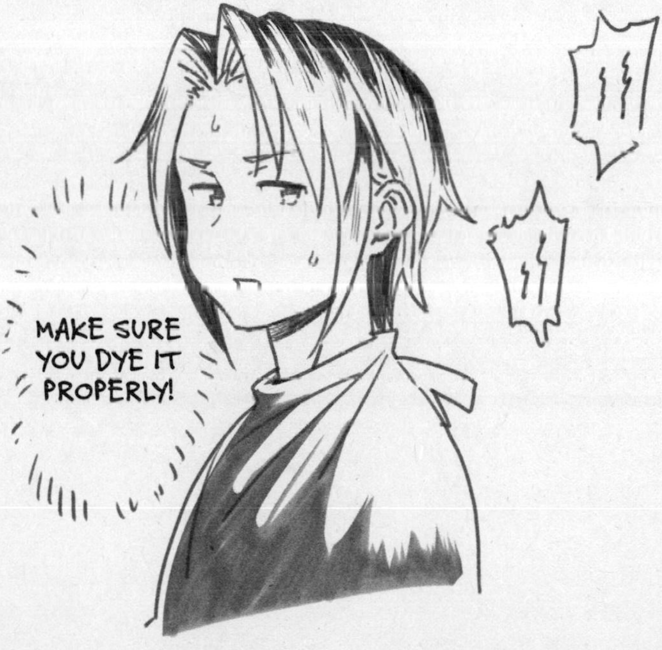
MAKE SURE YOU DYE IT PROPERLY!

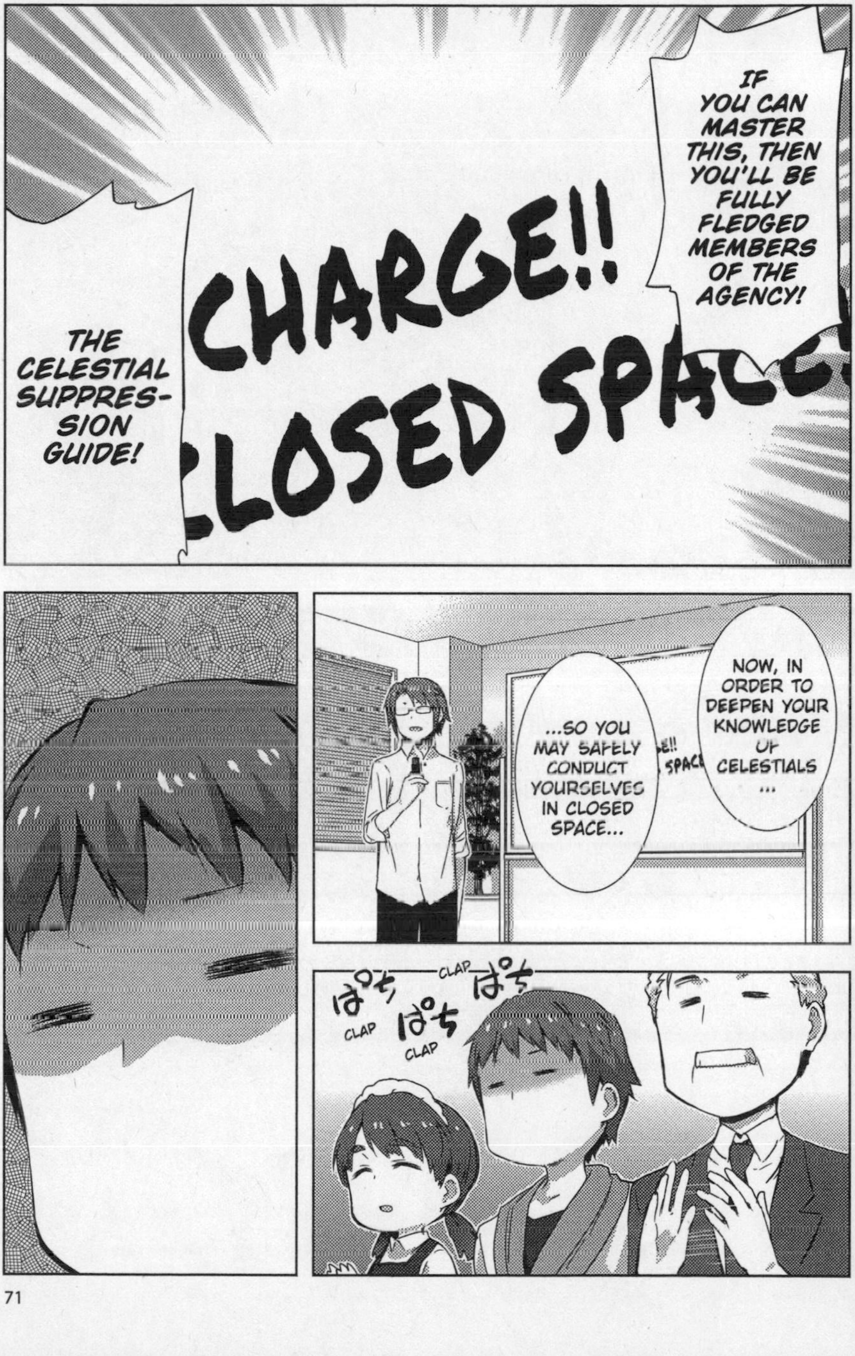
IF YOU CAN MASTER THIS, THEN YOU'LL BE FULLY FLEDGED MEMBERS OF THE AGENCY!
CHARGE!!
CLOSED SPAC
THE CELESTIAL SUPPRES-SION GUIDE!
NOW, IN ORDER TO DEEPEN YOUR KNOWLEDGE OF CELESTIALS ...
...SO YOU MAY SAFELY CONDUCT YOURSELVES IN CLOSED SPACE...
ぱち CLAP
ぱち CLAP
ぱち CLAP

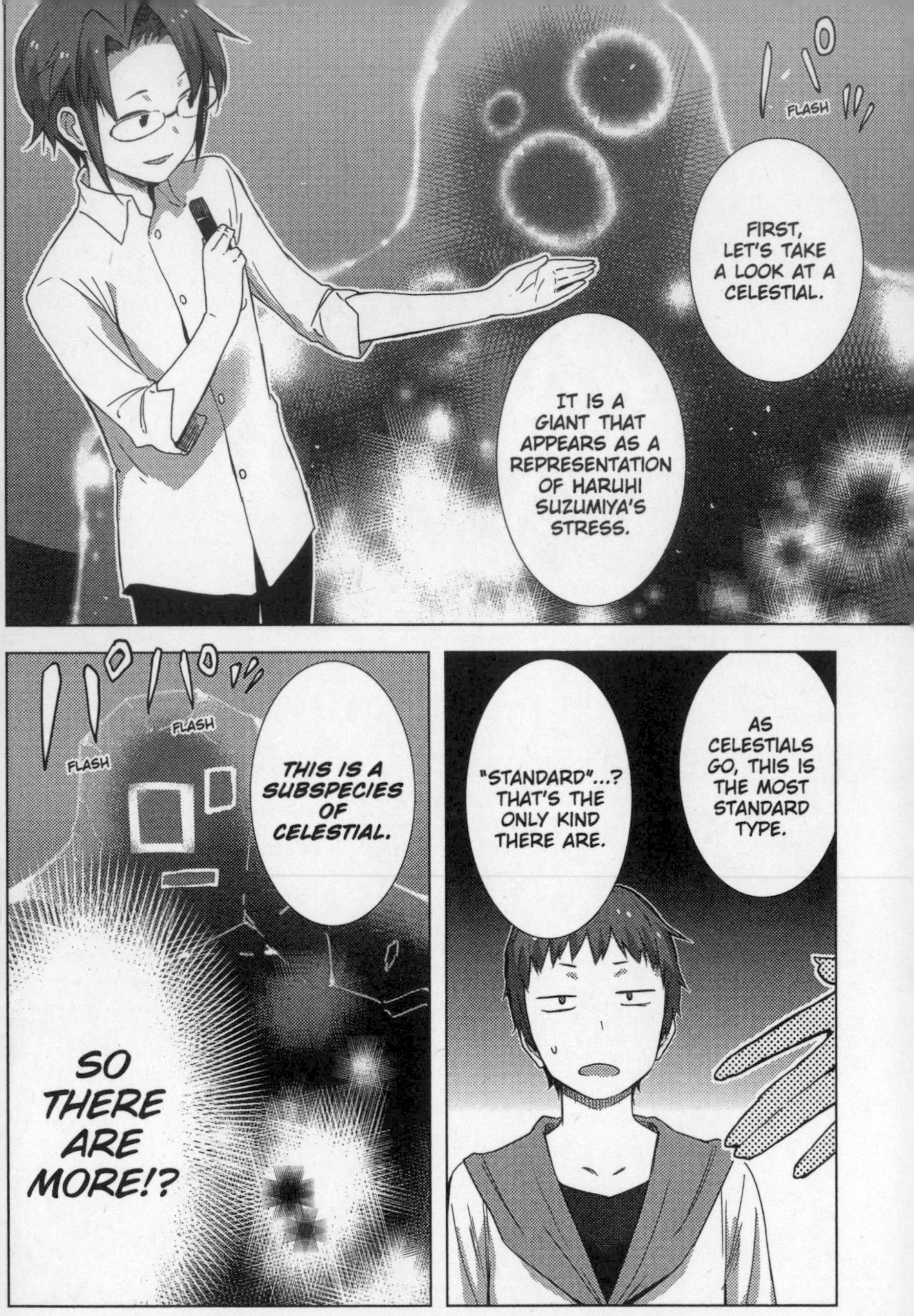
FLASH
FIRST, LET'S TAKE A LOOK AT A CELESTIAL.
IT IS A GIANT THAT APPEARS AS A REPRESENTATION OF HARUHI SUZUMIYA'S STRESS.
AS CELESTIALS GO, THIS IS THE MOST STANDARD TYPE.
"STANDARD"...? THAT'S THE ONLY KIND THERE ARE.
FLASH
FLASH
THIS IS A SUBSPECIES OF CELESTIAL.
SO THERE ARE MORE!?

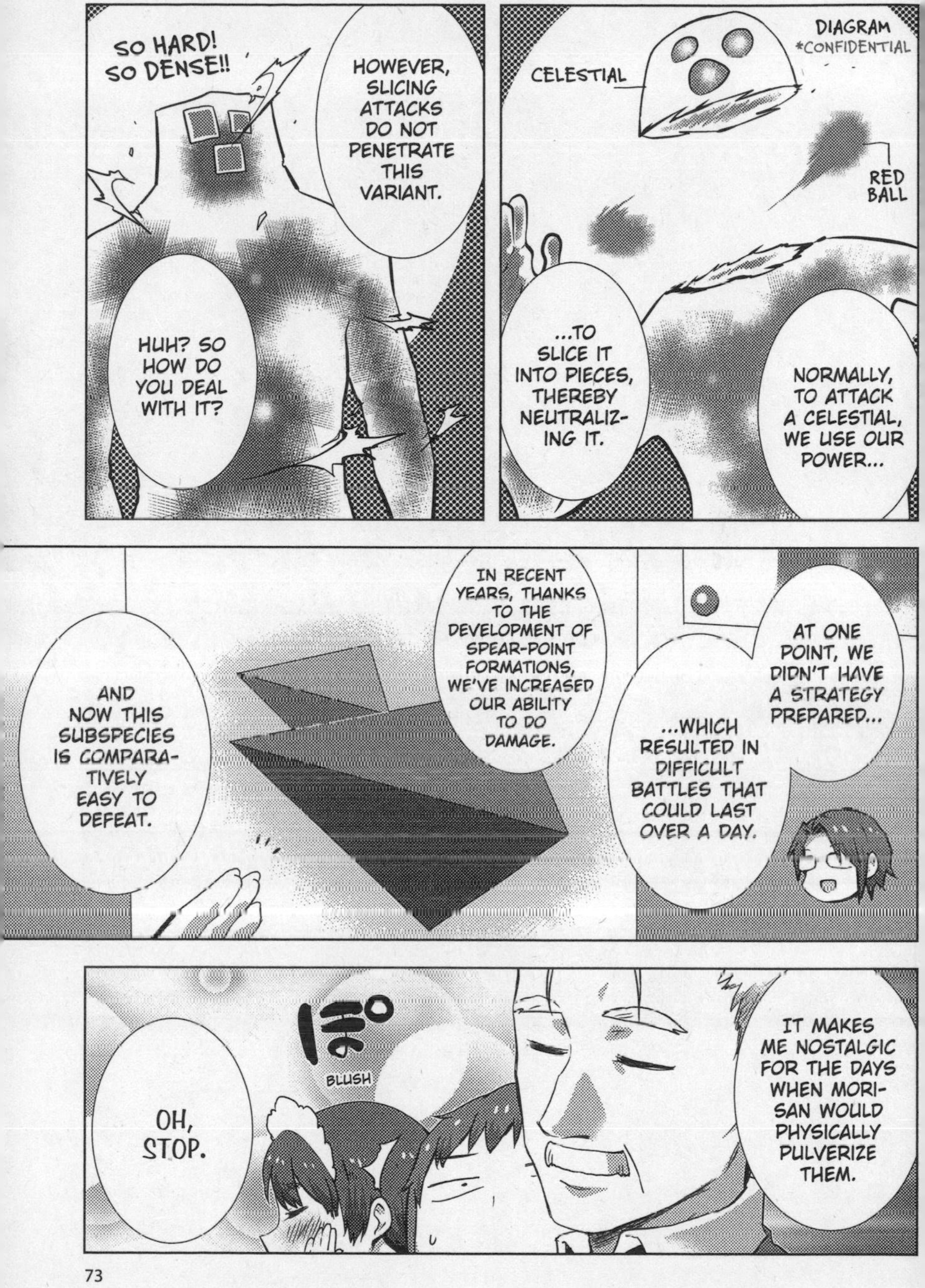
DIAGRAM
*CONFIDENTIAL
CELESTIAL
RED BALL
NORMALLY, TO ATTACK A CELESTIAL, WE USE OUR POWER...
...TO SLICE IT INTO PIECES, THEREBY NEUTRALIZING IT.
HOWEVER, SLICING ATTACKS DO NOT PENETRATE THIS VARIANT.
SO HARD! SO DENSE!!
HUH? SO HOW DO YOU DEAL WITH IT?
AT ONE POINT, WE DIDN'T HAVE A STRATEGY PREPARED...
...WHICH RESULTED IN DIFFICULT BATTLES THAT COULD LAST OVER A DAY.
IN RECENT YEARS, THANKS TO THE DEVELOPMENT OF SPEAR-POINT FORMATIONS, WE'VE INCREASED OUR ABILITY TO DO DAMAGE.
AND NOW THIS SUBSPECIES IS COMPARATIVELY EASY TO DEFEAT.
IT MAKES ME NOSTALGIC FOR THE DAYS WHEN MORI-SAN WOULD PHYSICALLY PULVERIZE THEM.
BLUSH
OH, STOP.

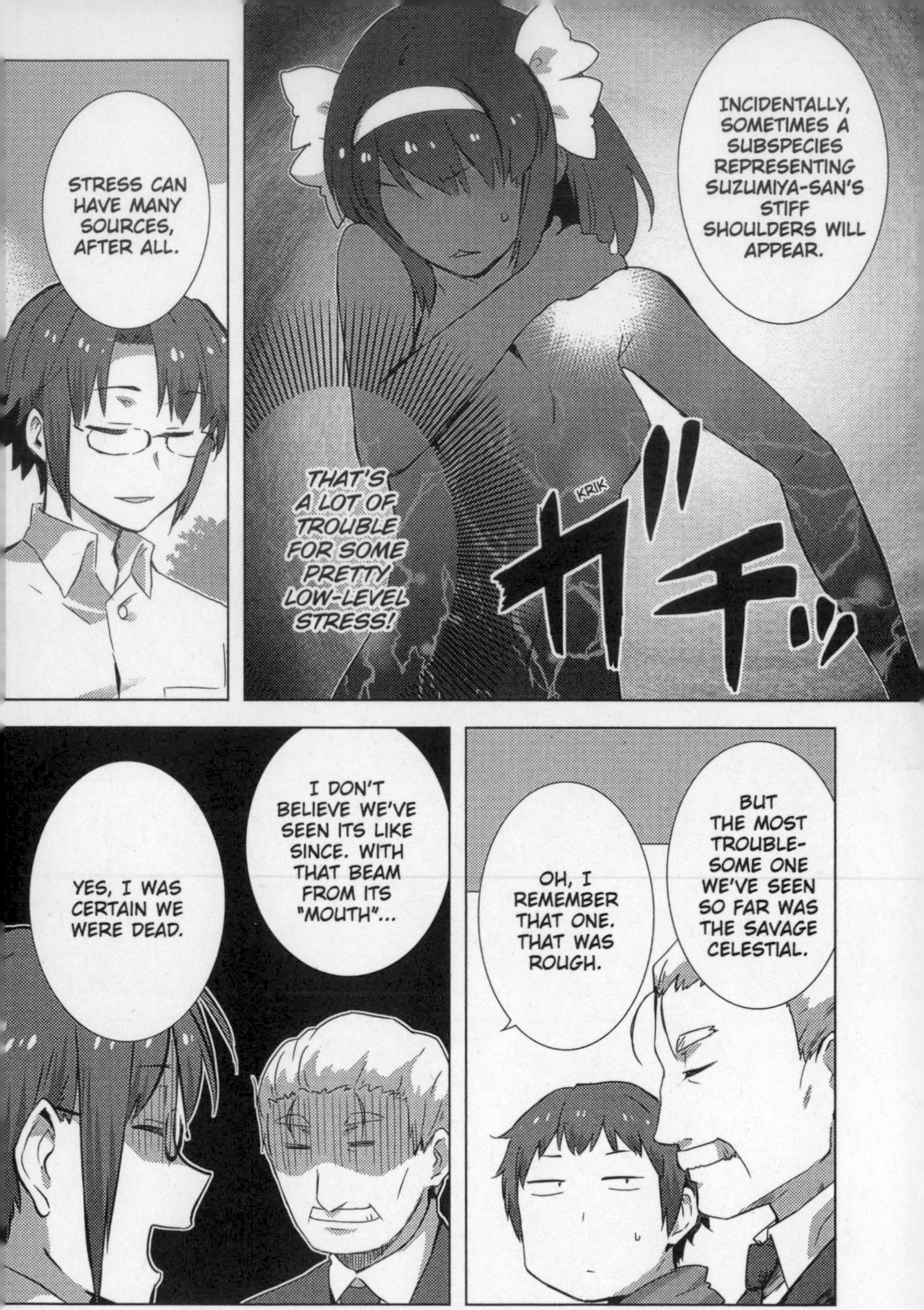
INCIDENTALLY, SOMETIMES A SUBSPECIES REPRESENTING SUZUMIYA-SAN'S STIFF SHOULDERS WILL APPEAR.
THAT'S A LOT OF TROUBLE FOR SOME PRETTY LOW-LEVEL STRESS!
ガチッ
KRIK
STRESS CAN HAVE MANY SOURCES, AFTER ALL.
BUT THE MOST TROUBLE-SOME ONE WE'VE SEEN SO FAR WAS THE SAVAGE CELESTIAL.
OH, I REMEMBER THAT ONE. THAT WAS ROUGH.
I DON'T BELIEVE WE'VE SEEN ITS LIKE SINCE. WITH THAT BEAM FROM ITS "MOUTH"...
YES, I WAS CERTAIN WE WERE DEAD.

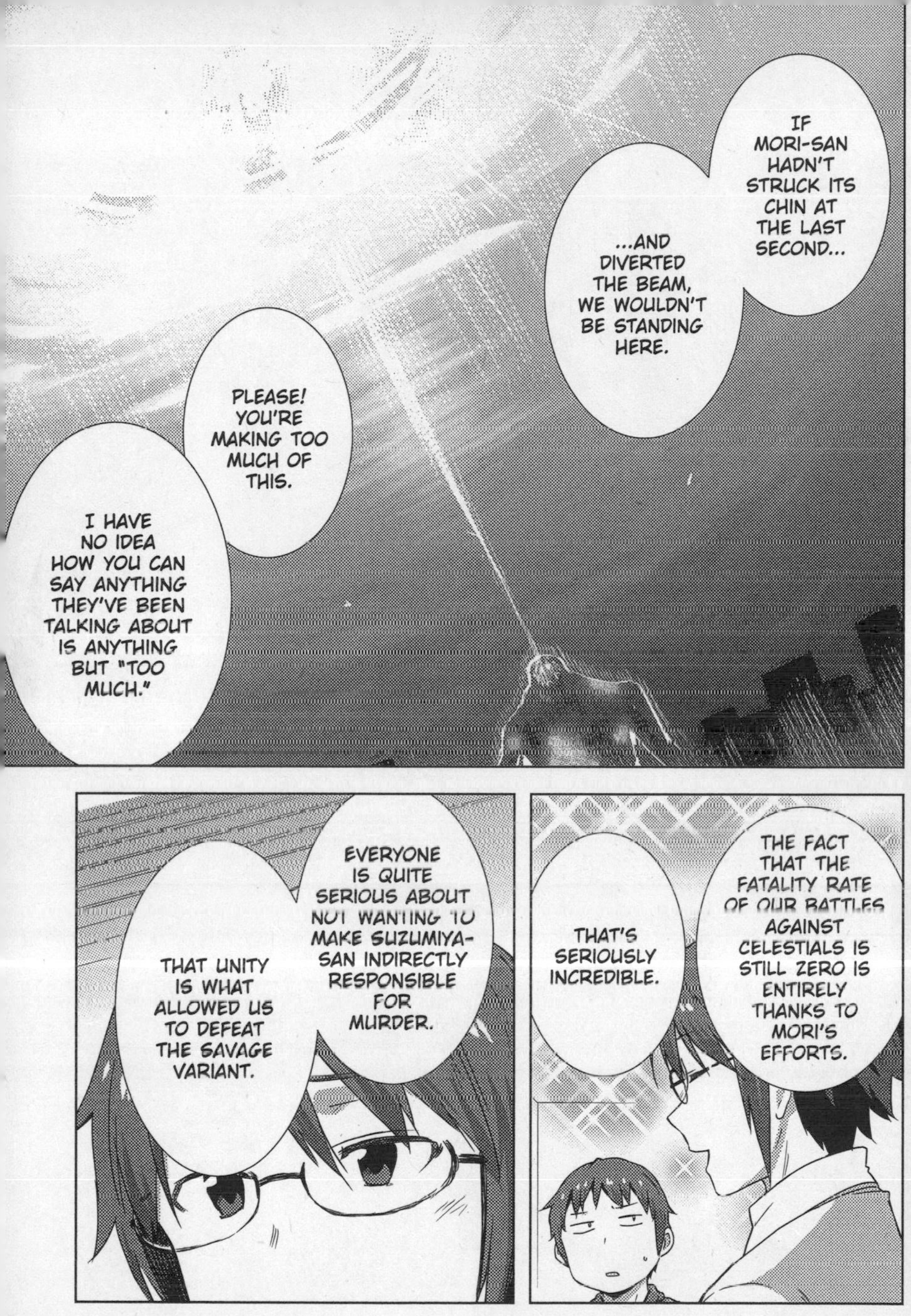
IF MORI-SAN HADN'T STRUCK ITS CHIN AT THE LAST SECOND...
...AND DIVERTED THE BEAM, WE WOULDN'T BE STANDING HERE.
PLEASE! YOU'RE MAKING TOO MUCH OF THIS.
I HAVE NO IDEA HOW YOU CAN SAY ANYTHING THEY'VE BEEN TALKING ABOUT IS ANYTHING BUT "TOO MUCH."
THE FACT THAT THE FATALITY RATE OF OUR BATTLES AGAINST CELESTIALS IS STILL ZERO IS ENTIRELY THANKS TO MORI'S EFFORTS.
THAT'S SERIOUSLY INCREDIBLE.
EVERYONE IS QUITE SERIOUS ABOUT NOT WANTING TO MAKE SUZUMIYA-SAN INDIRECTLY RESPONSIBLE FOR MURDER.
THAT UNITY IS WHAT ALLOWED US TO DEFEAT THE SAVAGE VARIANT.

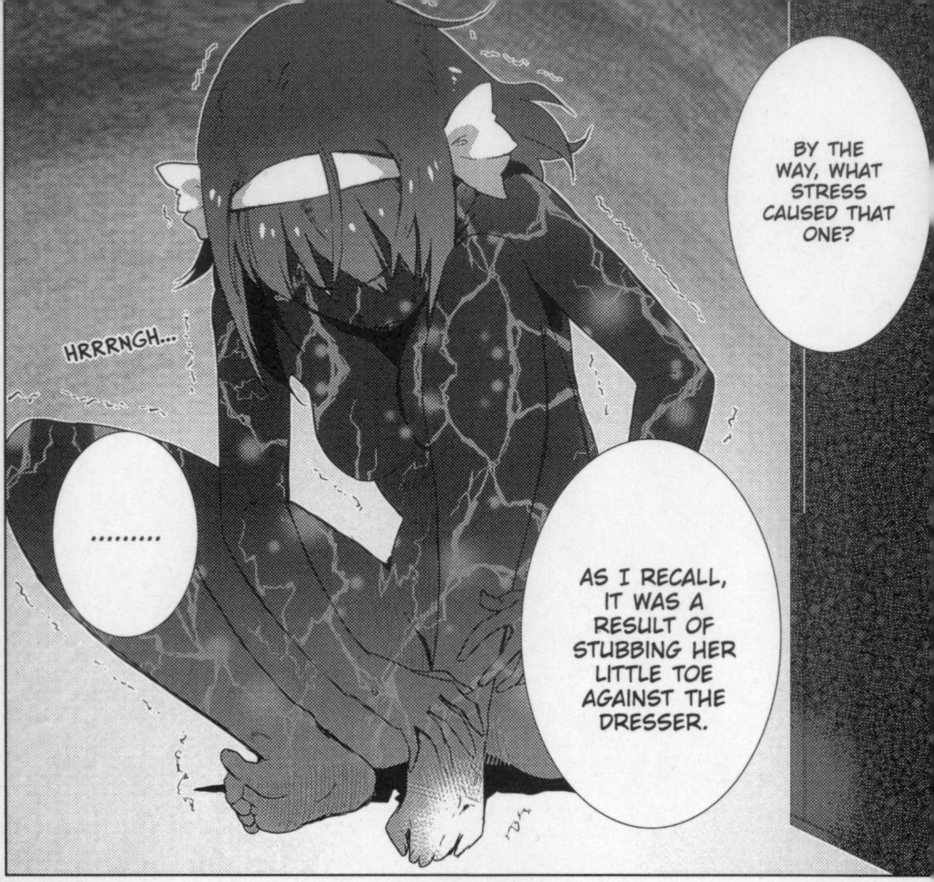
BY THE WAY, WHAT STRESS CAUSED THAT ONE?
HRRRNGH...
AS I RECALL, IT WAS A RESULT OF STUBBING HER LITTLE TOE AGAINST THE DRESSER.
....

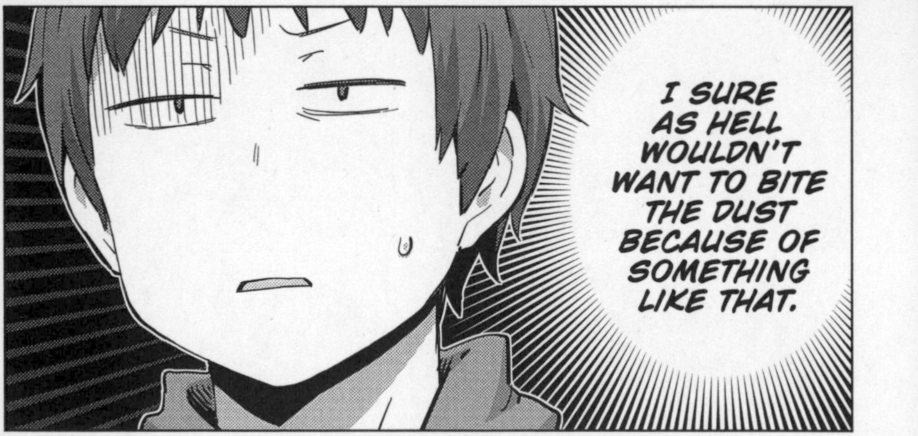
I SURE AS HELL WOULDN'T WANT TO BITE THE DUST BECAUSE OF SOMETHING LIKE THAT.

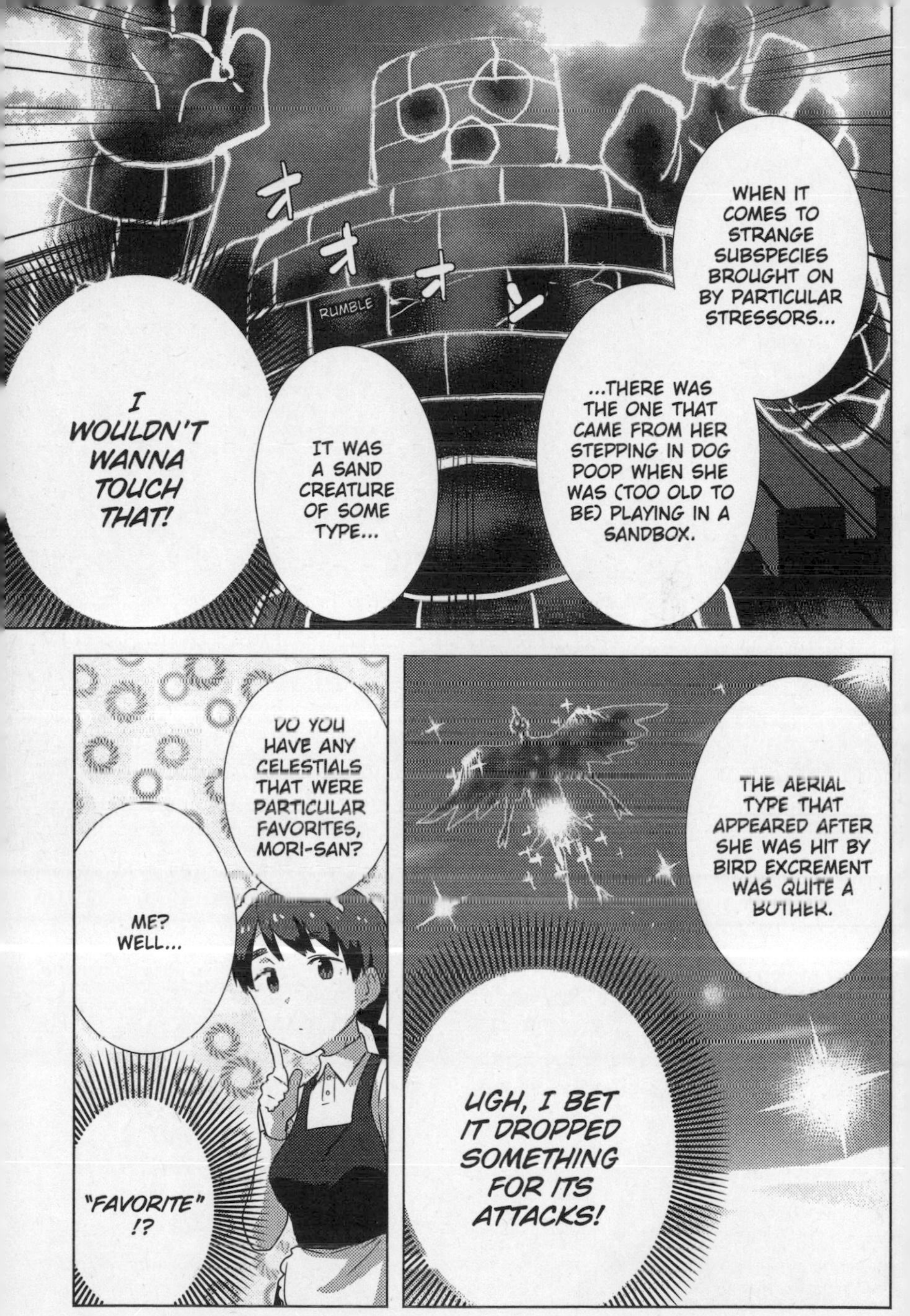
WHEN IT COMES TO STRANGE SUBSPECIES BROUGHT ON BY PARTICULAR STRESSORS...
オオオン
...THERE WAS THE ONE THAT CAME FROM HER STEPPING IN DOG POOP WHEN SHE WAS (TOO OLD TO BE) PLAYING IN A SANDBOX.
RUMBLE
IT WAS A SAND CREATURE OF SOME TYPE...
I WOULDN'T WANNA TOUCH THAT!
THE AERIAL TYPE THAT APPEARED AFTER SHE WAS HIT BY BIRD EXCREMENT WAS QUITE A BOTHER.
UGH, I BET IT DROPPED SOMETHING FOR ITS ATTACKS!
DO YOU HAVE ANY CELESTIALS THAT WERE PARTICULAR FAVORITES, MORI-SAN?
ME? WELL...
"FAVORITE" !?

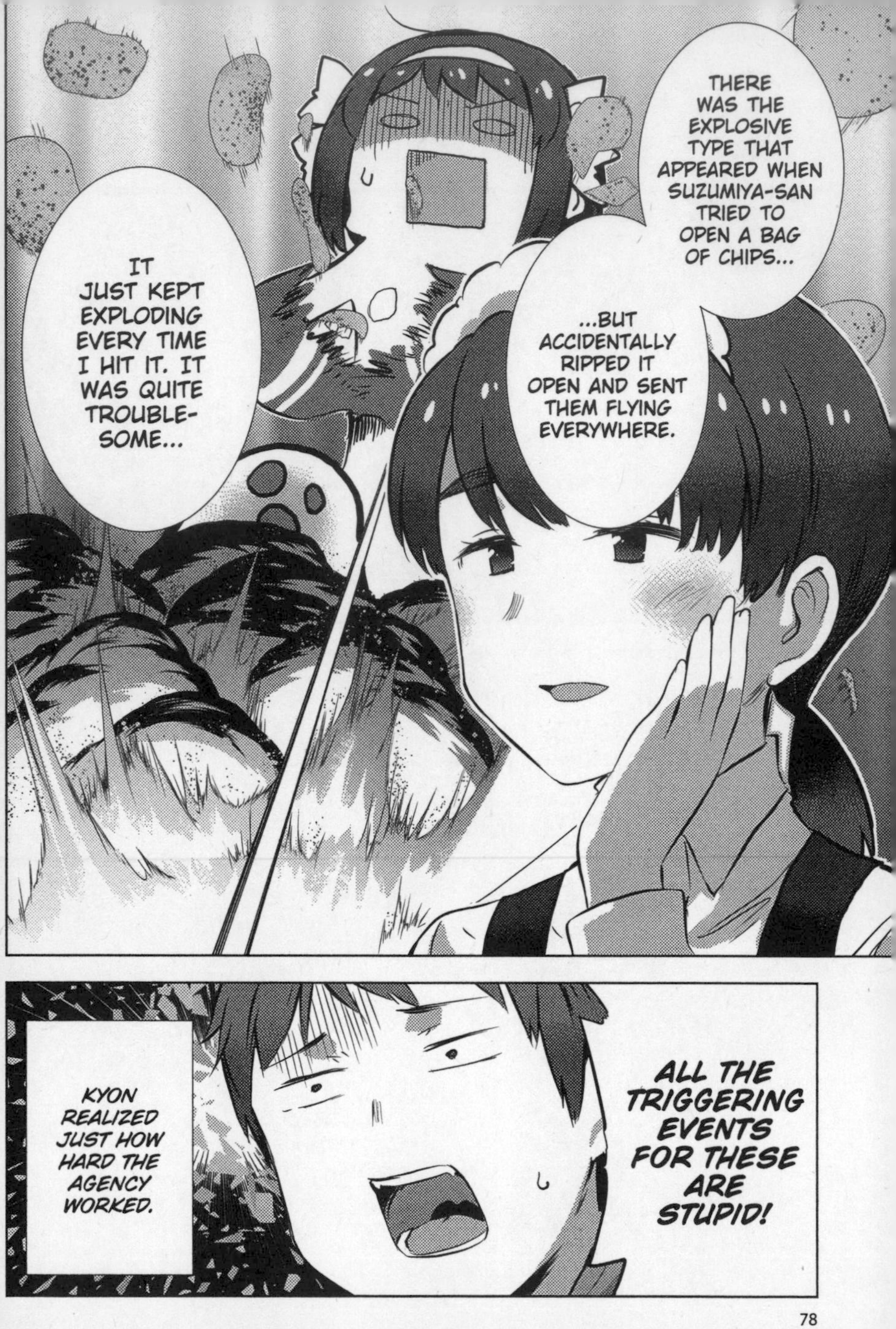
THERE WAS THE EXPLOSIVE TYPE THAT APPEARED WHEN SUZUMIYA-SAN TRIED TO OPEN A BAG OF CHIPS...
...BUT ACCIDENTALLY RIPPED IT OPEN AND SENT THEM FLYING EVERYWHERE.
IT JUST KEPT EXPLODING EVERY TIME I HIT IT. IT WAS QUITE TROUBLE-SOME...
ALL THE TRIGGERING EVENTS FOR THESE ARE STUPID!
KYON REALIZED JUST HOW HARD THE AGENCY WORKED.

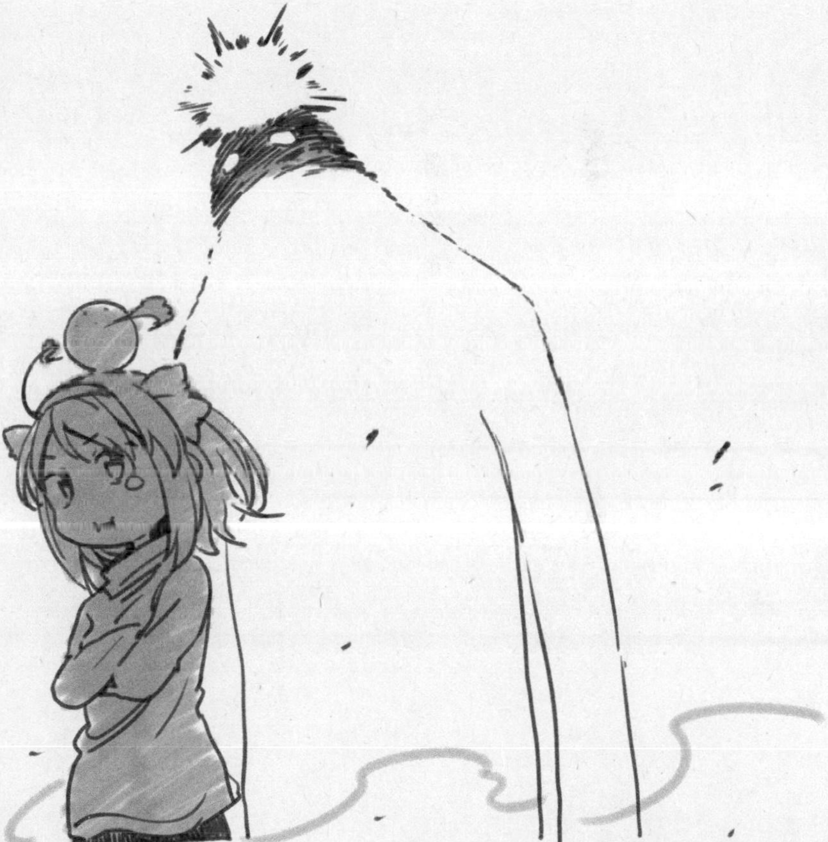

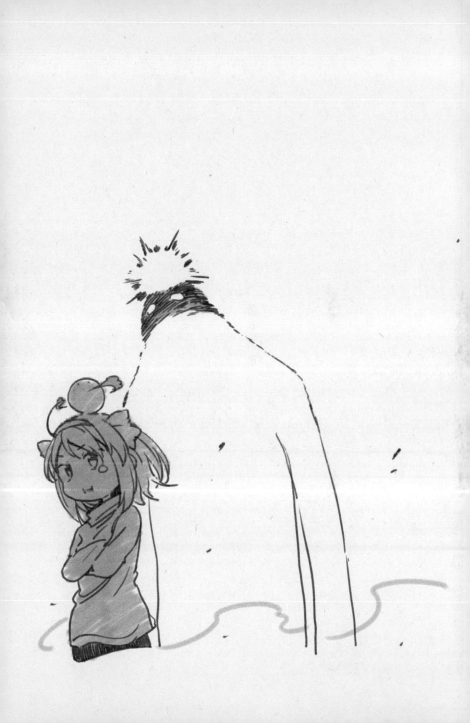

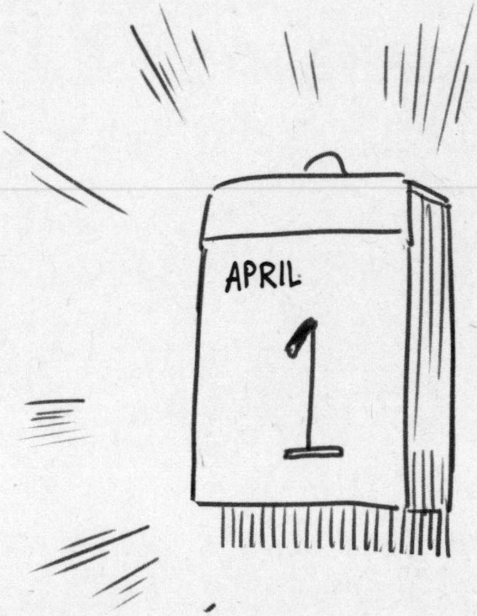
APRIL
1

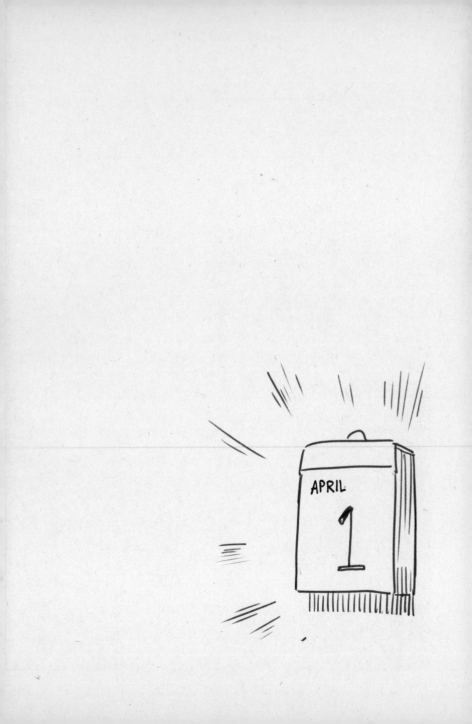

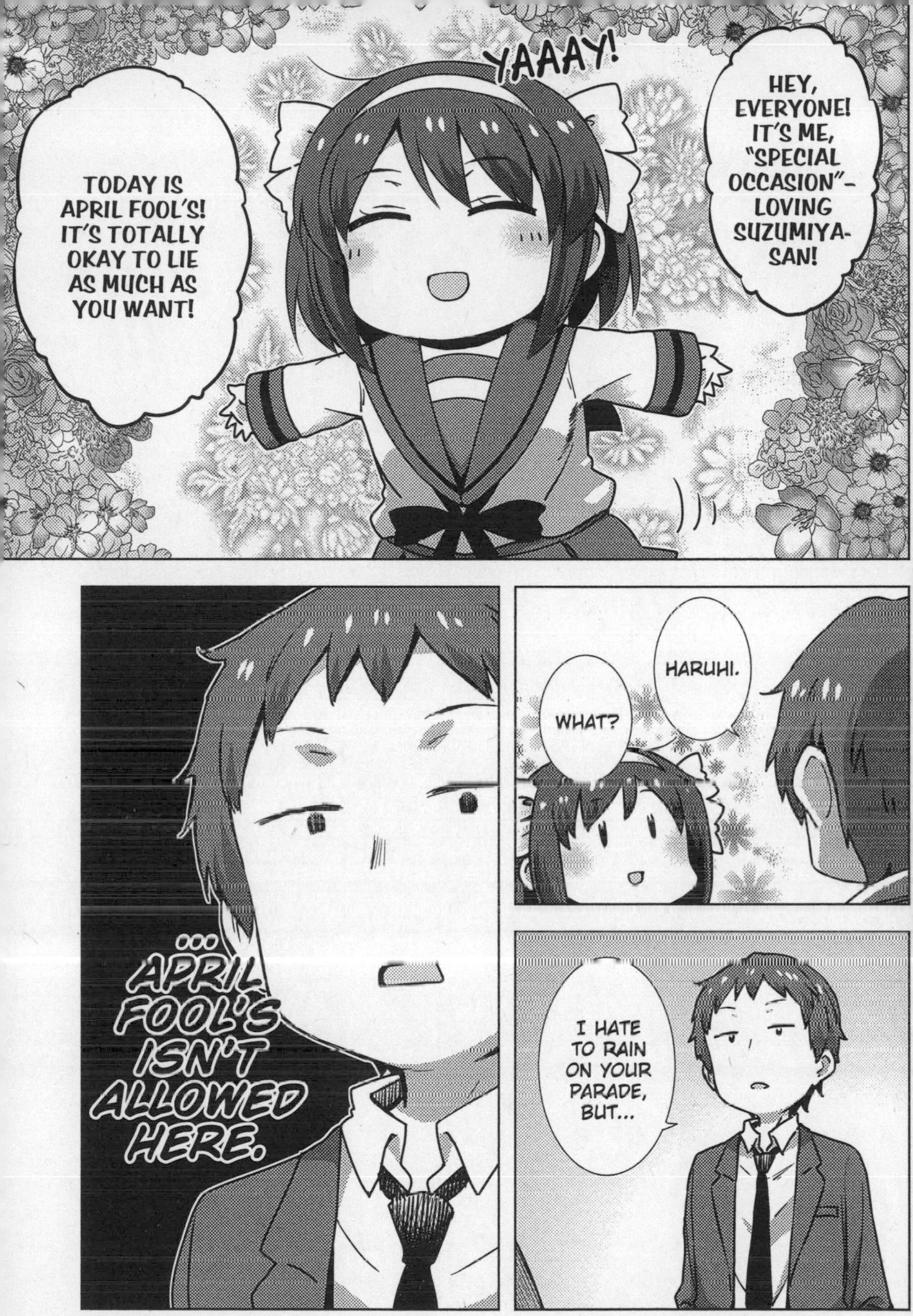
HEY, EVERYONE! IT'S ME, "SPECIAL OCCASION"-LOVING SUZUMIYA-SAN!
YAAAY!
TODAY IS APRIL FOOL'S! IT'S TOTALLY OKAY TO LIE AS MUCH AS YOU WANT!
HARUHI.
WHAT?
I HATE TO RAIN ON YOUR PARADE, BUT...
...APRIL FOOL'S ISN'T ALLOWED HERE.

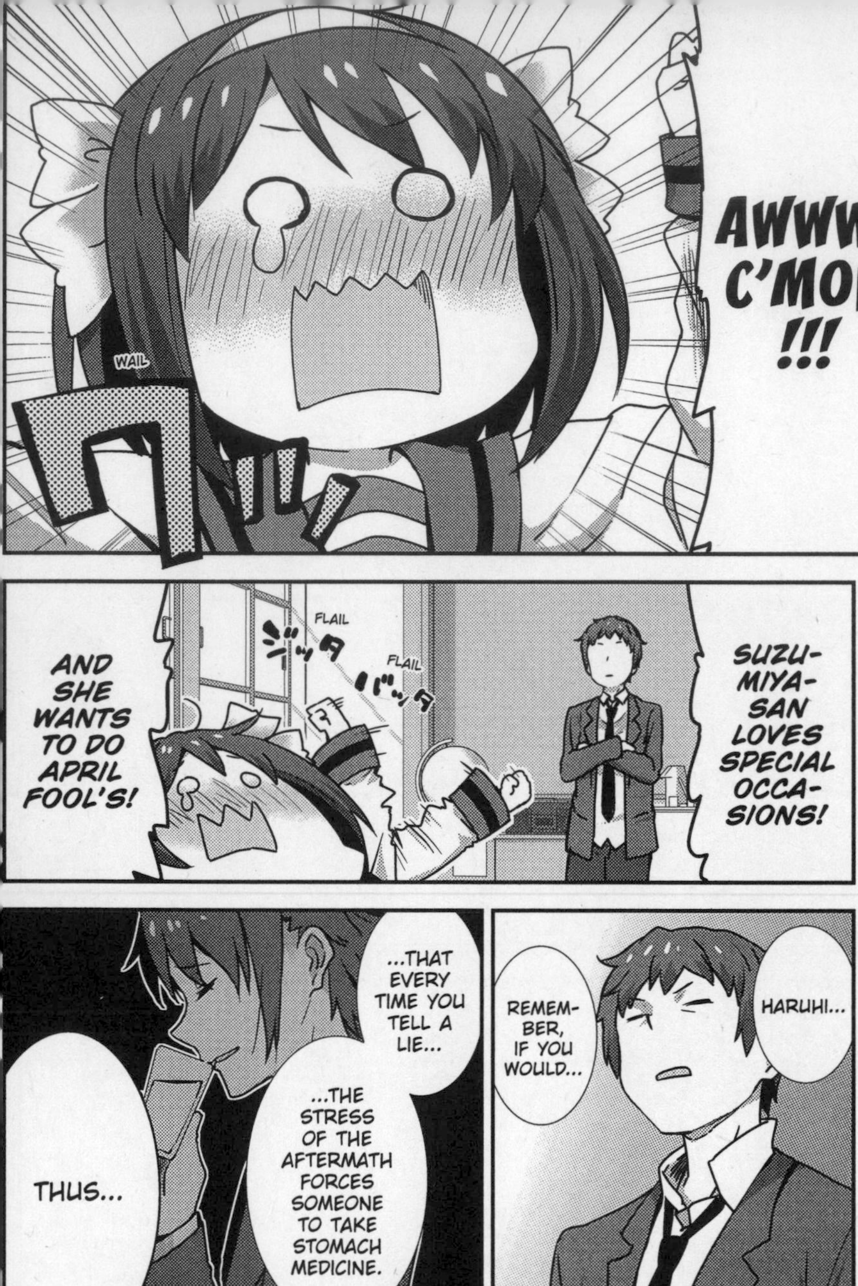
AWWW, C'MON!!!
WAIL
SUZU-MIYA-SAN LOVES SPECIAL OCCA-SIONS!
FLAIL
FLAIL
AND SHE WANTS TO DO APRIL FOOL'S!
HARUHI...
REMEM-BER, IF YOU WOULD...
...THAT EVERY TIME YOU TELL A LIE...
...THE STRESS OF THE AFTERMATH FORCES SOMEONE TO TAKE STOMACH MEDICINE.
THUS...

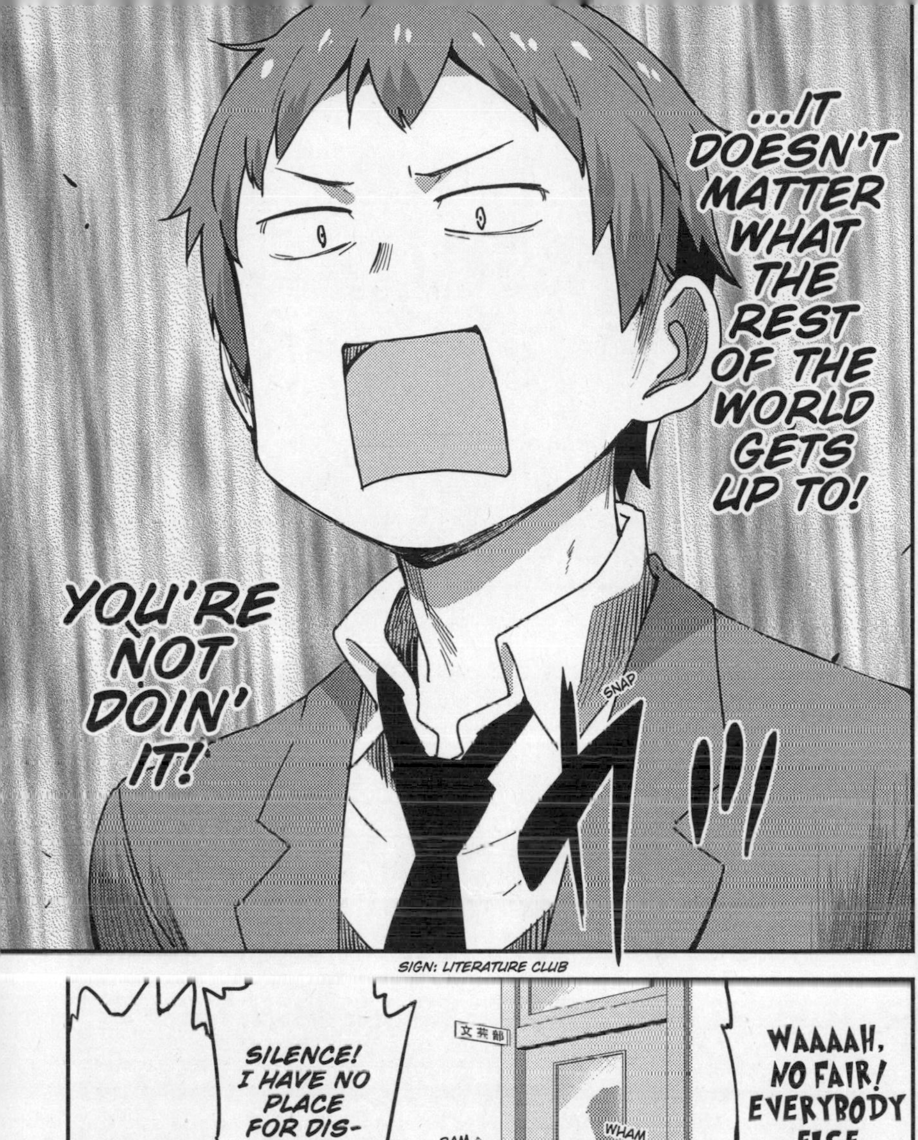
...IT DOESN'T MATTER WHAT THE REST OF THE WORLD GETS UP TO!
YOU'RE NOT DOIN' IT!
SNAP

SIGN: LITERATURE CLUB

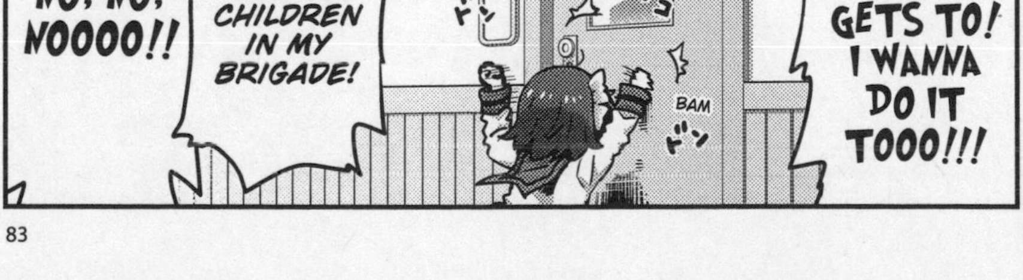
WAAAAH, NO FAIR! EVERYBODY ELSE GETS TO! I WANNA DO IT TOOO!!!
文芸部
WHAM
BAM
BAM
SILENCE! I HAVE NO PLACE FOR DIS-OBEDIENT CHILDREN IN MY BRIGADE!
NO, NO, NOOOO!!

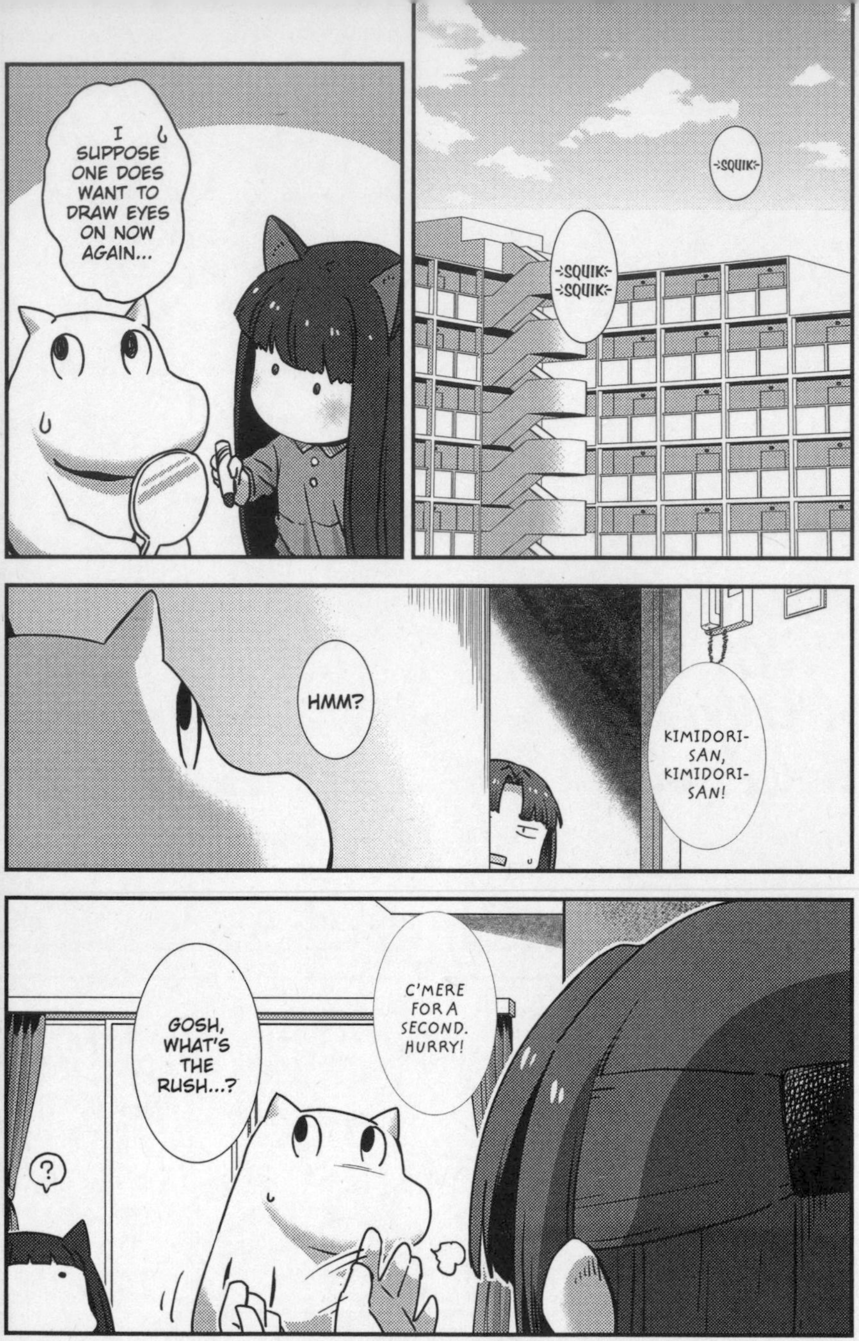

SQUIK
SQUIK SQUIK
I SUPPOSE ONE DOES WANT TO DRAW EYES ON NOW AGAIN...
KIMIDORI-SAN, KIMIDORI-SAN!
HMM?
C'MERE FOR A SECOND. HURRY!
GOSH, WHAT'S THE RUSH...?
?

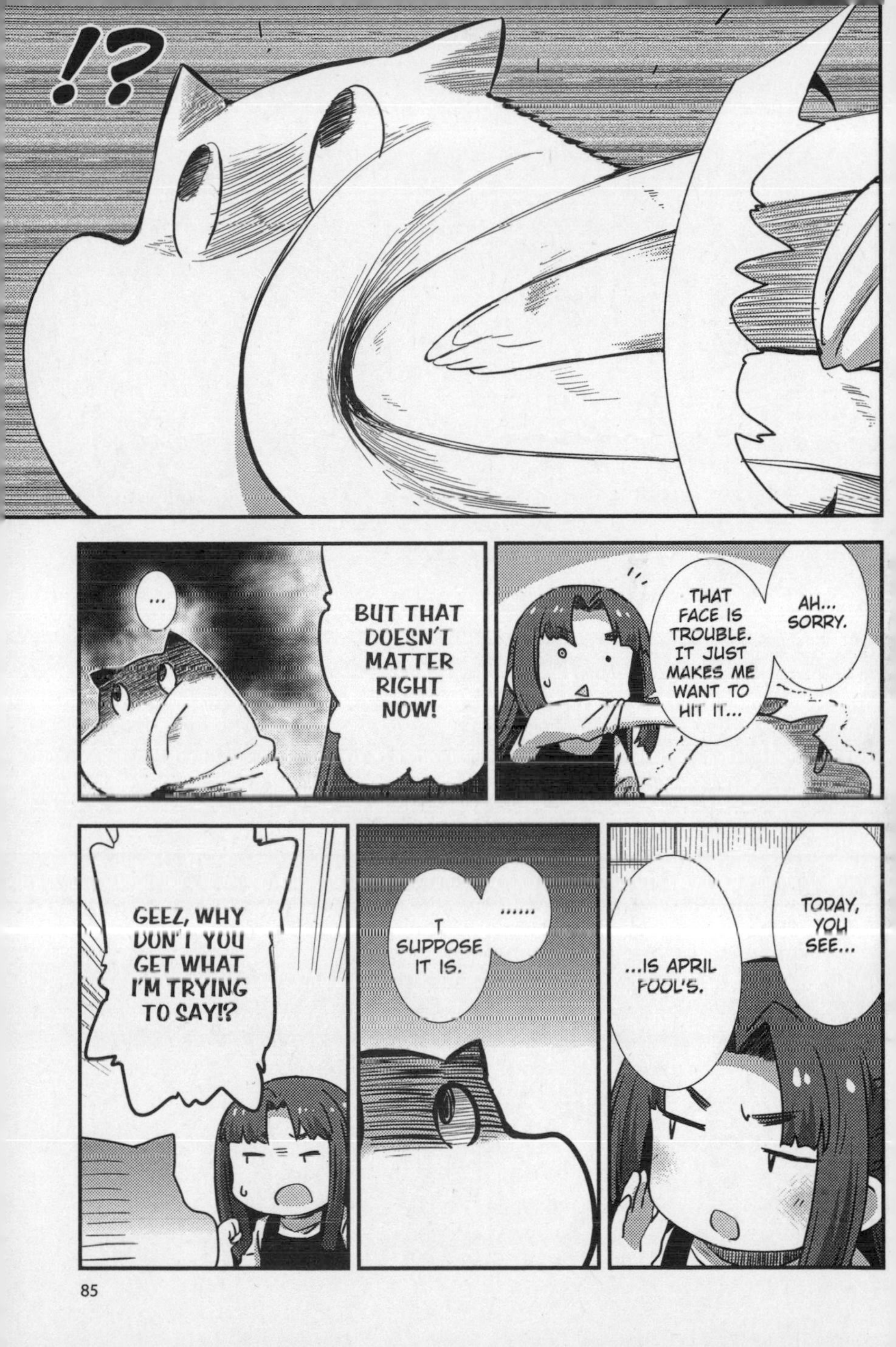
!?
AH... SORRY.
THAT FACE IS TROUBLE. IT JUST MAKES ME WANT TO HIT IT...
BUT THAT DOESN'T MATTER RIGHT NOW!
...
TODAY, YOU SEE...
...IS APRIL FOOL'S.
......
I SUPPOSE IT IS.
GEEZ, WHY DON'T YOU GET WHAT I'M TRYING TO SAY!?

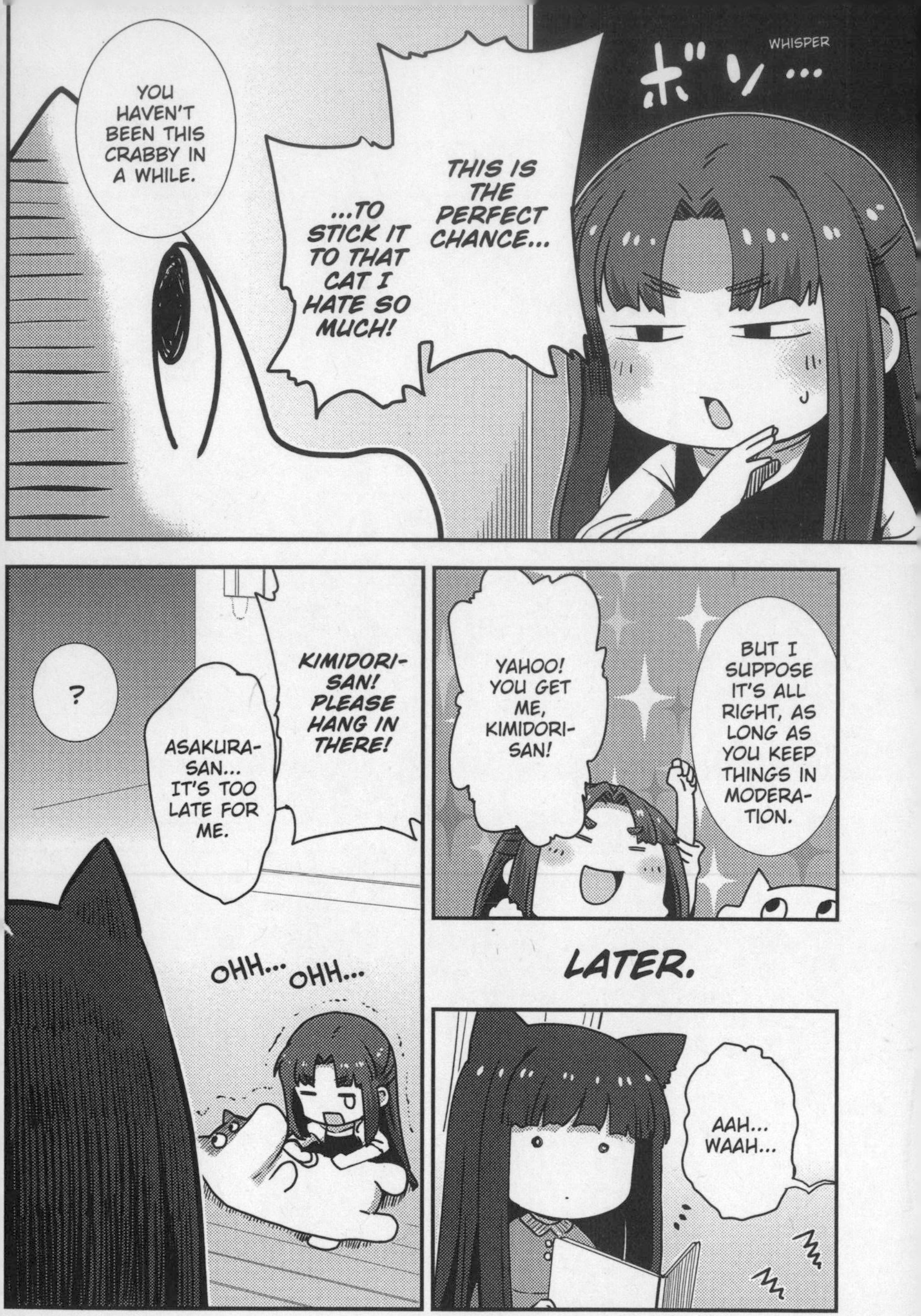
WHISPER
ボソ…
THIS IS THE PERFECT CHANCE...
...TO STICK IT TO THAT CAT I HATE SO MUCH!
YOU HAVEN'T BEEN THIS CRABBY IN A WHILE.
BUT I SUPPOSE IT'S ALL RIGHT, AS LONG AS YOU KEEP THINGS IN MODERA-TION.
YAHOO! YOU GET ME, KIMIDORI-SAN!
LATER.
AAH... WAAH...
KIMIDORI-SAN! PLEASE HANG IN THERE!
ASAKURA-SAN... IT'S TOO LATE FOR ME.
?
OHH... OHH...

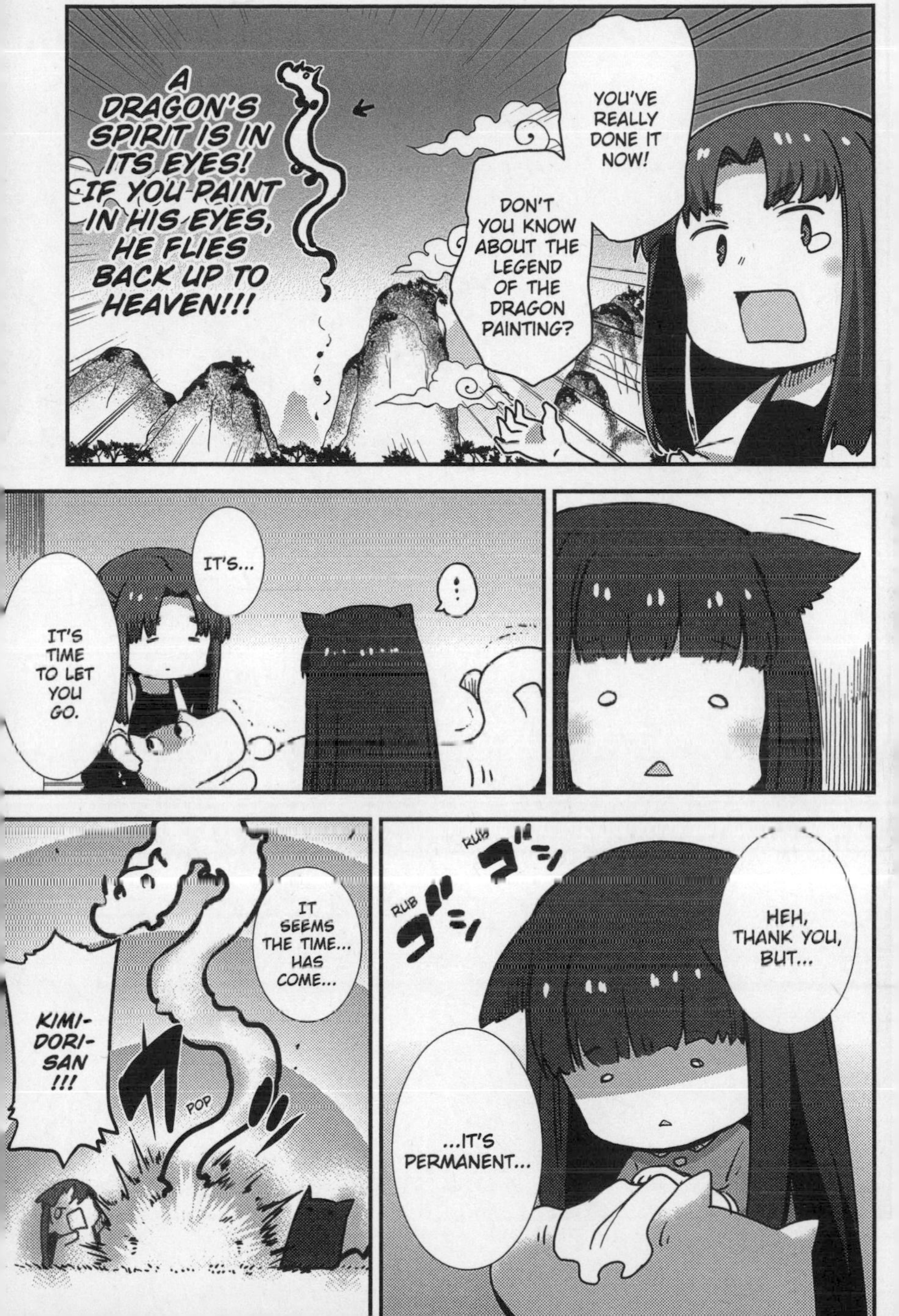
YOU'VE REALLY DONE IT NOW!
DON'T YOU KNOW ABOUT THE LEGEND OF THE DRAGON PAINTING?
A DRAGON'S SPIRIT IS IN ITS EYES! IF YOU PAINT IN HIS EYES, HE FLIES BACK UP TO HEAVEN!!!
...
IT'S...
IT'S TIME TO LET YOU GO.
RUB
RUB
HEH, THANK YOU, BUT...
...IT'S PERMANENT...
IT SEEMS THE TIME... HAS COME...
KIMI-DORI-SAN!!!
POP

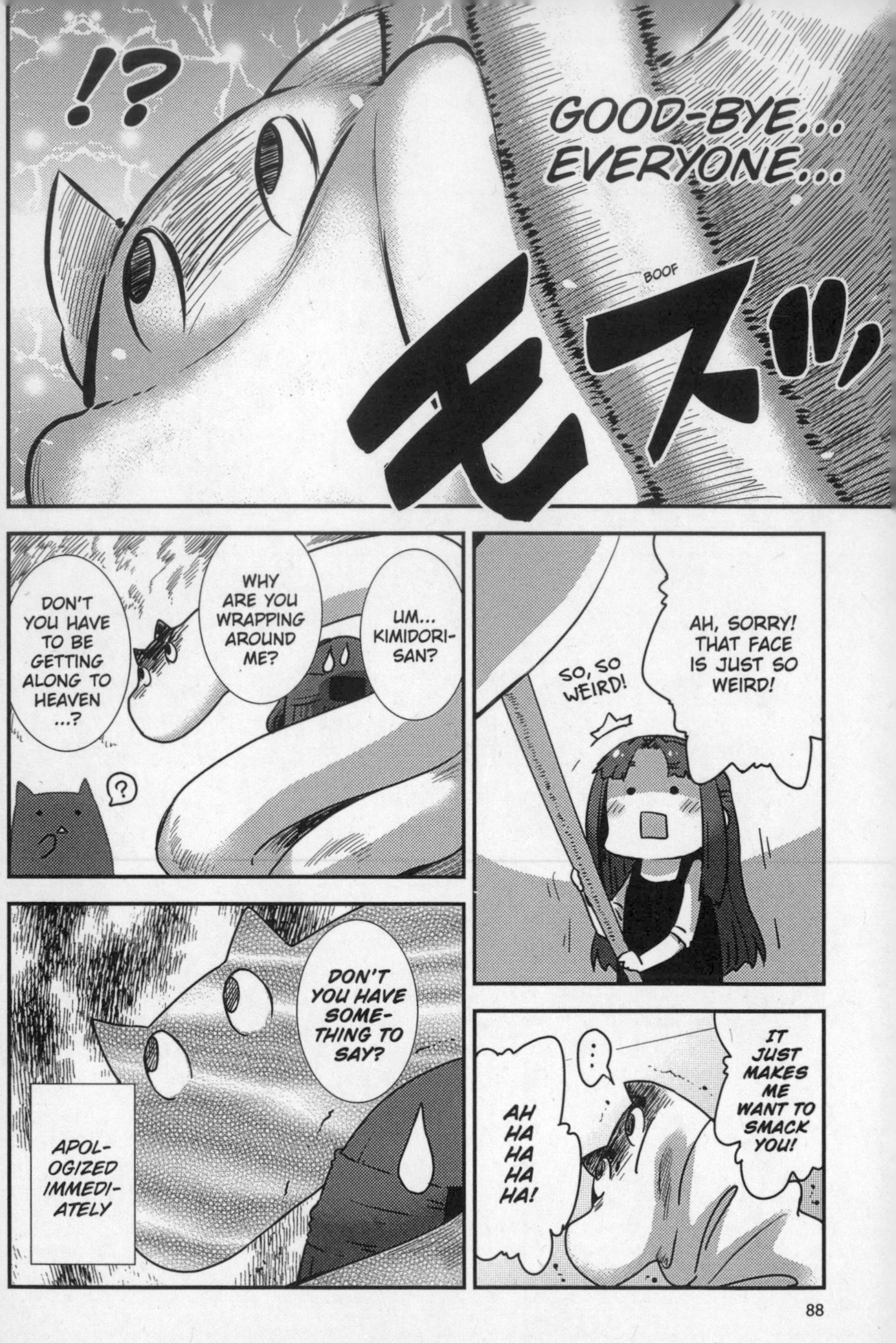
GOOD-BYE... EVERYONE...
!?
BOOF
AH, SORRY! THAT FACE IS JUST SO WEIRD!
SO, SO WEIRD!
UM... KIMIDORI-SAN?
WHY ARE YOU WRAPPING AROUND ME?
DON'T YOU HAVE TO BE GETTING ALONG TO HEAVEN ...?
?
IT JUST MAKES ME WANT TO SMACK YOU!
...
AH HA HA HA HA!
DON'T YOU HAVE SOME-THING TO SAY?
APOL-OGIZED IMMEDI-ATELY

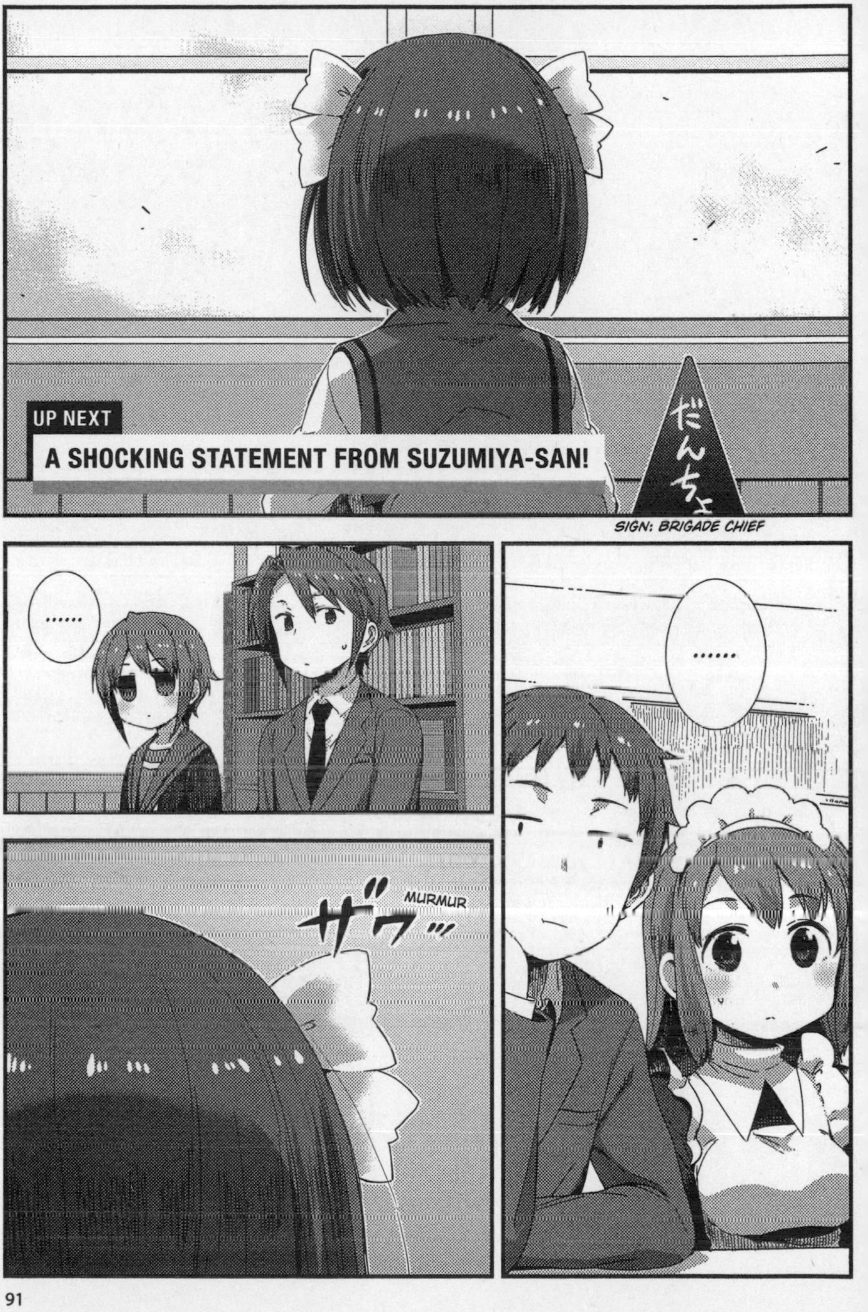
UP NEXT
A SHOCKING STATEMENT FROM SUZUMIYA-SAN!
だんちょ
SIGN: BRIGADE CHIEF
......
......
ザワ
MURMUR

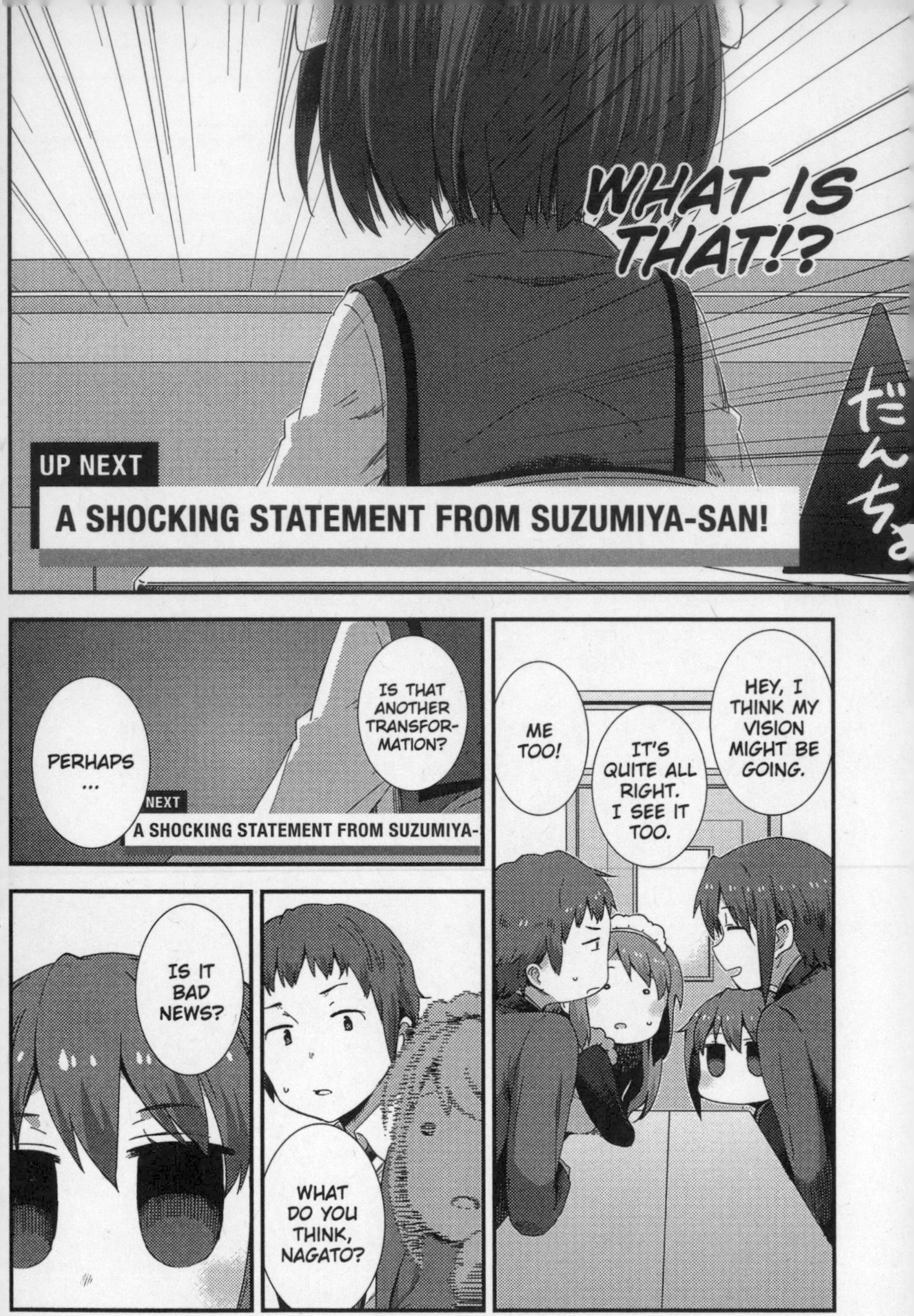
WHAT IS THAT!?
UP NEXT
A SHOCKING STATEMENT FROM SUZUMIYA-SAN!
HEY, I THINK MY VISION MIGHT BE GOING.
ME TOO!
IT'S QUITE ALL RIGHT. I SEE IT TOO.
IS THAT ANOTHER TRANSFORMATION?
PERHAPS...
NEXT
A SHOCKING STATEMENT FROM SUZUMIYA-
WHAT DO YOU THINK, NAGATO?
IS IT BAD NEWS?

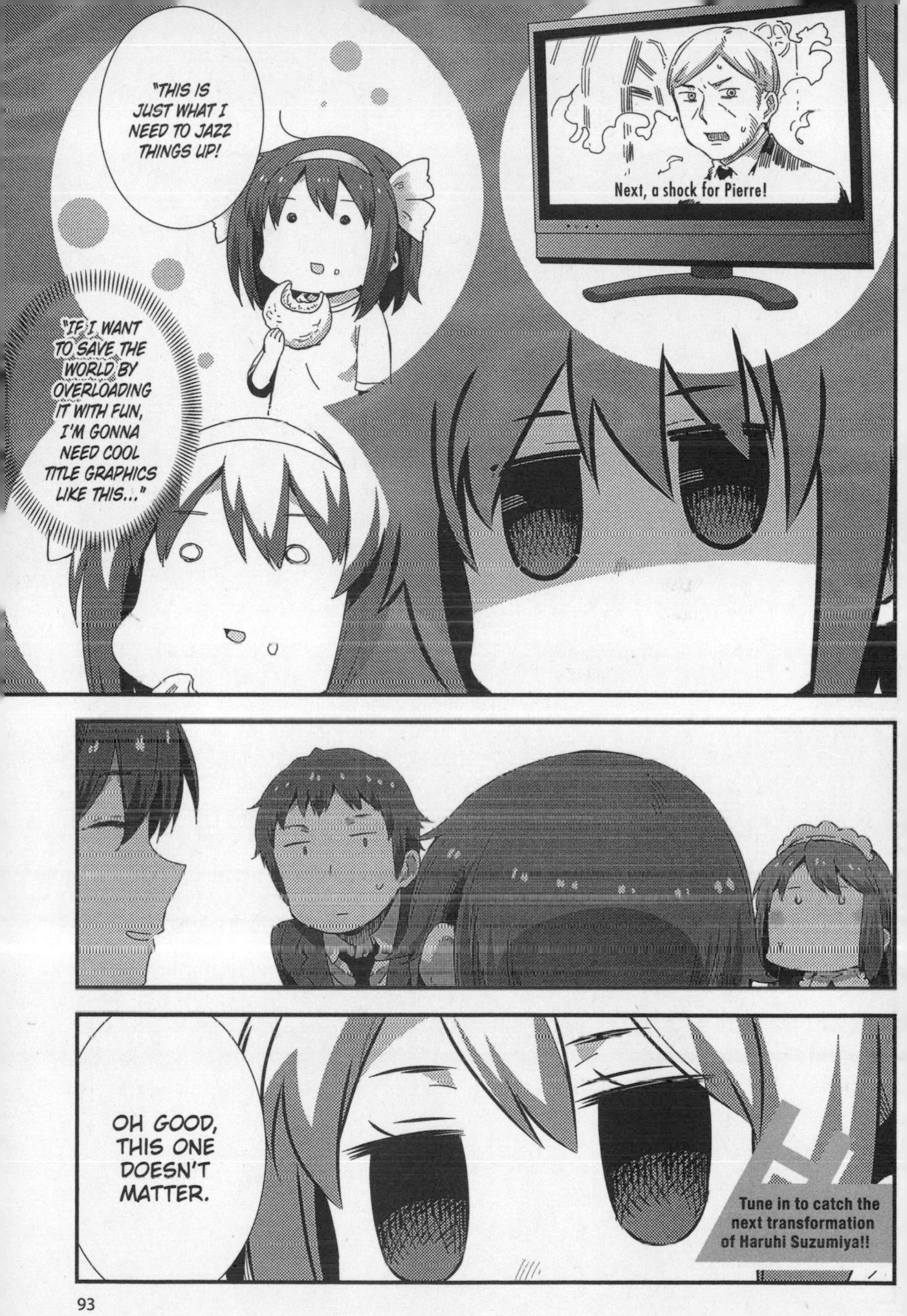
Next, a shock for Pierre!
"THIS IS JUST WHAT I NEED TO JAZZ THINGS UP!
"IF I WANT TO SAVE THE WORLD BY OVERLOADING IT WITH FUN, I'M GONNA NEED COOL TITLE GRAPHICS LIKE THIS..."
OH GOOD, THIS ONE DOESN'T MATTER.
Tune in to catch the next transformation of Haruhi Suzumiya!!

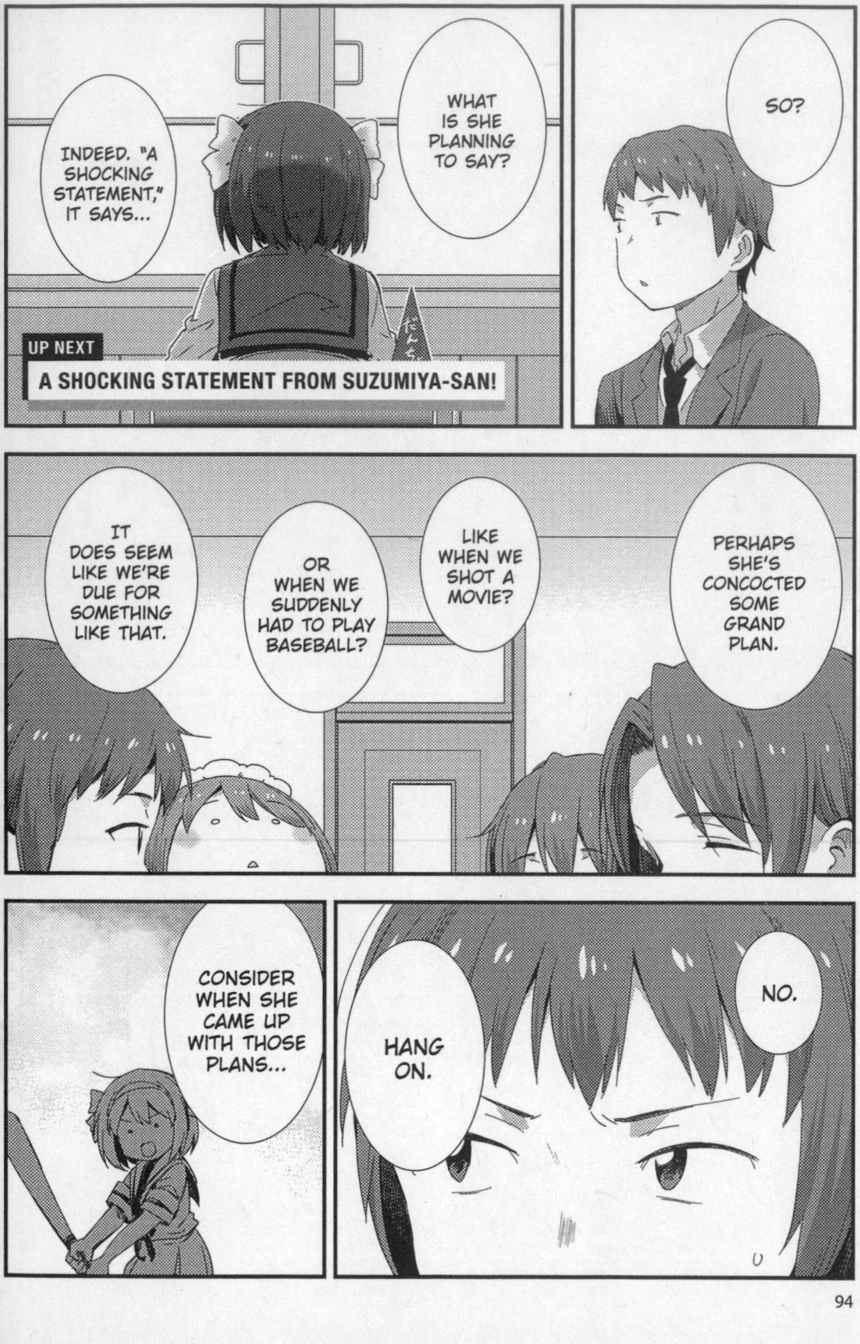
SO?
WHAT IS SHE PLANNING TO SAY?
INDEED. "A SHOCKING STATEMENT," IT SAYS...
UP NEXT
A SHOCKING STATEMENT FROM SUZUMIYA-SAN!
PERHAPS SHE'S CONCOCTED SOME GRAND PLAN.
LIKE WHEN WE SHOT A MOVIE?
OR WHEN WE SUDDENLY HAD TO PLAY BASEBALL?
IT DOES SEEM LIKE WE'RE DUE FOR SOMETHING LIKE THAT.
NO.
HANG ON.
CONSIDER WHEN SHE CAME UP WITH THOSE PLANS...

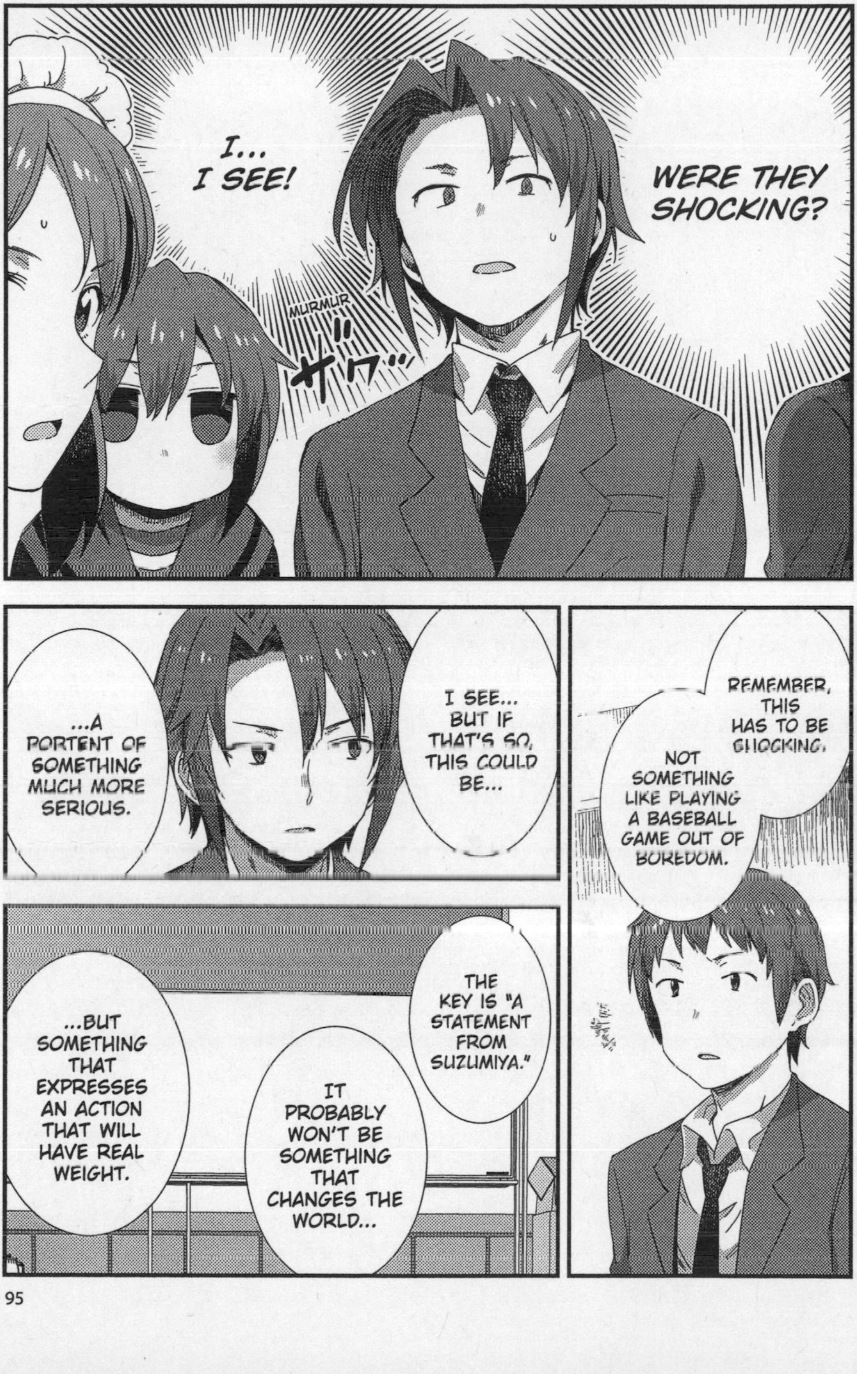
WERE THEY SHOCKING?
I... I SEE!
MURMUR
REMEMBER, THIS HAS TO BE SHOCKING.
NOT SOMETHING LIKE PLAYING A BASEBALL GAME OUT OF BOREDOM.
I SEE... BUT IF THAT'S SO, THIS COULD BE...
...A PORTENT OF SOMETHING MUCH MORE SERIOUS.
THE KEY IS "A STATEMENT FROM SUZUMIYA."
IT PROBABLY WON'T BE SOMETHING THAT CHANGES THE WORLD...
...BUT SOMETHING THAT EXPRESSES AN ACTION THAT WILL HAVE REAL WEIGHT.

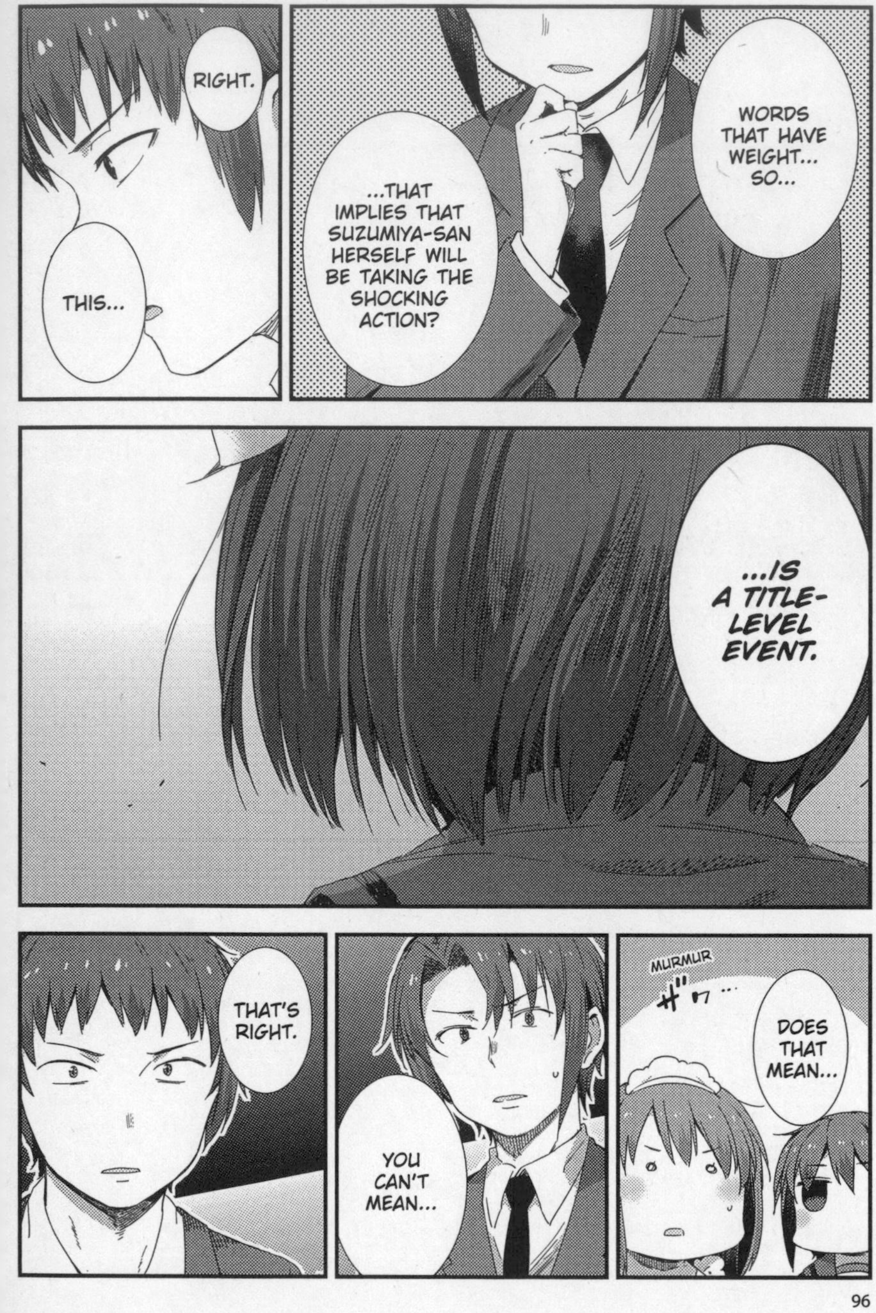
WORDS THAT HAVE WEIGHT... SO...
...THAT IMPLIES THAT SUZUMIYA-SAN HERSELF WILL BE TAKING THE SHOCKING ACTION?
RIGHT.
THIS...
...IS A TITLE-LEVEL EVENT.
MURMUR
DOES THAT MEAN...
YOU CAN'T MEAN...
THAT'S RIGHT.

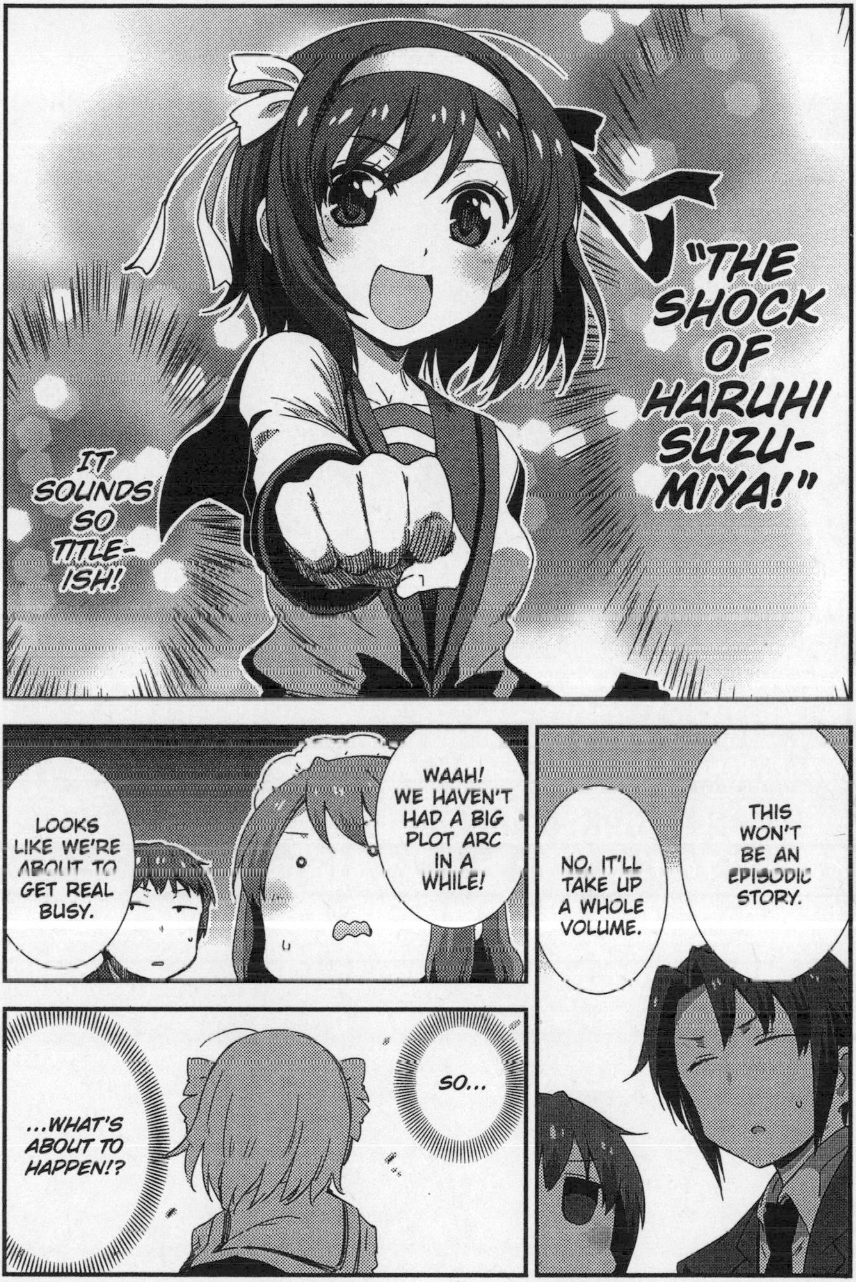
"THE SHOCK OF HARUHI SUZUMIYA!"
IT SOUNDS SO TITLE-ISH!
THIS WON'T BE AN EPISODIC STORY.
NO, IT'LL TAKE UP A WHOLE VOLUME.
WAAH! WE HAVEN'T HAD A BIG PLOT ARC IN A WHILE!
LOOKS LIKE WE'RE ABOUT TO GET REAL BUSY.
SO...
...WHAT'S ABOUT TO HAPPEN!?

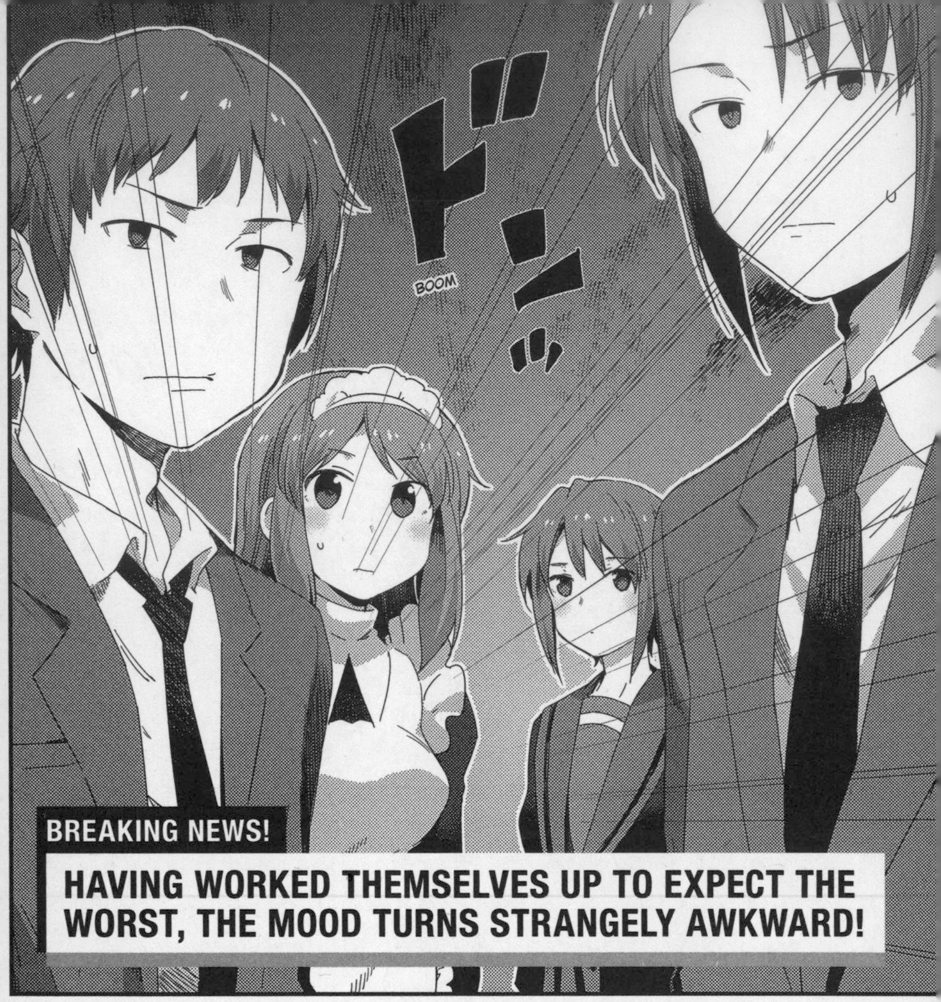
BOOM
BREAKING NEWS!
HAVING WORKED THEMSELVES UP TO EXPECT THE WORST, THE MOOD TURNS STRANGELY AWKWARD!
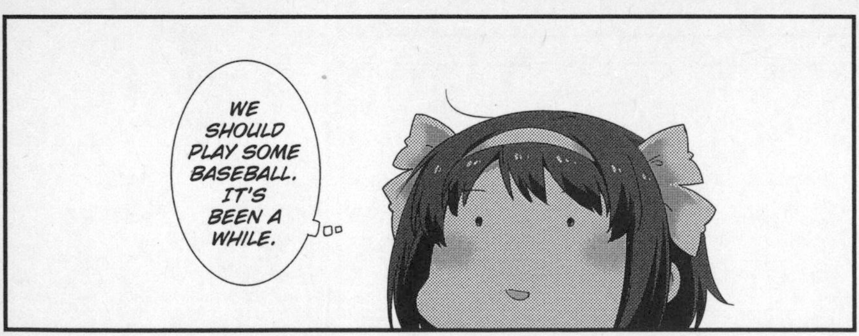
WE SHOULD PLAY SOME BASEBALL. IT'S BEEN A WHILE.

HIYAAH!

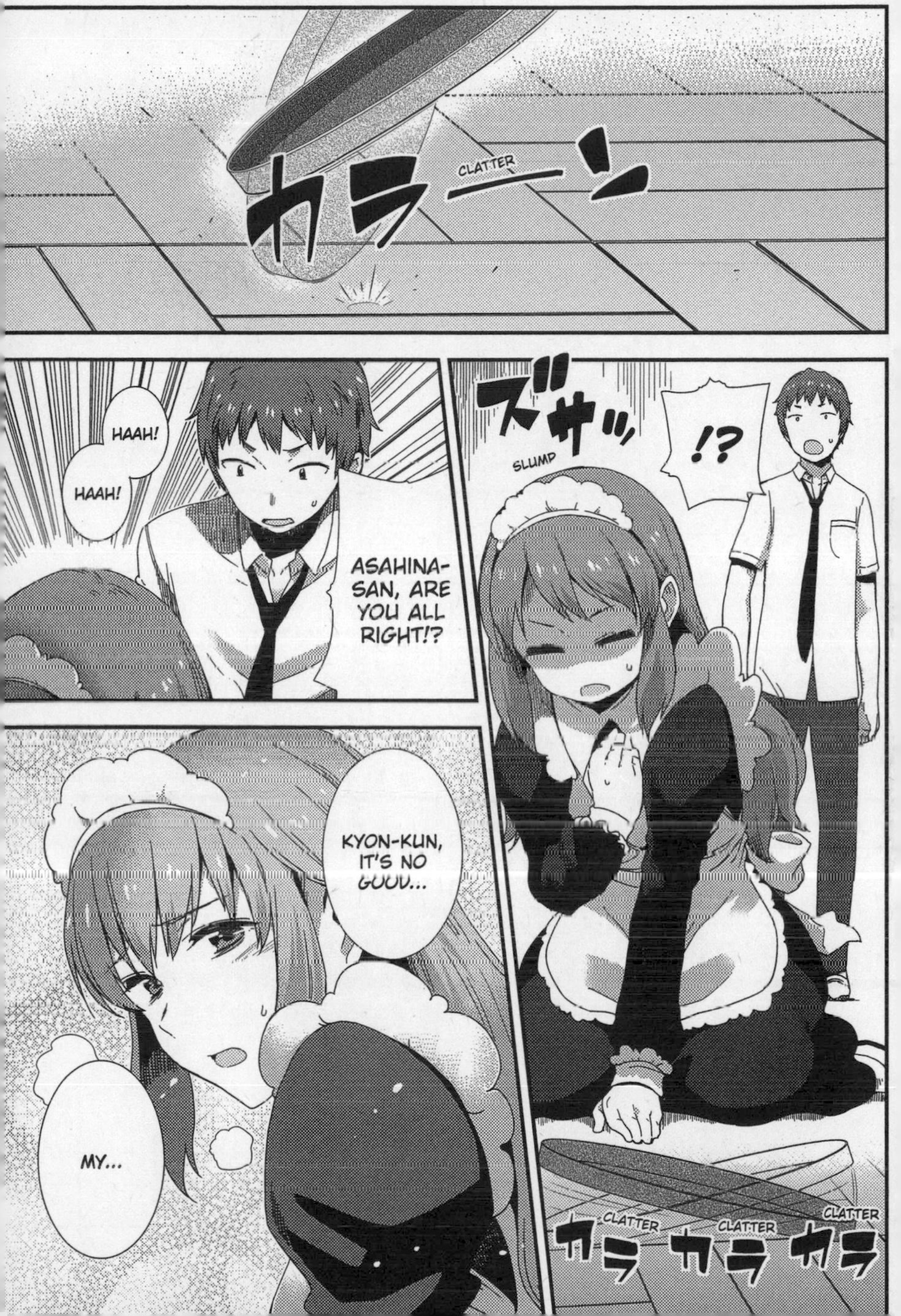
カラーン
CLATTER
ズサッ
SLUMP
!?
カラ カラ カラ
CLATTER CLATTER CLATTER
HAAH!
HAAH!
ASAHINA-SAN, ARE YOU ALL RIGHT!?
KYON-KUN, IT'S NO GOOD...
MY...

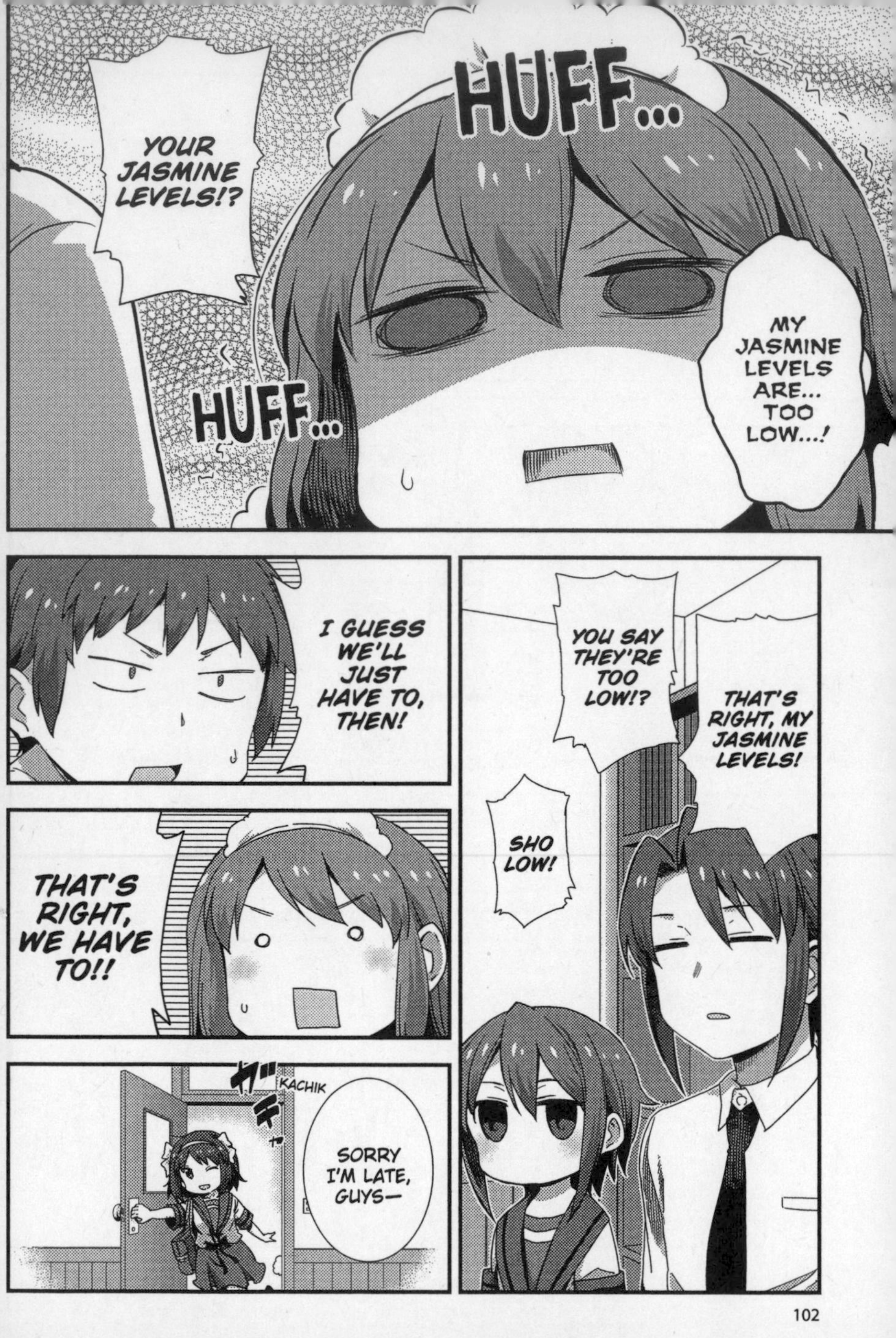

HUFF...
MY JASMINE LEVELS ARE... TOO LOW...!
HUFF...
YOUR JASMINE LEVELS!?
YOU SAY THEY'RE TOO LOW!?
THAT'S RIGHT, MY JASMINE LEVELS!
SHO LOW!
I GUESS WE'LL JUST HAVE TO, THEN!
THAT'S RIGHT, WE HAVE TO!!
KACHIK
SORRY I'M LATE, GUYS—

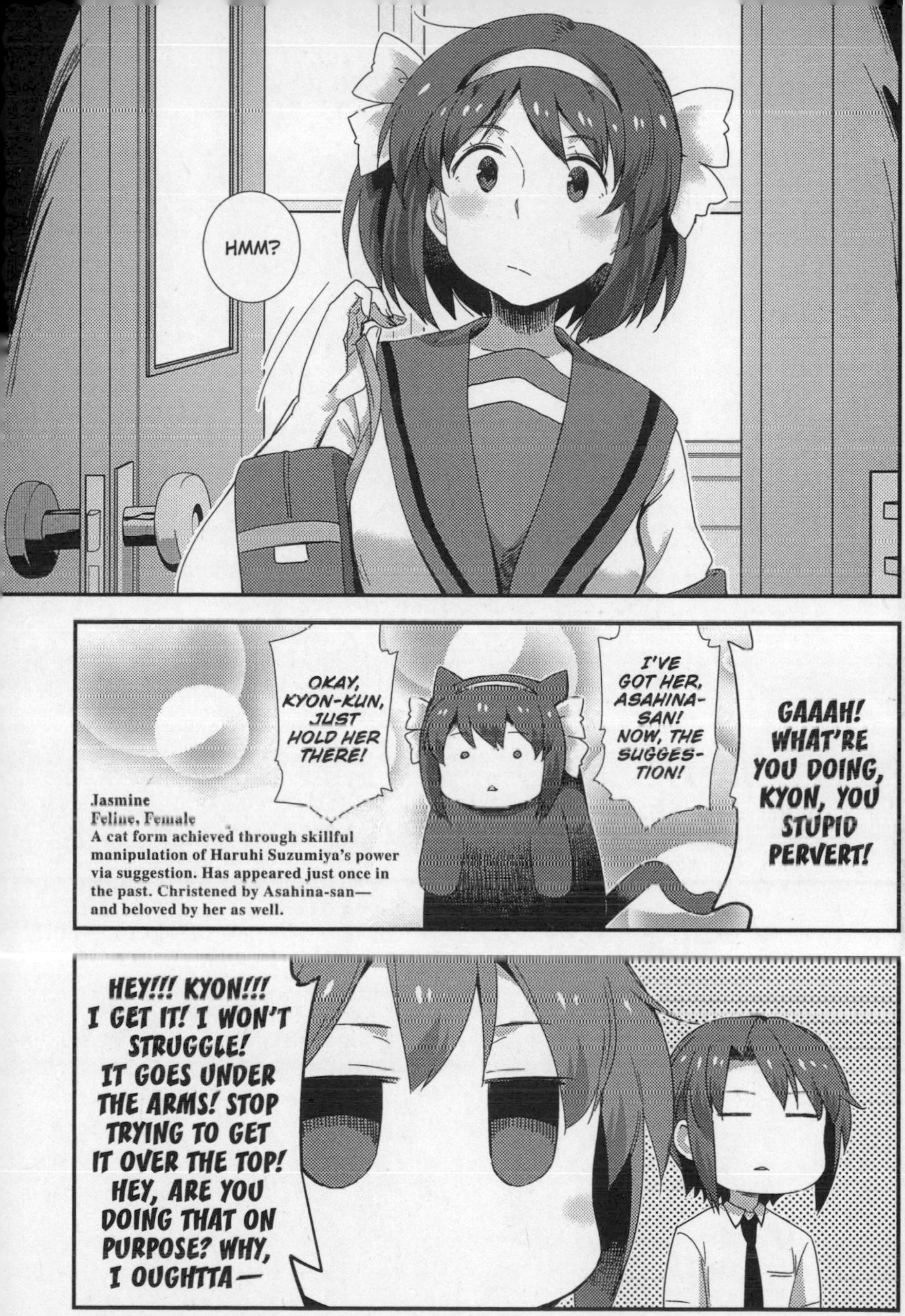
HMM?
GAAAH! WHAT'RE YOU DOING, KYON, YOU STUPID PERVERT!
I'VE GOT HER, ASAHINA-SAN! NOW, THE SUGGES-TION!
OKAY, KYON-KUN, JUST HOLD HER THERE!
Jasmine
Feline, Female
A cat form achieved through skillful manipulation of Haruhi Suzumiya's power via suggestion. Has appeared just once in the past. Christened by Asahina-san—and beloved by her as well.
HEY!!! KYON!!! I GET IT! I WON'T STRUGGLE! IT GOES UNDER THE ARMS! STOP TRYING TO GET IT OVER THE TOP! HEY, ARE YOU DOING THAT ON PURPOSE? WHY, I OUGHTTA—

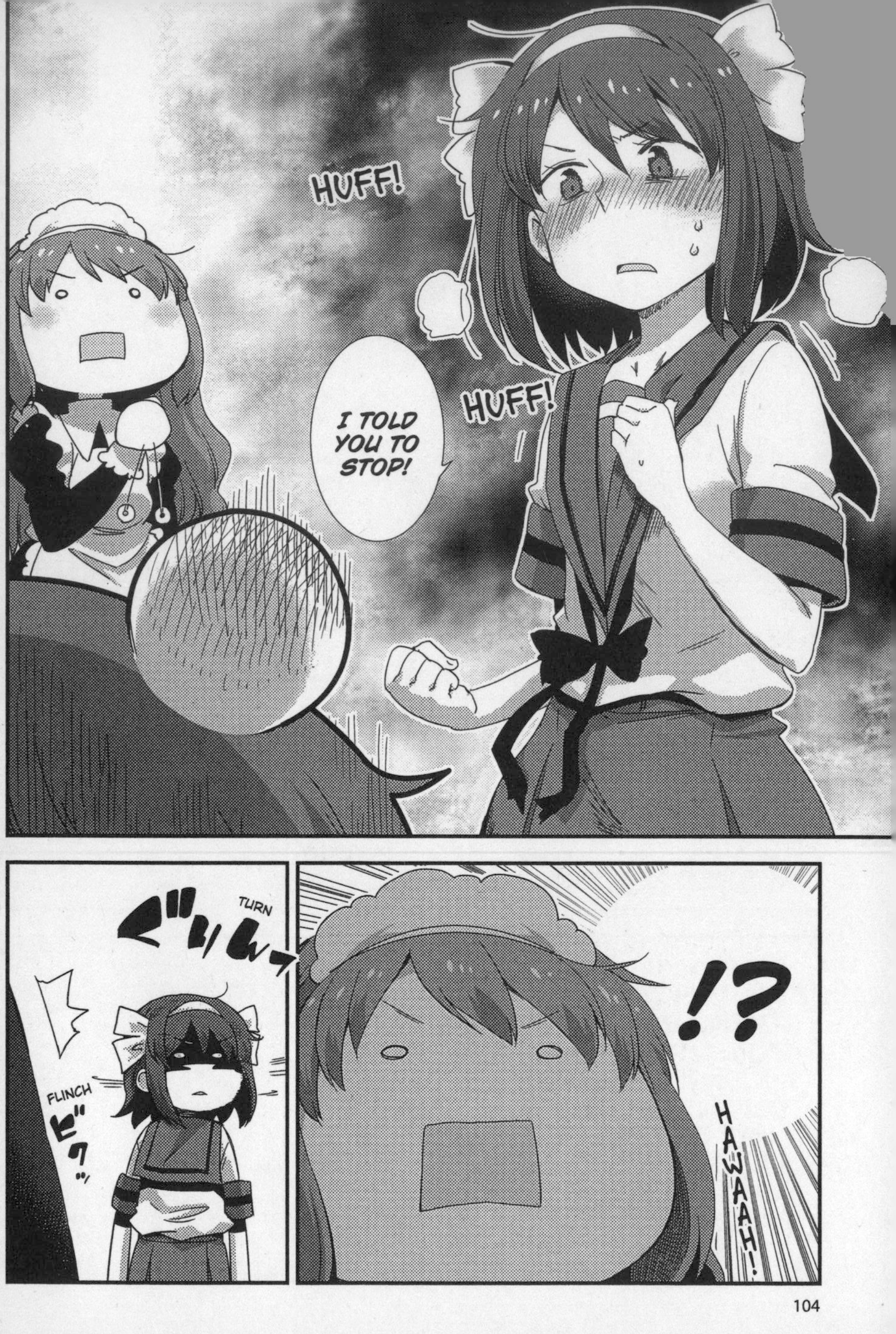
HUFF!
HUFF!
I TOLD YOU TO STOP!
!?
HAWAAH!
TURN
ぐりんっ
FLINCH
ビクッ

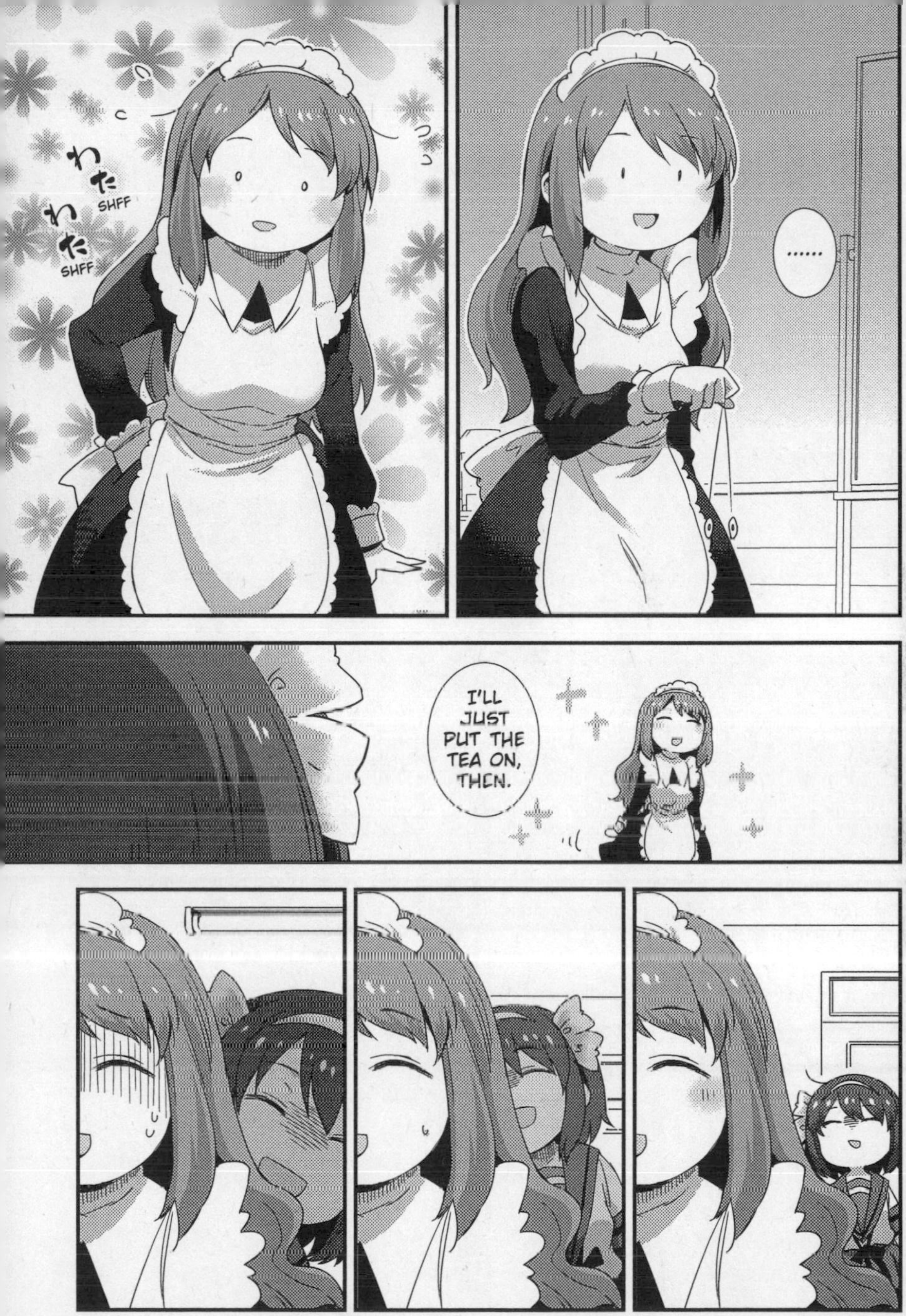
......
わた
SHFF
わた
SHFF
I'LL JUST PUT THE TEA ON, THEN.

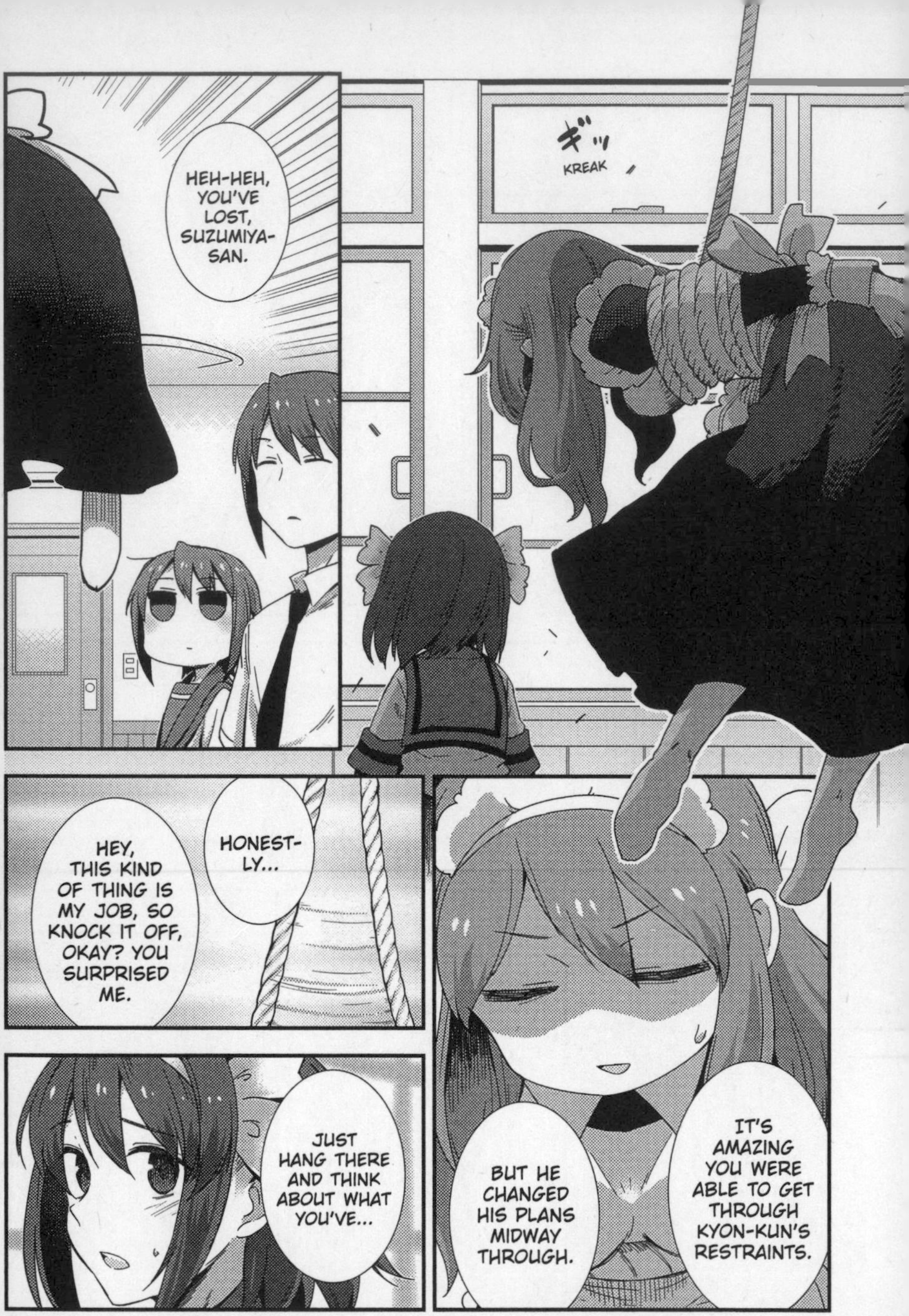
ギッ
KREAK
HEH-HEH, YOU'VE LOST, SUZUMIYA-SAN.
IT'S AMAZING YOU WERE ABLE TO GET THROUGH KYON-KUN'S RESTRAINTS.
BUT HE CHANGED HIS PLANS MIDWAY THROUGH.
HONEST-LY...
HEY, THIS KIND OF THING IS MY JOB, SO KNOCK IT OFF, OKAY? YOU SURPRISED ME.
JUST HANG THERE AND THINK ABOUT WHAT YOU'VE...

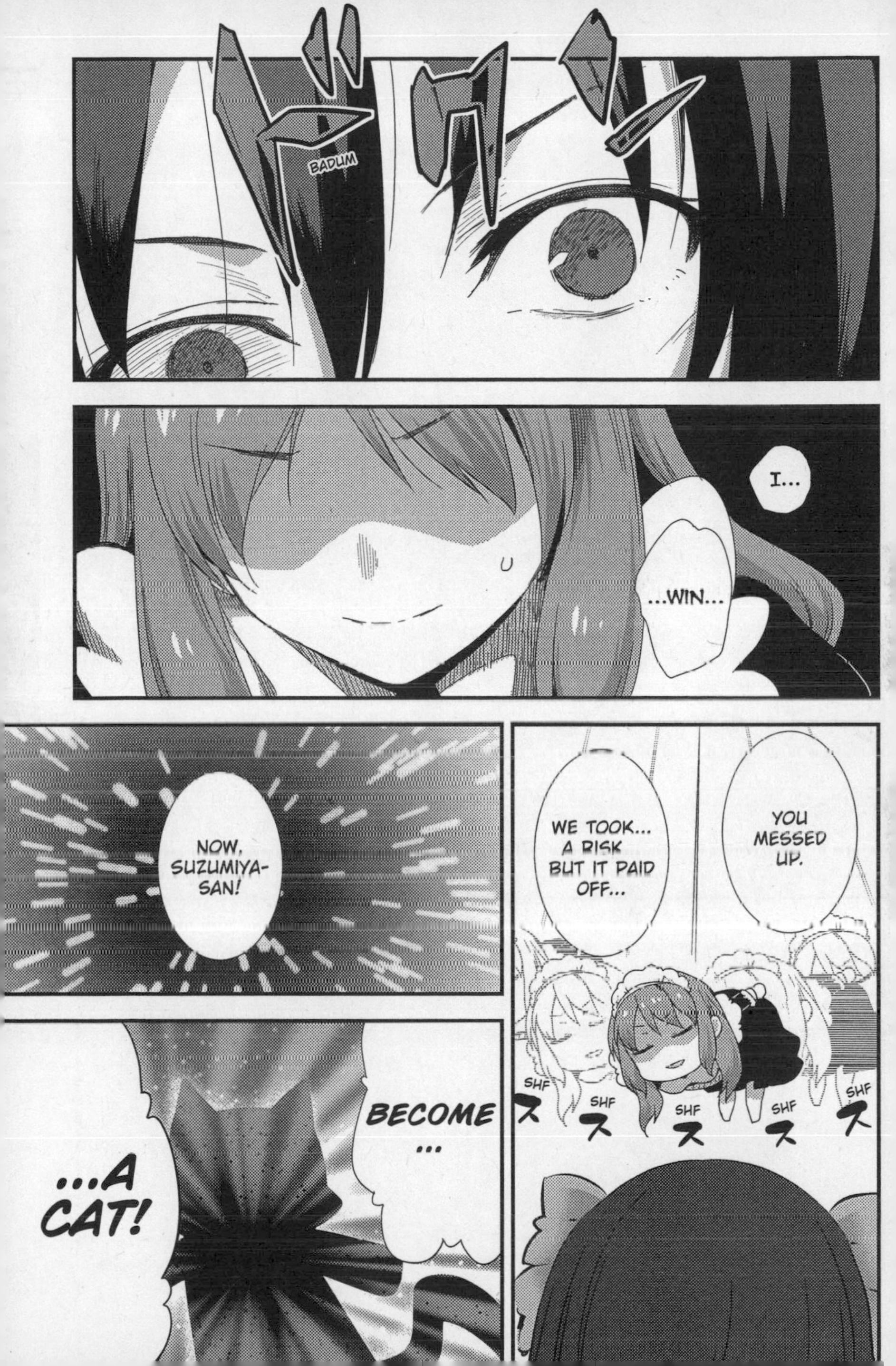
BADUM
I...
...WIN...
YOU MESSED UP.
WE TOOK... A RISK BUT IT PAID OFF...
SHF
SHF
SHF
SHF
SHF
NOW, SUZUMIYA-SAN!
BECOME...
...A CAT!

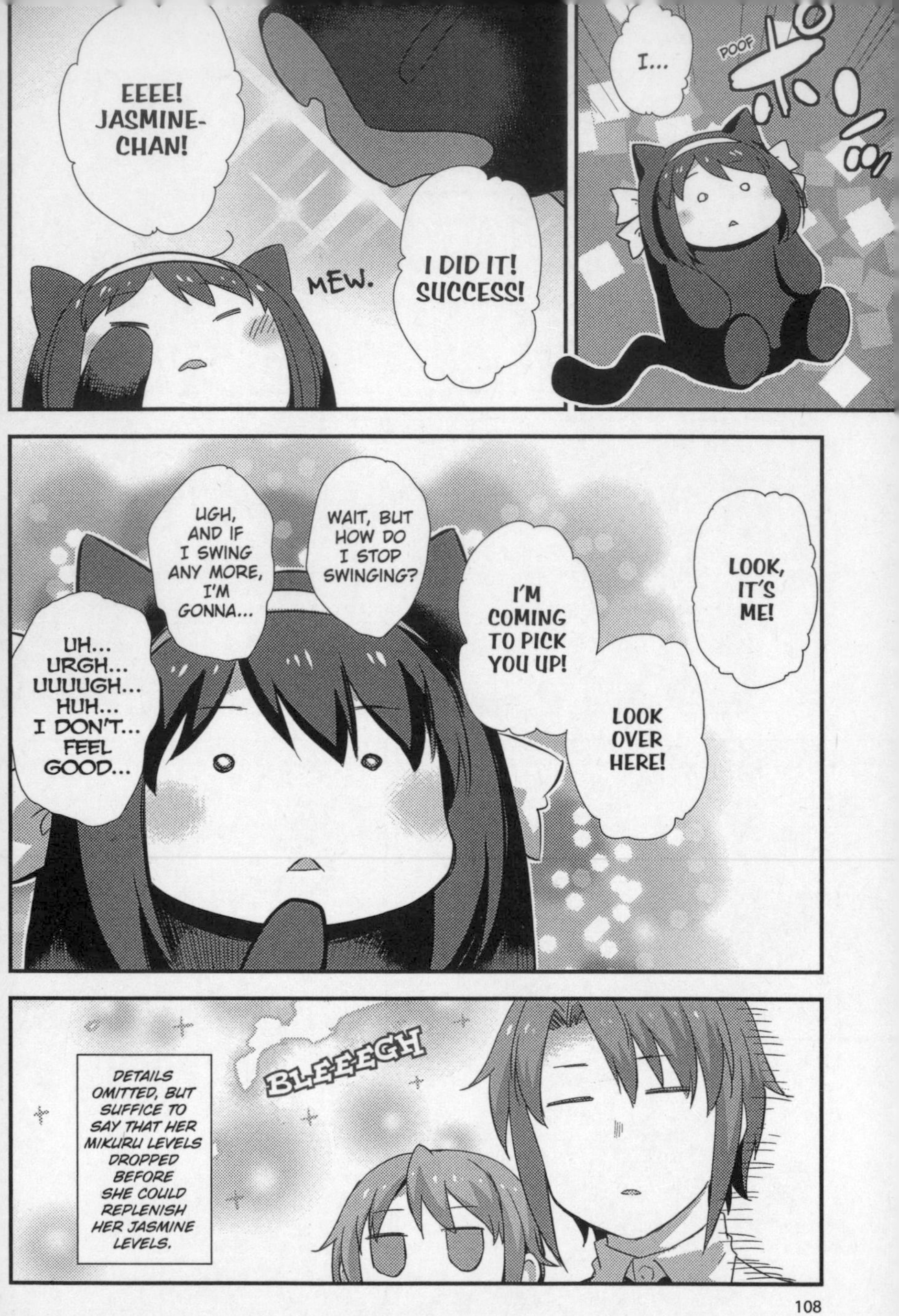
POOF
I...
I DID IT! SUCCESS!
MEW.
EEEE! JASMINE-CHAN!
LOOK, IT'S ME!
LOOK OVER HERE!
I'M COMING TO PICK YOU UP!
WAIT, BUT HOW DO I STOP SWINGING?
UGH, AND IF I SWING ANY MORE, I'M GONNA...
UH... URGH... UUUUGH... HUH... I DON'T... FEEL GOOD...
BLEEEGH
DETAILS OMITTED, BUT SUFFICE TO SAY THAT HER MIKURU LEVELS DROPPED BEFORE SHE COULD REPLENISH HER JASMINE LEVELS.

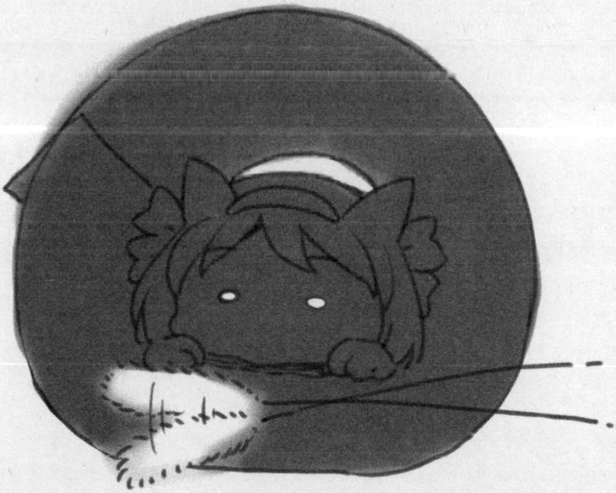

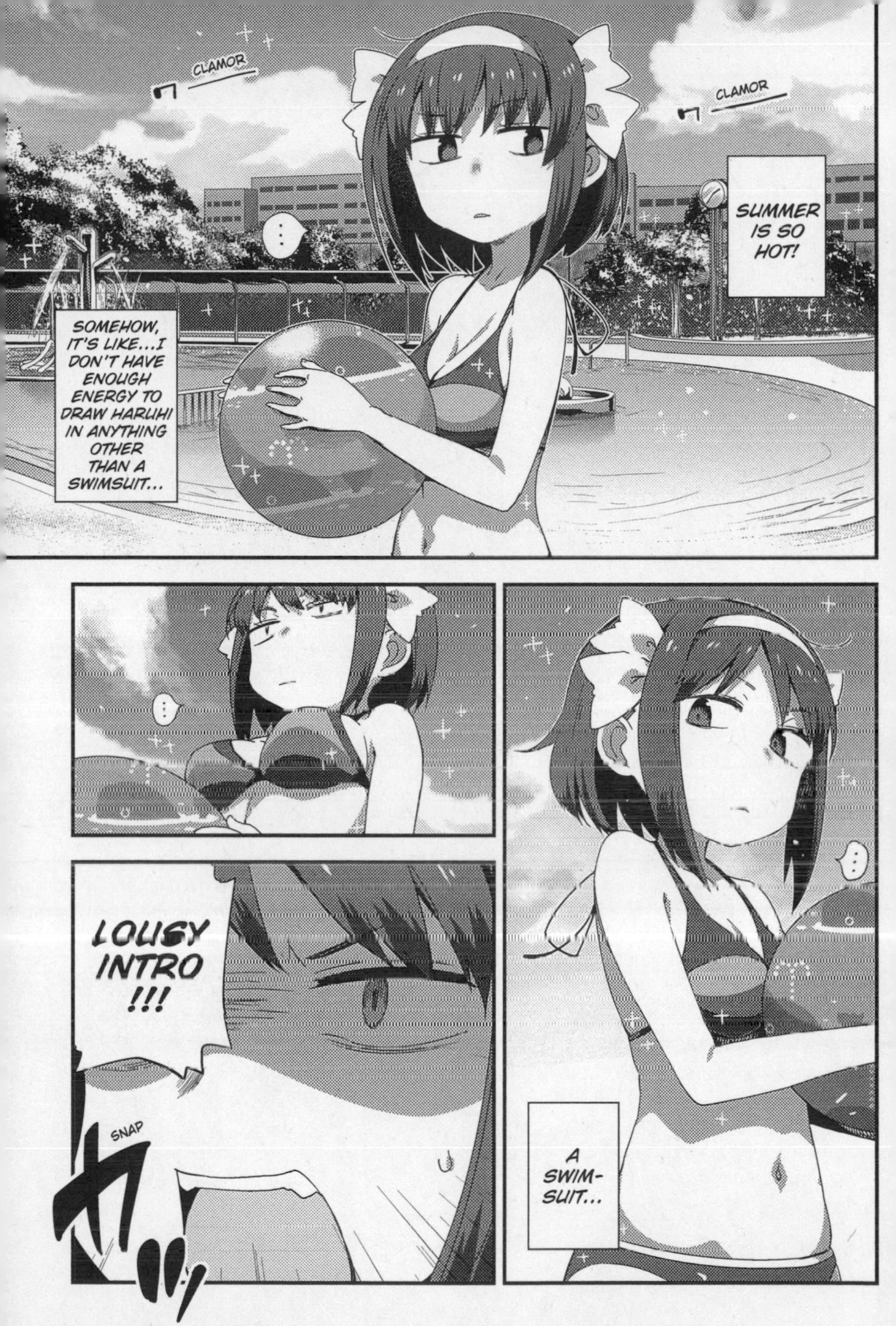
CLAMOR
SUMMER IS SO HOT!
CLAMOR
...
SOMEHOW, IT'S LIKE...I DON'T HAVE ENOUGH ENERGY TO DRAW HARUHI IN ANYTHING OTHER THAN A SWIMSUIT...
...
A SWIM-SUIT...
...
LOUSY INTRO !!!
SNAP

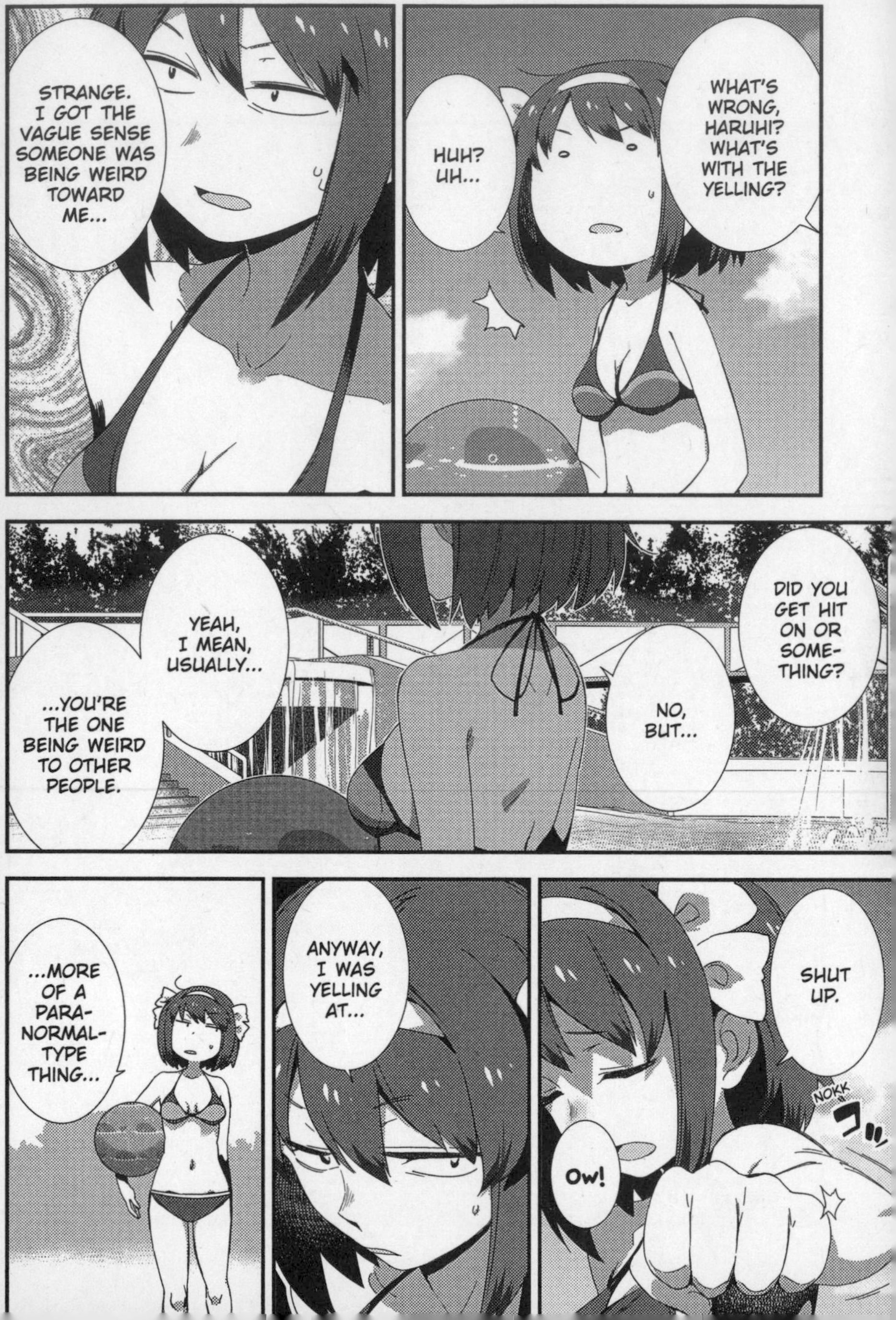
WHAT'S WRONG, HARUHI? WHAT'S WITH THE YELLING?
HUH? UH...
STRANGE. I GOT THE VAGUE SENSE SOMEONE WAS BEING WEIRD TOWARD ME...
DID YOU GET HIT ON OR SOME-THING?
NO, BUT...
YEAH, I MEAN, USUALLY...
...YOU'RE THE ONE BEING WEIRD TO OTHER PEOPLE.
SHUT UP.
NOKK
Ow!
ANYWAY, I WAS YELLING AT...
...MORE OF A PARA-NORMAL-TYPE THING...

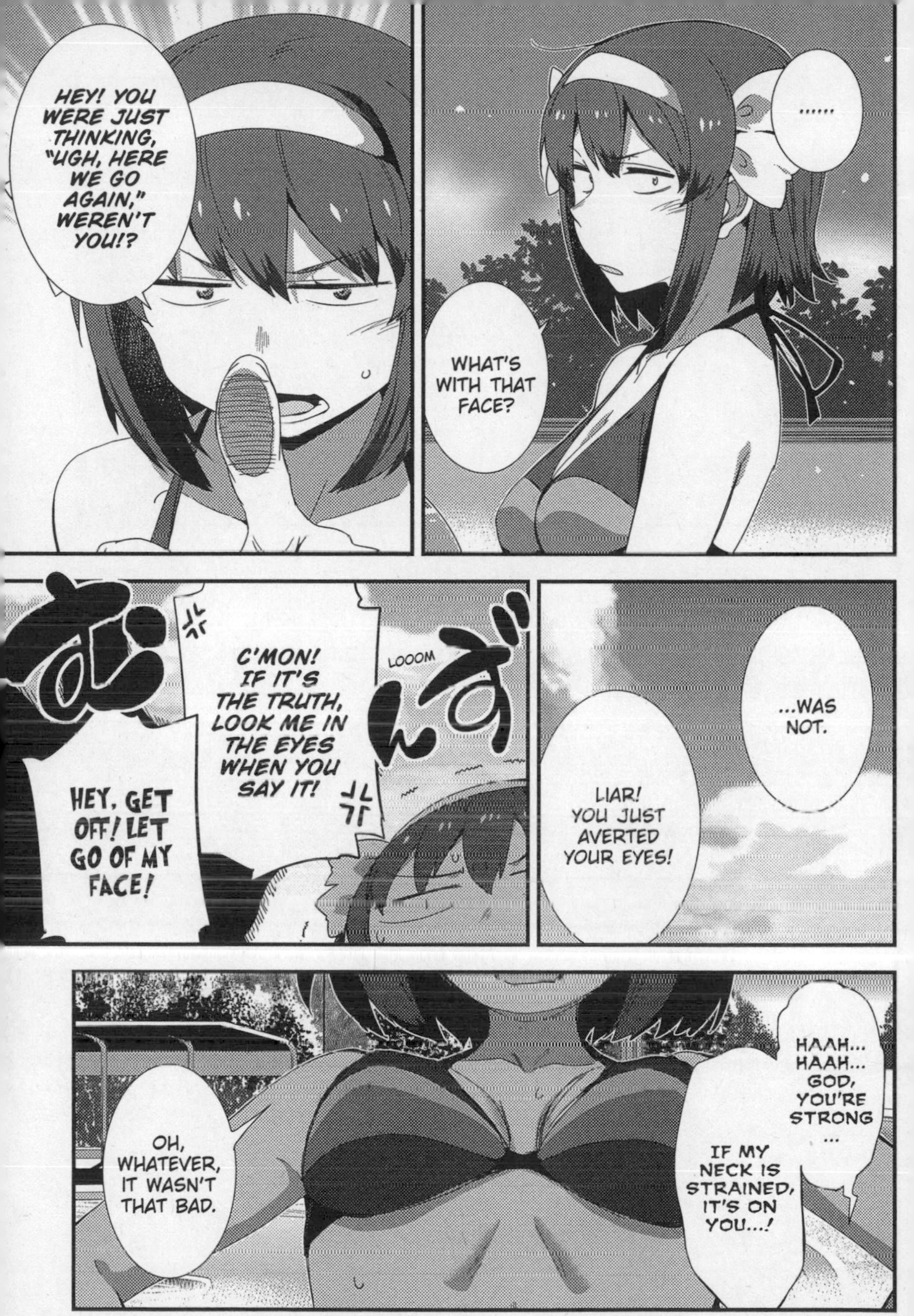
......
WHAT'S WITH THAT FACE?
HEY! YOU WERE JUST THINKING, "UGH, HERE WE GO AGAIN," WEREN'T YOU!?
...WAS NOT.
LIAR! YOU JUST AVERTED YOUR EYES!
LOOOM
C'MON! IF IT'S THE TRUTH, LOOK ME IN THE EYES WHEN YOU SAY IT!
HEY, GET OFF! LET GO OF MY FACE!
HAAH... HAAH... GOD, YOU'RE STRONG...
IF MY NECK IS STRAINED, IT'S ON YOU...!
OH, WHATEVER, IT WASN'T THAT BAD.

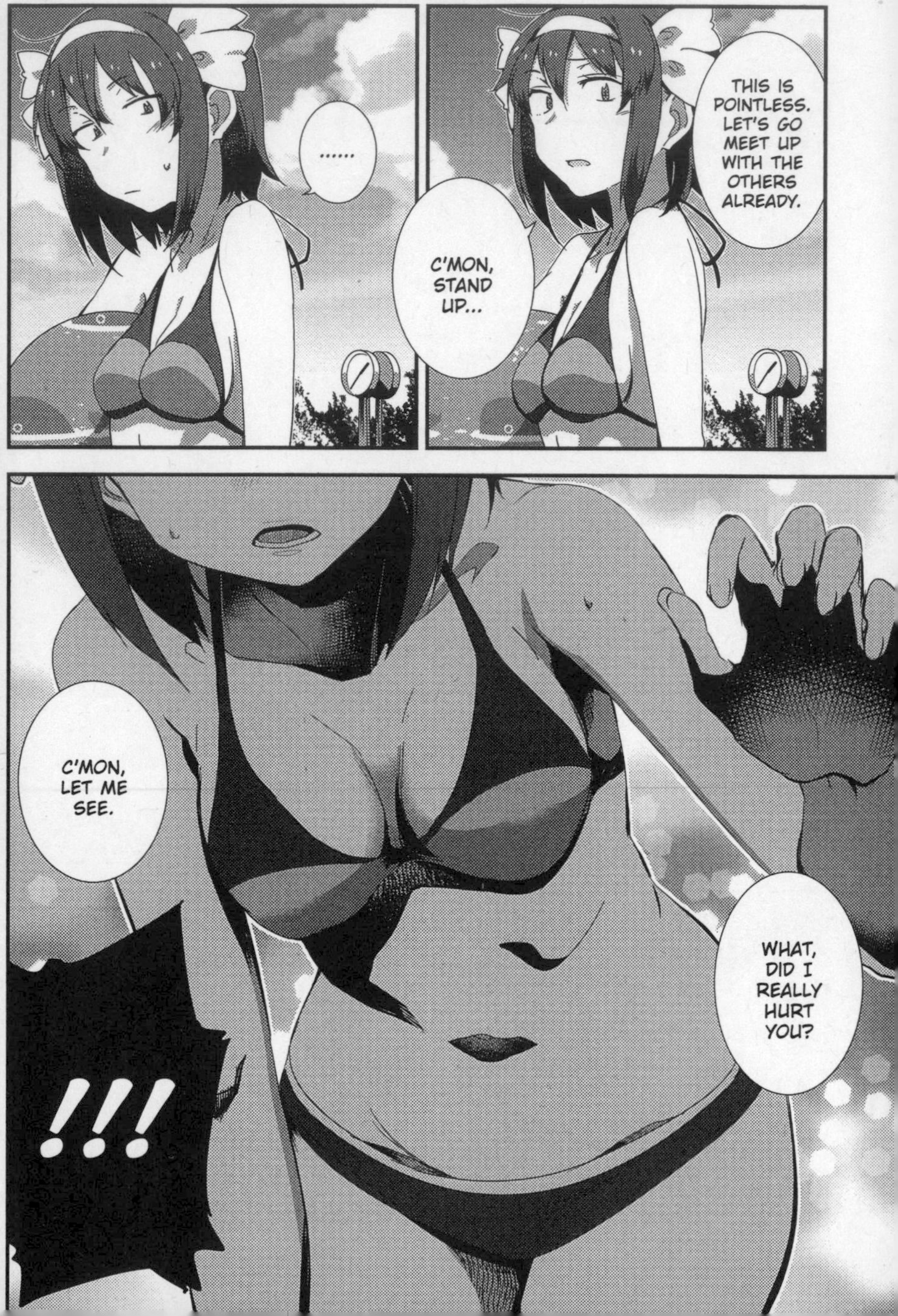
THIS IS POINTLESS. LET'S GO MEET UP WITH THE OTHERS ALREADY.
C'MON, STAND UP...
......
WHAT, DID I REALLY HURT YOU?
C'MON, LET ME SEE.
!!!

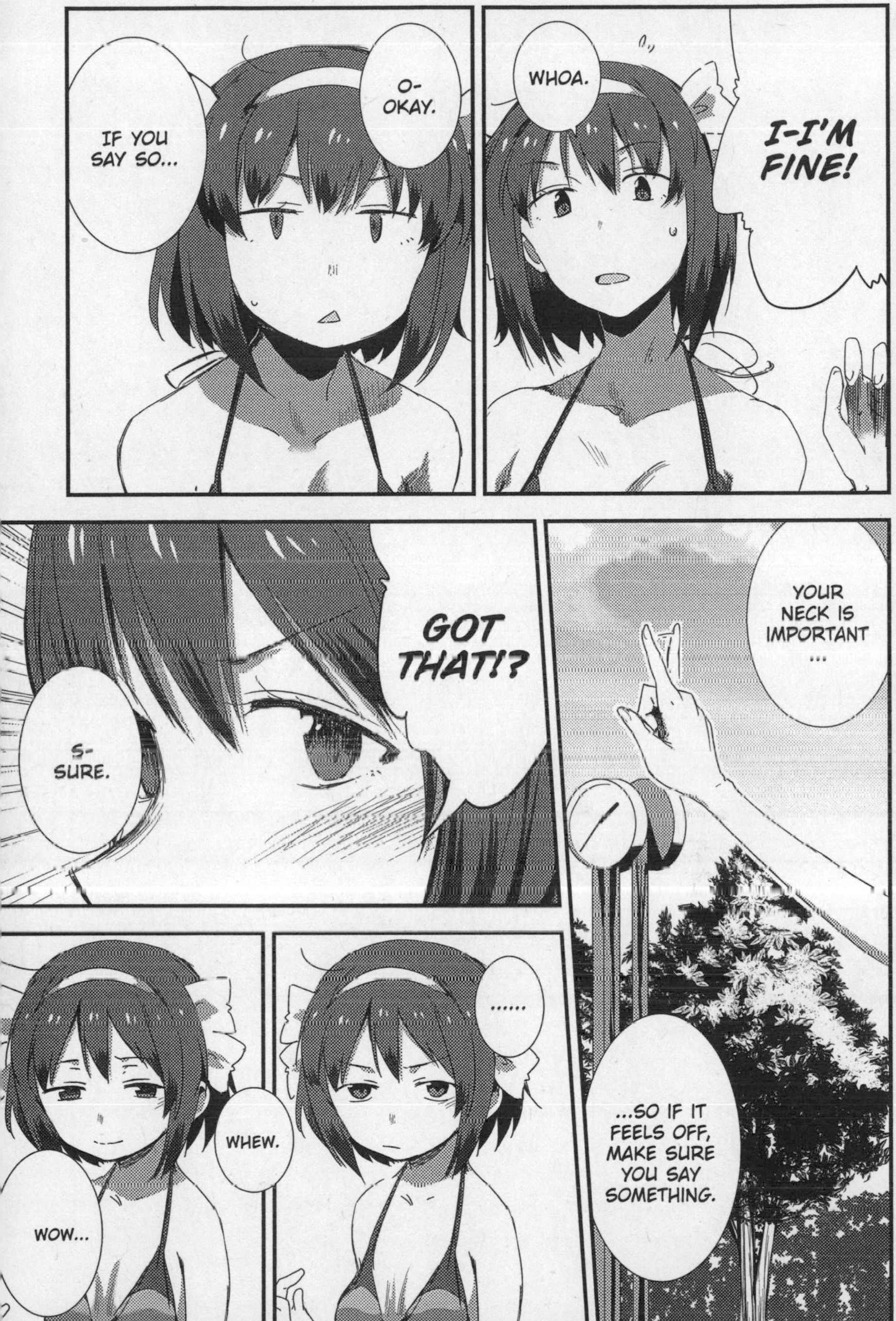
I-I'M FINE!
WHOA.
O-OKAY.
IF YOU SAY SO...
YOUR NECK IS IMPORTANT ...
...SO IF IT FEELS OFF, MAKE SURE YOU SAY SOMETHING.
GOT THAT!?
S-SURE.
......
WHEW.
WOW...

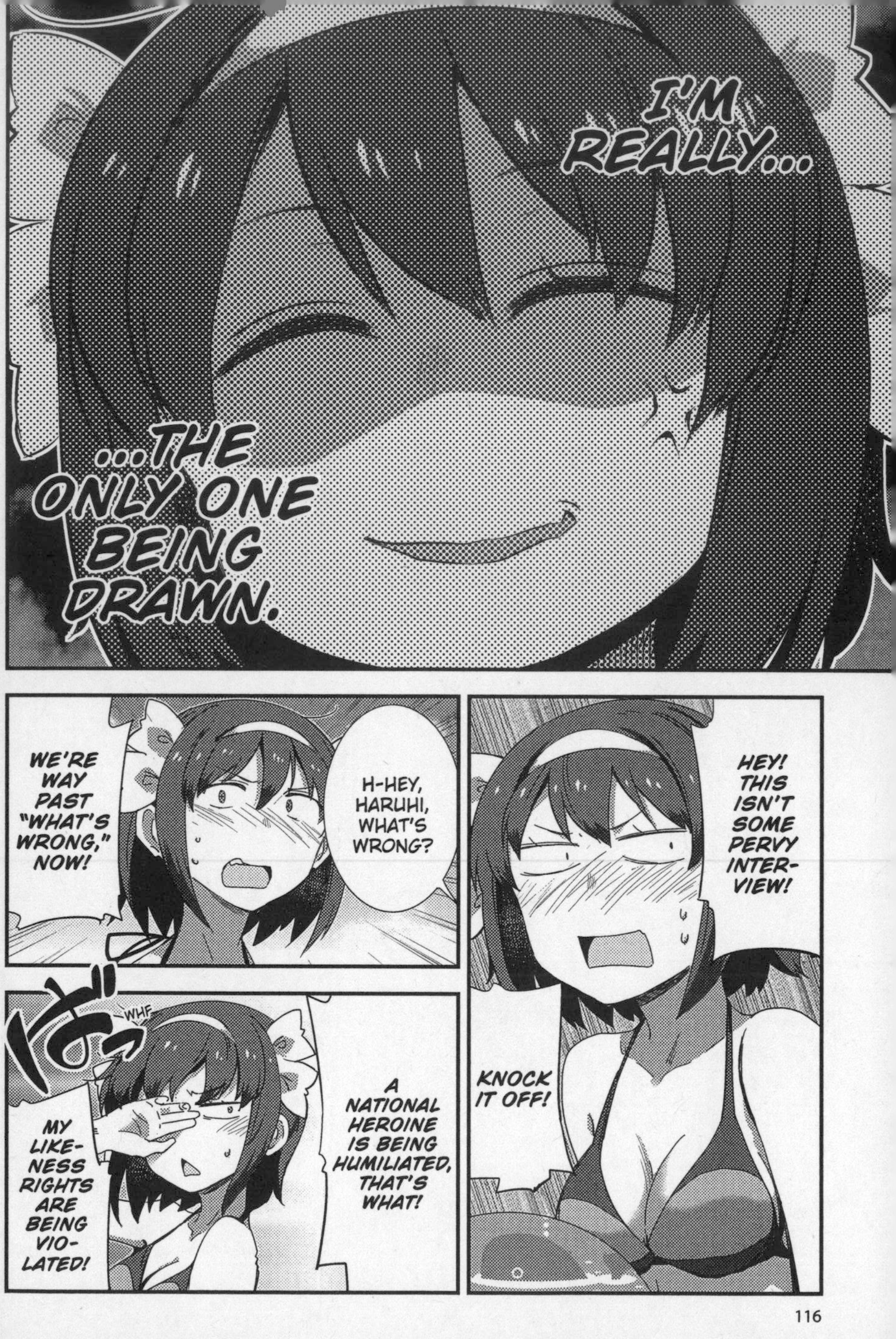
I'M REALLY...
...THE ONLY ONE BEING DRAWN.
HEY! THIS ISN'T SOME PERVY INTER-VIEW!
KNOCK IT OFF!
H-HEY, HARUHI, WHAT'S WRONG?
WE'RE WAY PAST "WHAT'S WRONG," NOW!
WHF
A NATIONAL HEROINE IS BEING HUMILIATED, THAT'S WHAT!
MY LIKE-NESS RIGHTS ARE BEING VIO-LATED!

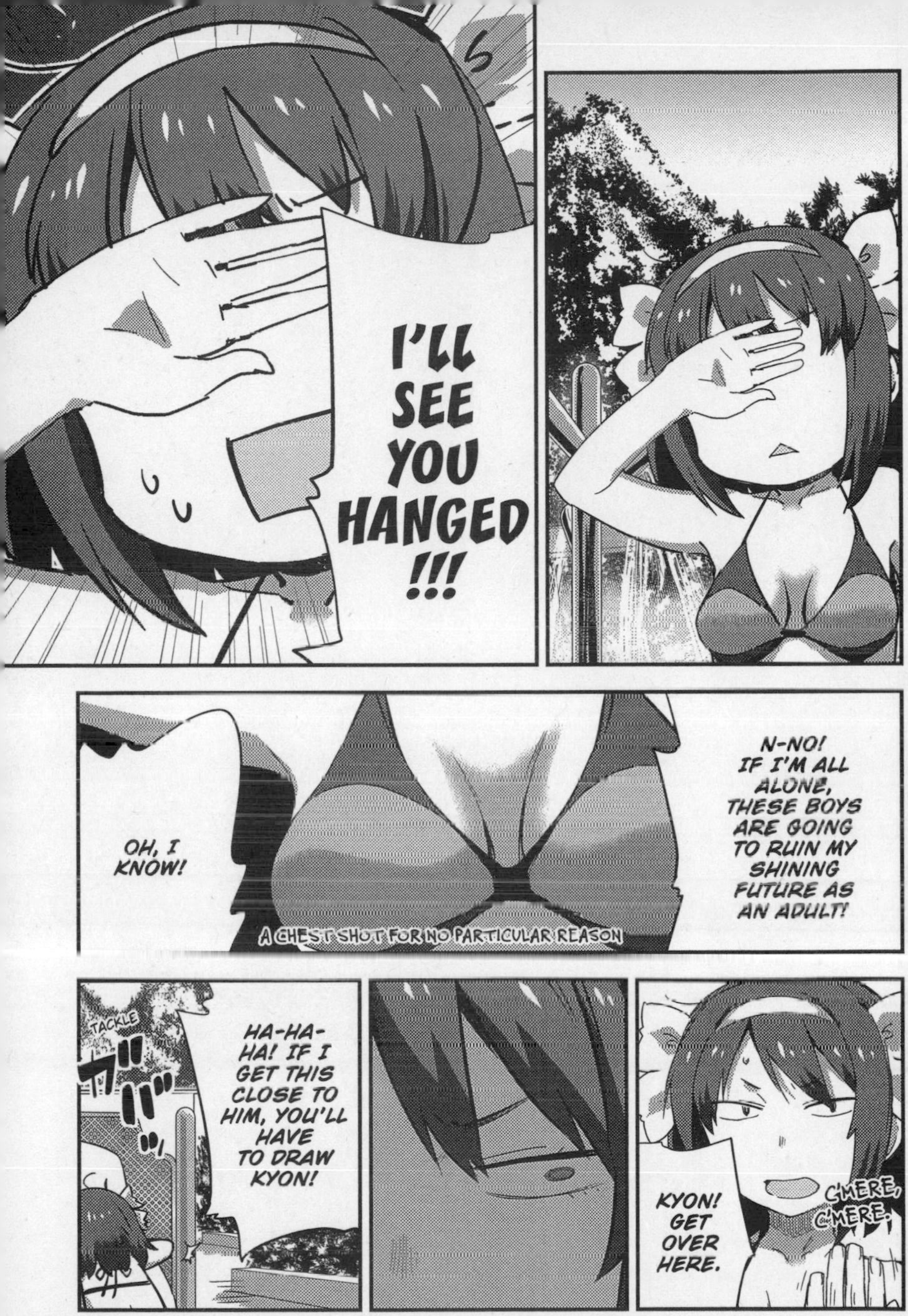
I'LL SEE YOU HANGED!!!
N-NO! IF I'M ALL ALONE, THESE BOYS ARE GOING TO RUIN MY SHINING FUTURE AS AN ADULT!
OH, I KNOW!
A CHEST SHOT FOR NO PARTICULAR REASON
C'MERE, C'MERE.
KYON! GET OVER HERE.
HA-HA-HA! IF I GET THIS CLOSE TO HIM, YOU'LL HAVE TO DRAW KYON!
TACKLE

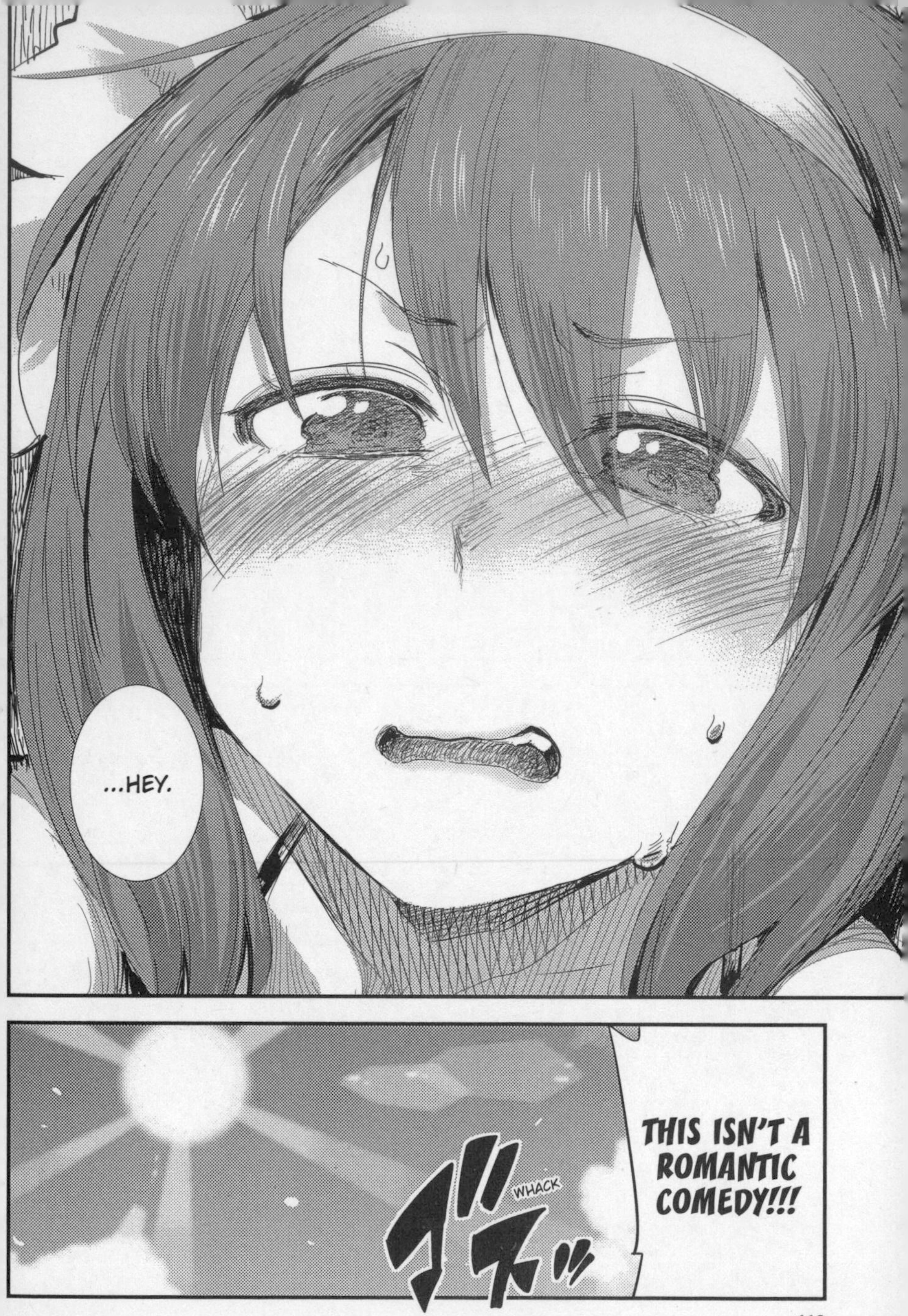
...HEY.
THIS ISN'T A ROMANTIC COMEDY!!!
ゴスッ
WHACK

HEY,
PAL.

I WANT
TO DO AN
"ARTIST'S
CHOICE"
CHAPTER.

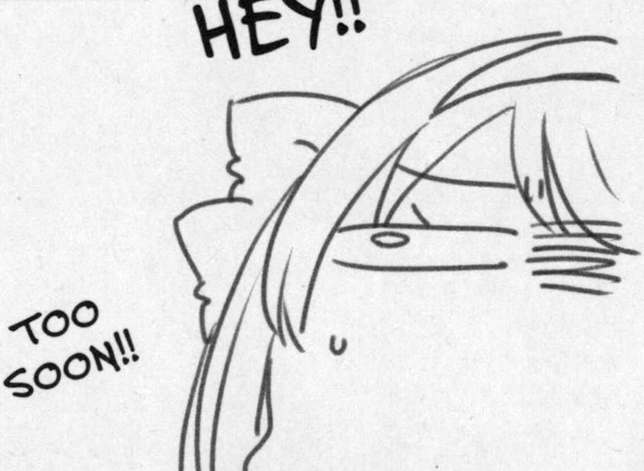
HEY!!
TOO SOON!!

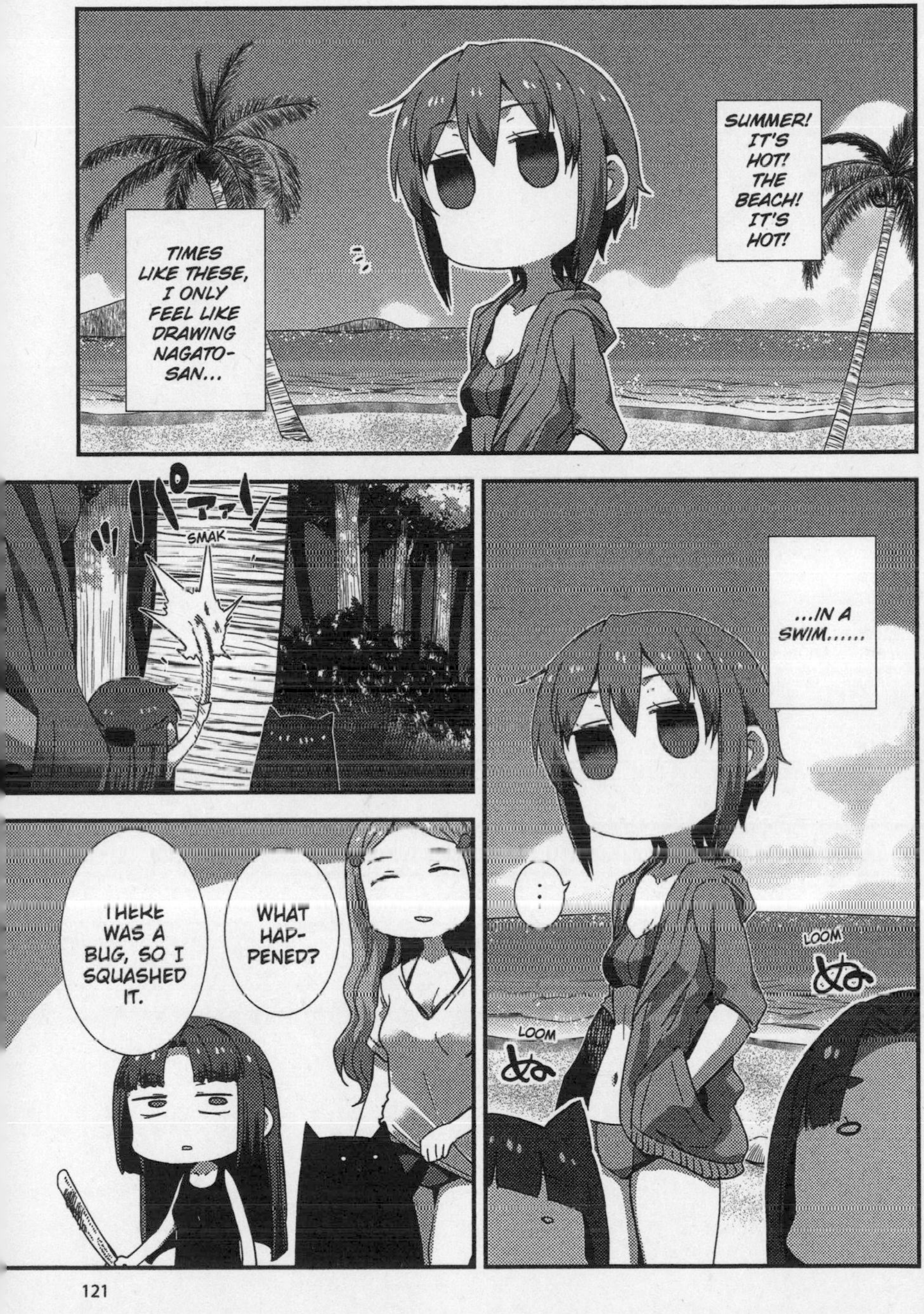
SUMMER! IT'S HOT! THE BEACH! IT'S HOT!
TIMES LIKE THESE, I ONLY FEEL LIKE DRAWING NAGATO-SAN...
...IN A SWIM......
...
LOOM
ぬ
LOOM
ぬ
SMAK
WHAT HAPPENED?
THERE WAS A BUG, SO I SQUASHED IT.

SUMMER AND BALLOONS

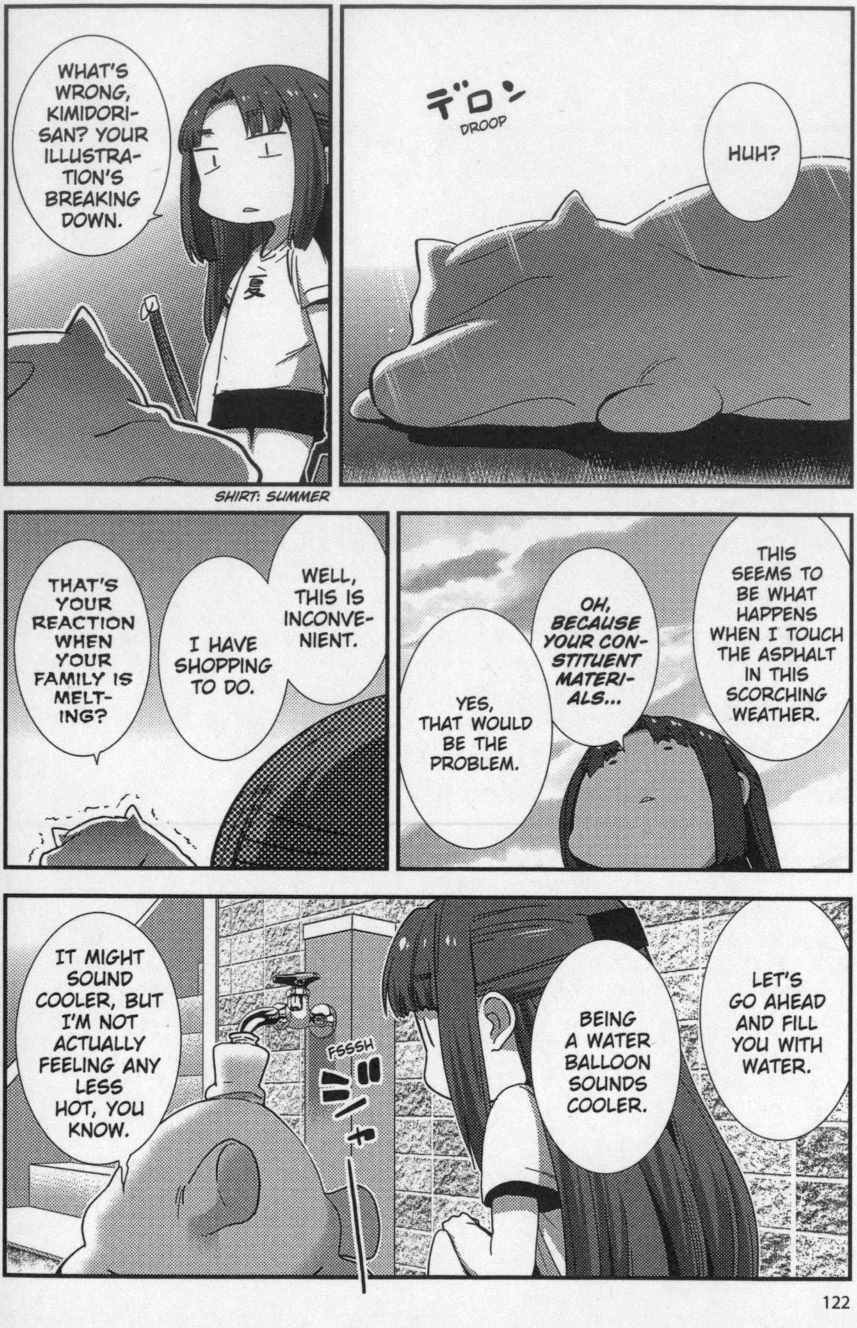

デロン
DROOP
HUH?
WHAT'S WRONG, KIMIDORI-SAN? YOUR ILLUSTRATION'S BREAKING DOWN.
SHIRT: SUMMER
THIS SEEMS TO BE WHAT HAPPENS WHEN I TOUCH THE ASPHALT IN THIS SCORCHING WEATHER.
OH, BECAUSE YOUR CONSTITUENT MATERIALS...
YES, THAT WOULD BE THE PROBLEM.
WELL, THIS IS INCONVENIENT.
I HAVE SHOPPING TO DO.
THAT'S YOUR REACTION WHEN YOUR FAMILY IS MELTING?
LET'S GO AHEAD AND FILL YOU WITH WATER.
BEING A WATER BALLOON SOUNDS COOLER.
FSSSH
IT MIGHT SOUND COOLER, BUT I'M NOT ACTUALLY FEELING ANY LESS HOT, YOU KNOW.

SUMMER AND WATER BALLOONS

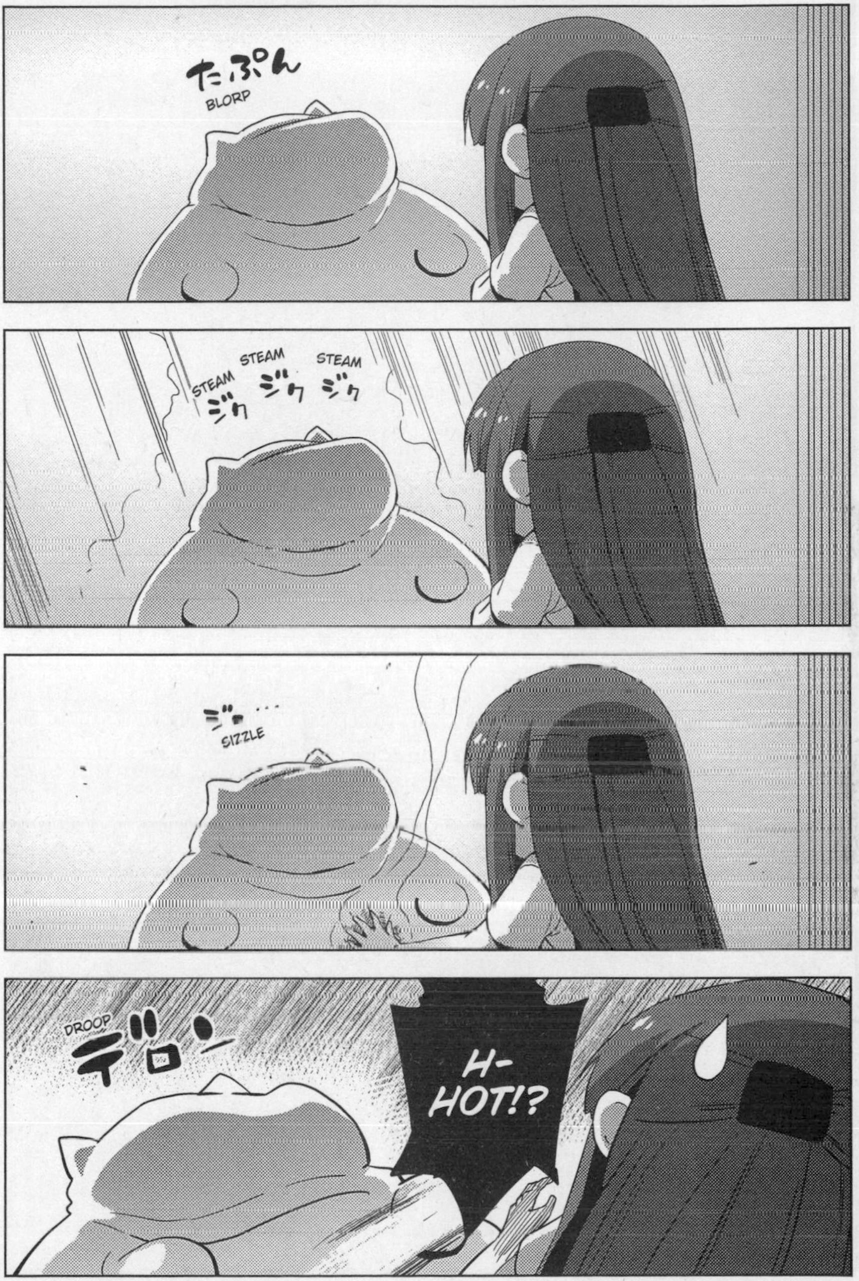
たぷん
BLORP
ジク
STEAM
ジク
STEAM
ジク
STEAM
ジュ…
SIZZLE
H-HOT!?
デロー
DROOP

FROZEN TREATS

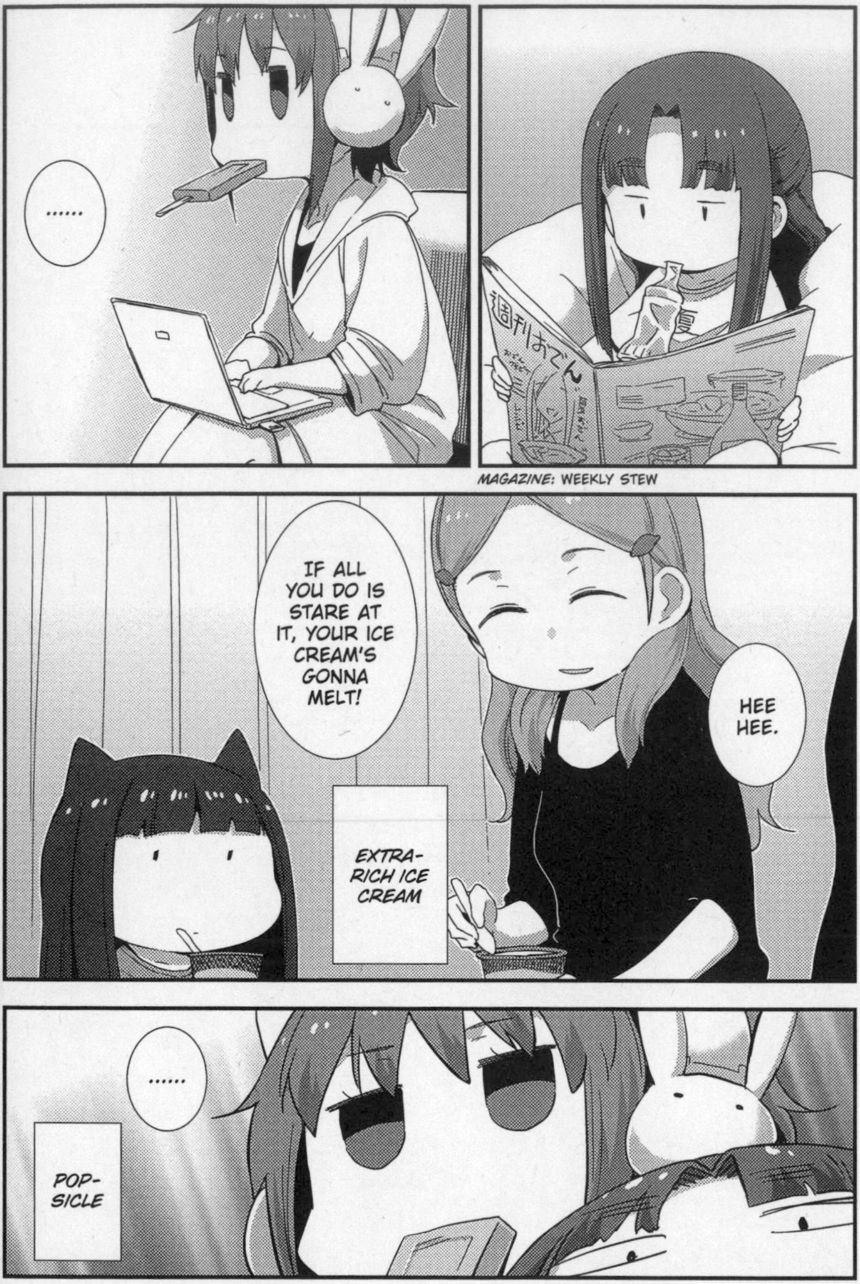

MAGAZINE: WEEKLY STEW
......
IF ALL YOU DO IS STARE AT IT, YOUR ICE CREAM'S GONNA MELT!
HEE HEE.
EXTRA-RICH ICE CREAM
......
POP-SICLE

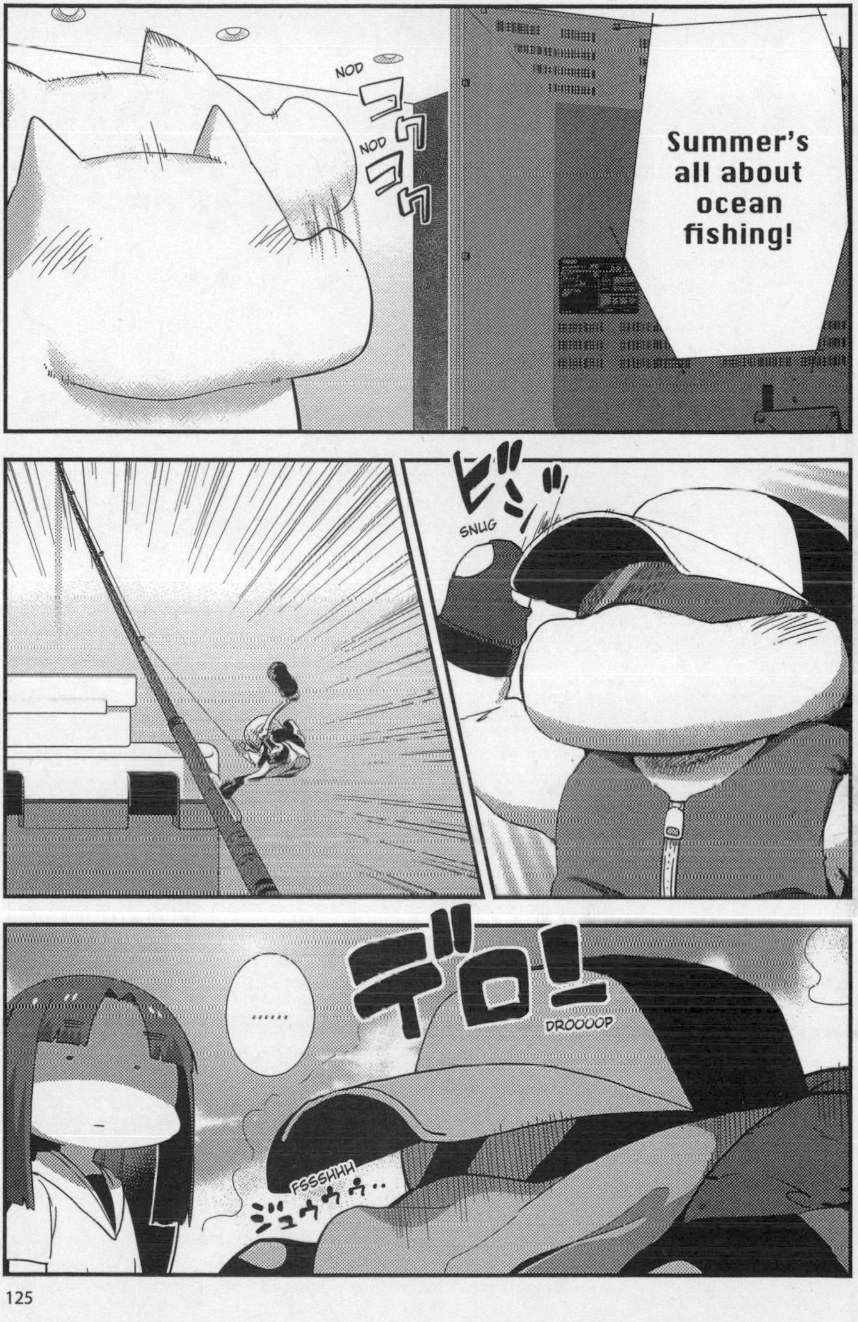
Summer's all about ocean fishing!
NOD
NOD
SNUG
DROOOOP
......
FSSSHHH

SUMMER

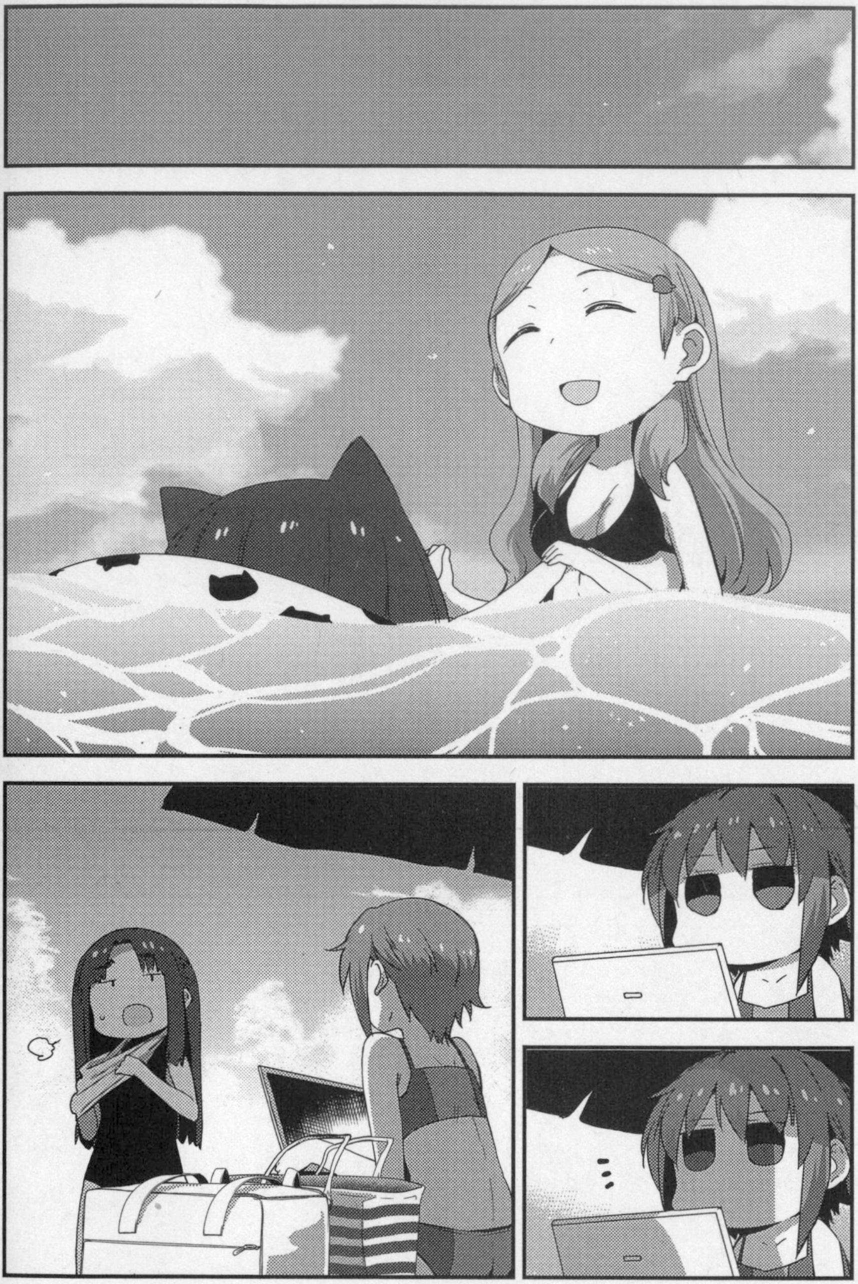

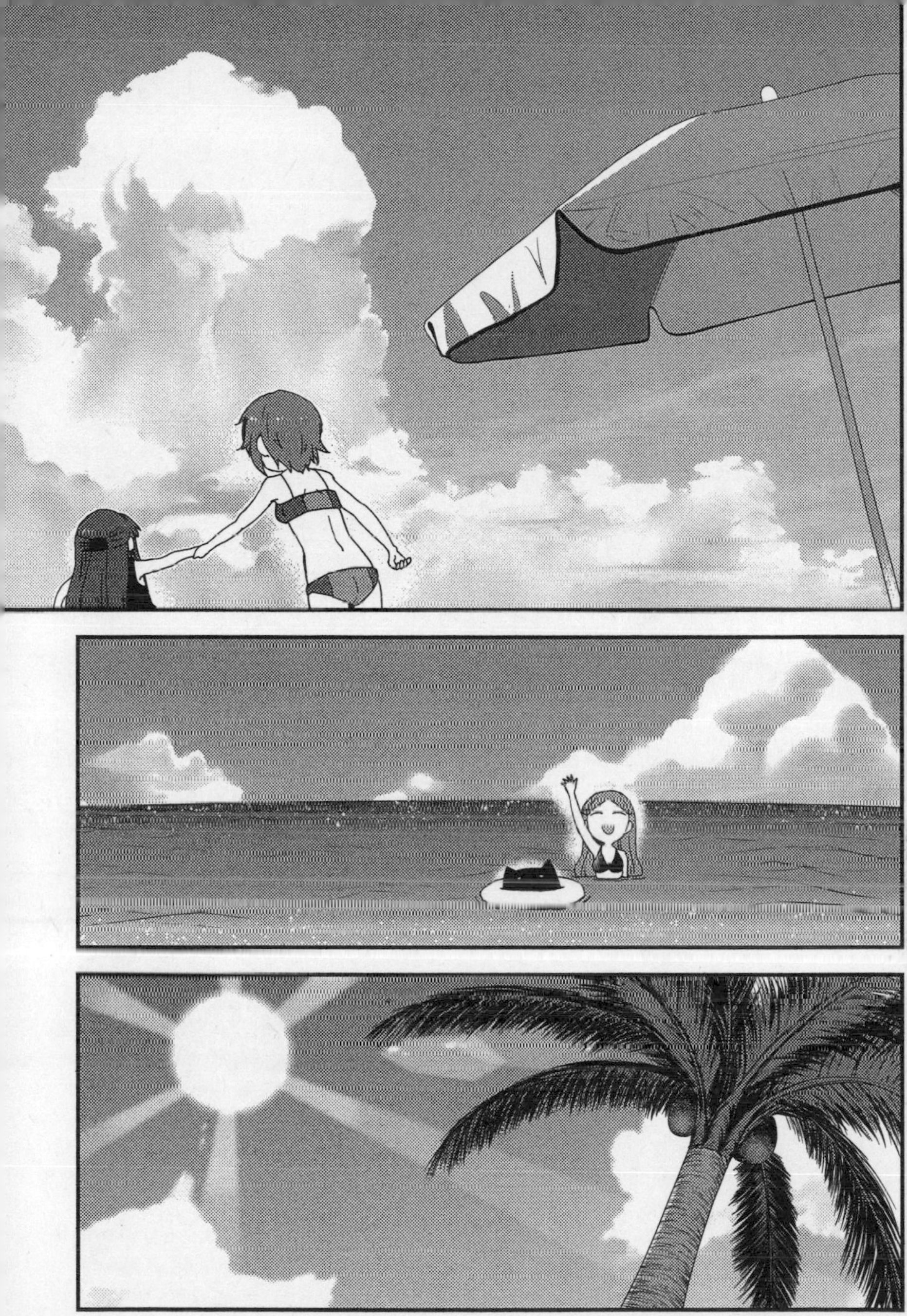

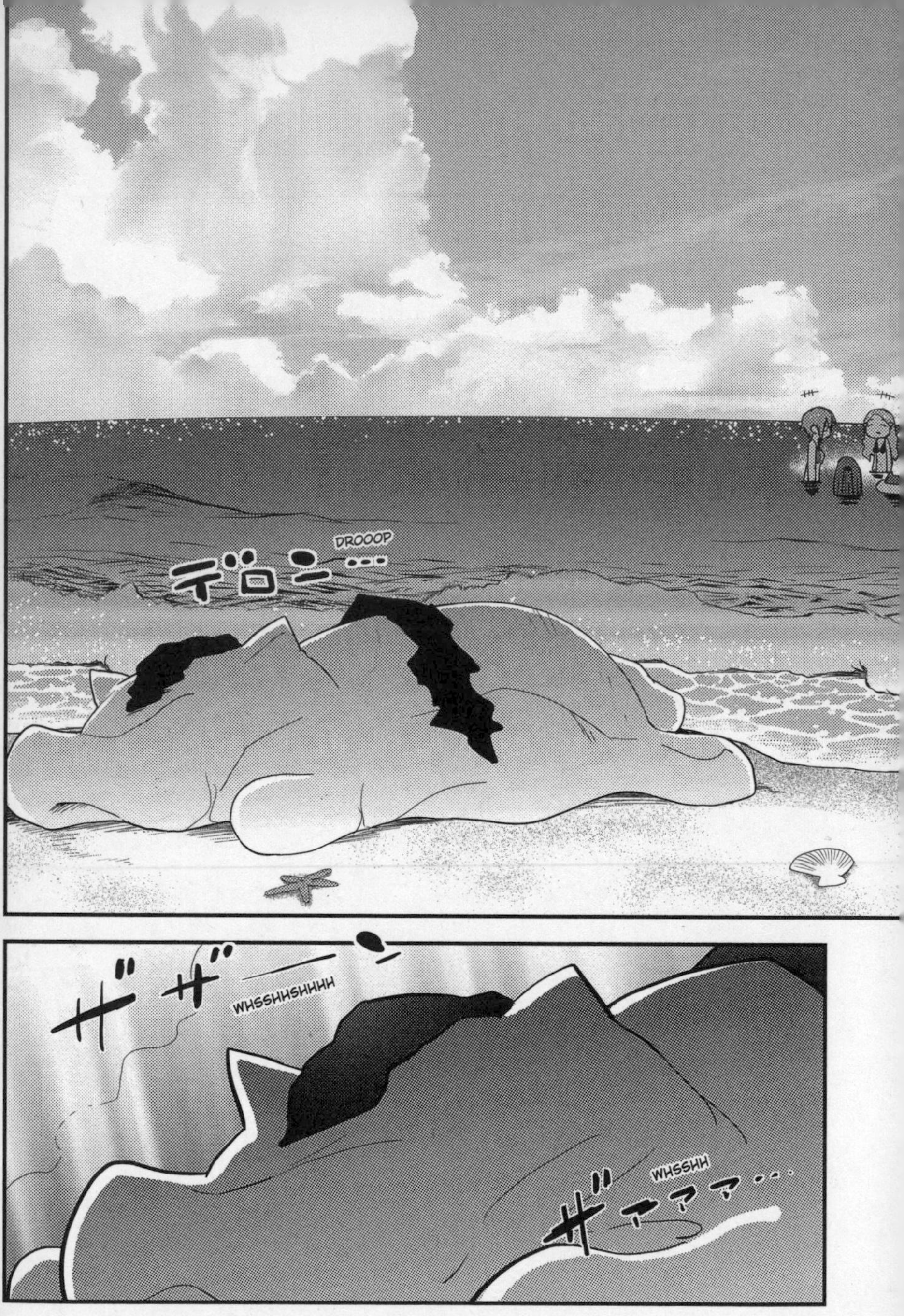
DROOOP
デロ～…
WHSSHHSHHHH
ザザーン
WHSSHH
ザァァァ…

IF THERE ARE
ANY JOKES
ABOUT THE
MATERIAL, ALL
I CAN DO IS
APOLOGIZE.

NOW, TO THE
ISLAND!

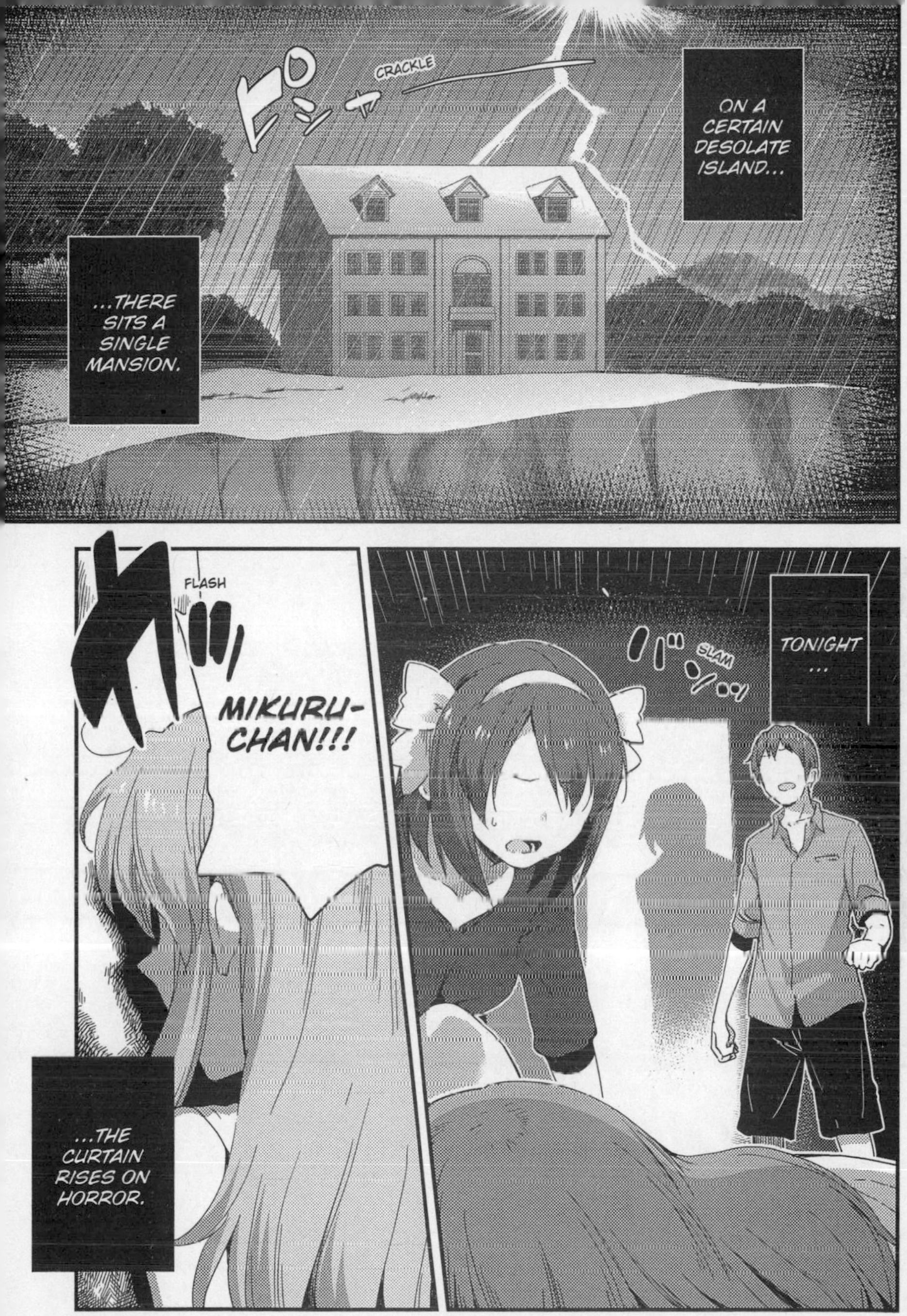
ON A CERTAIN DESOLATE ISLAND...
CRACKLE
...THERE SITS A SINGLE MANSION.
TONIGHT...
SLAM
FLASH
MIKURU-CHAN!!!
...THE CURTAIN RISES ON HORROR.

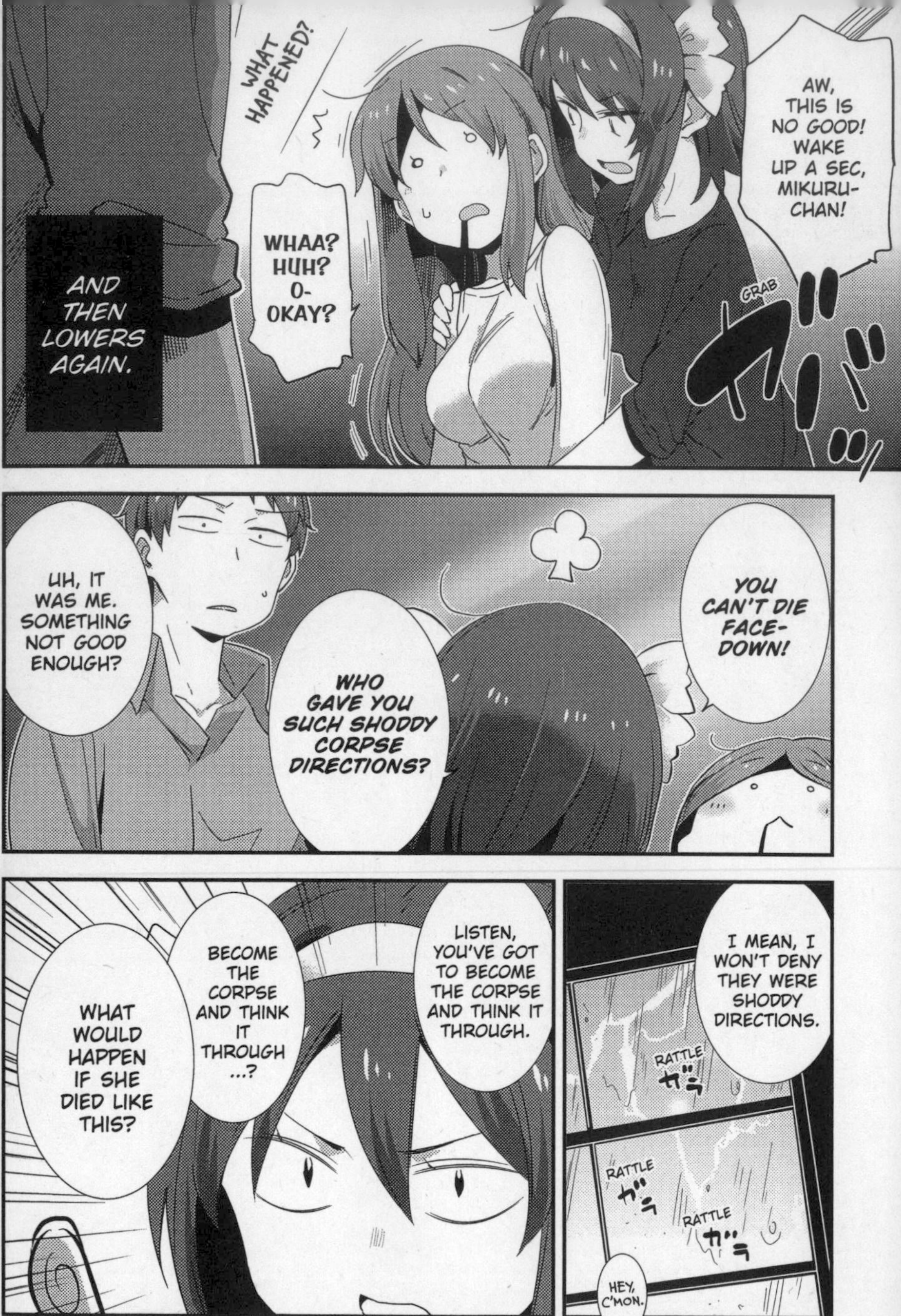
AW, THIS IS NO GOOD! WAKE UP A SEC, MIKURU-CHAN!
GRAB
WHAT HAPPENED?
WHAA? HUH? O-OKAY?
AND THEN LOWERS AGAIN.
YOU CAN'T DIE FACE-DOWN!
WHO GAVE YOU SUCH SHODDY CORPSE DIRECTIONS?
UH, IT WAS ME. SOMETHING NOT GOOD ENOUGH?
I MEAN, I WON'T DENY THEY WERE SHODDY DIRECTIONS.
RATTLE
RATTLE
RATTLE
HEY, C'MON.
LISTEN, YOU'VE GOT TO BECOME THE CORPSE AND THINK IT THROUGH.
BECOME THE CORPSE AND THINK IT THROUGH ...?
WHAT WOULD HAPPEN IF SHE DIED LIKE THIS?

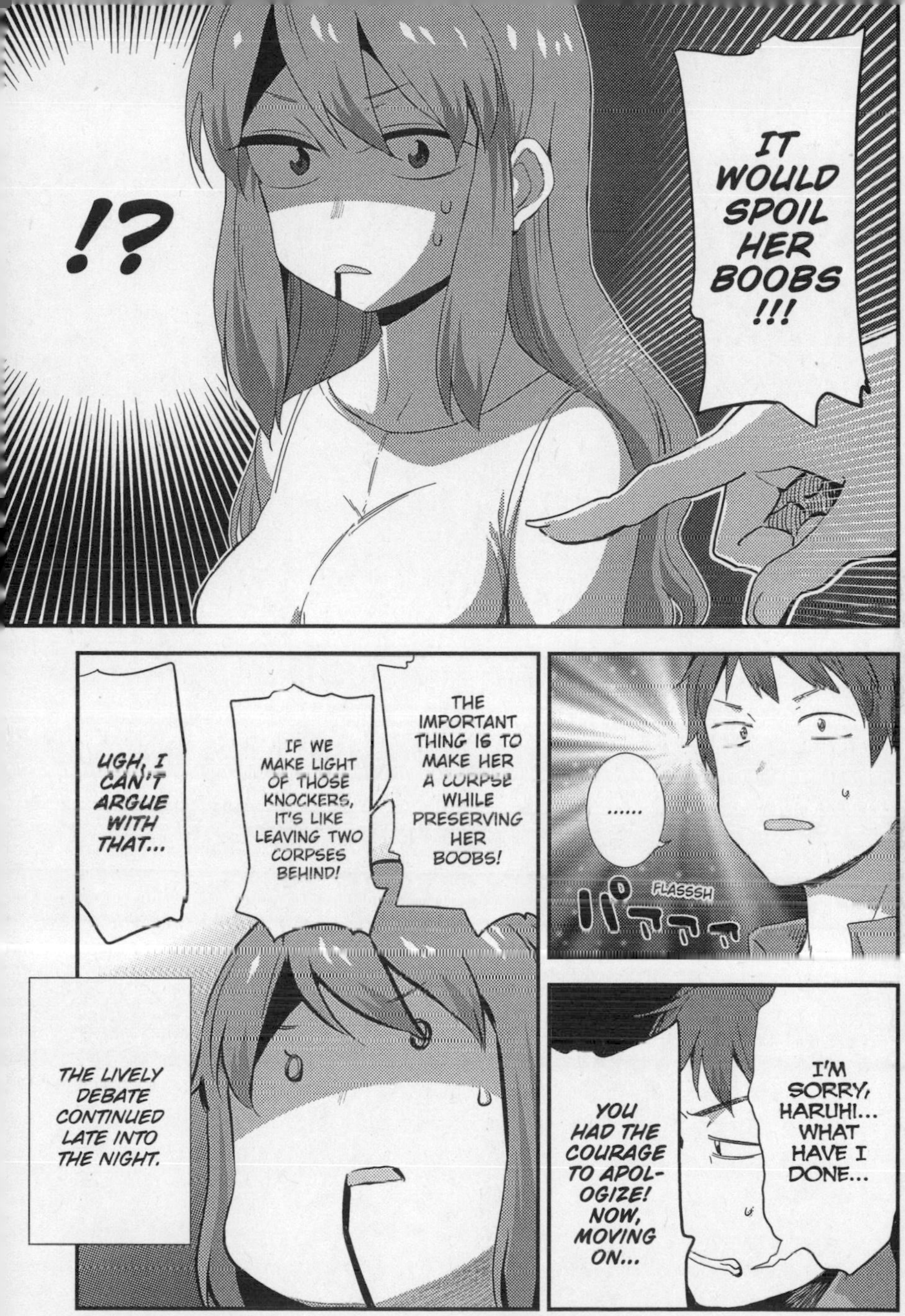
IT WOULD SPOIL HER BOOBS!!!
!?
......
FLASSSH
I'M SORRY, HARUHI... WHAT HAVE I DONE...
YOU HAD THE COURAGE TO APOLOGIZE! NOW, MOVING ON...
THE IMPORTANT THING IS TO MAKE HER A CORPSE WHILE PRESERVING HER BOOBS!
IF WE MAKE LIGHT OF THOSE KNOCKERS, IT'S LIKE LEAVING TWO CORPSES BEHIND!
UGH, I CAN'T ARGUE WITH THAT...
THE LIVELY DEBATE CONTINUED LATE INTO THE NIGHT.

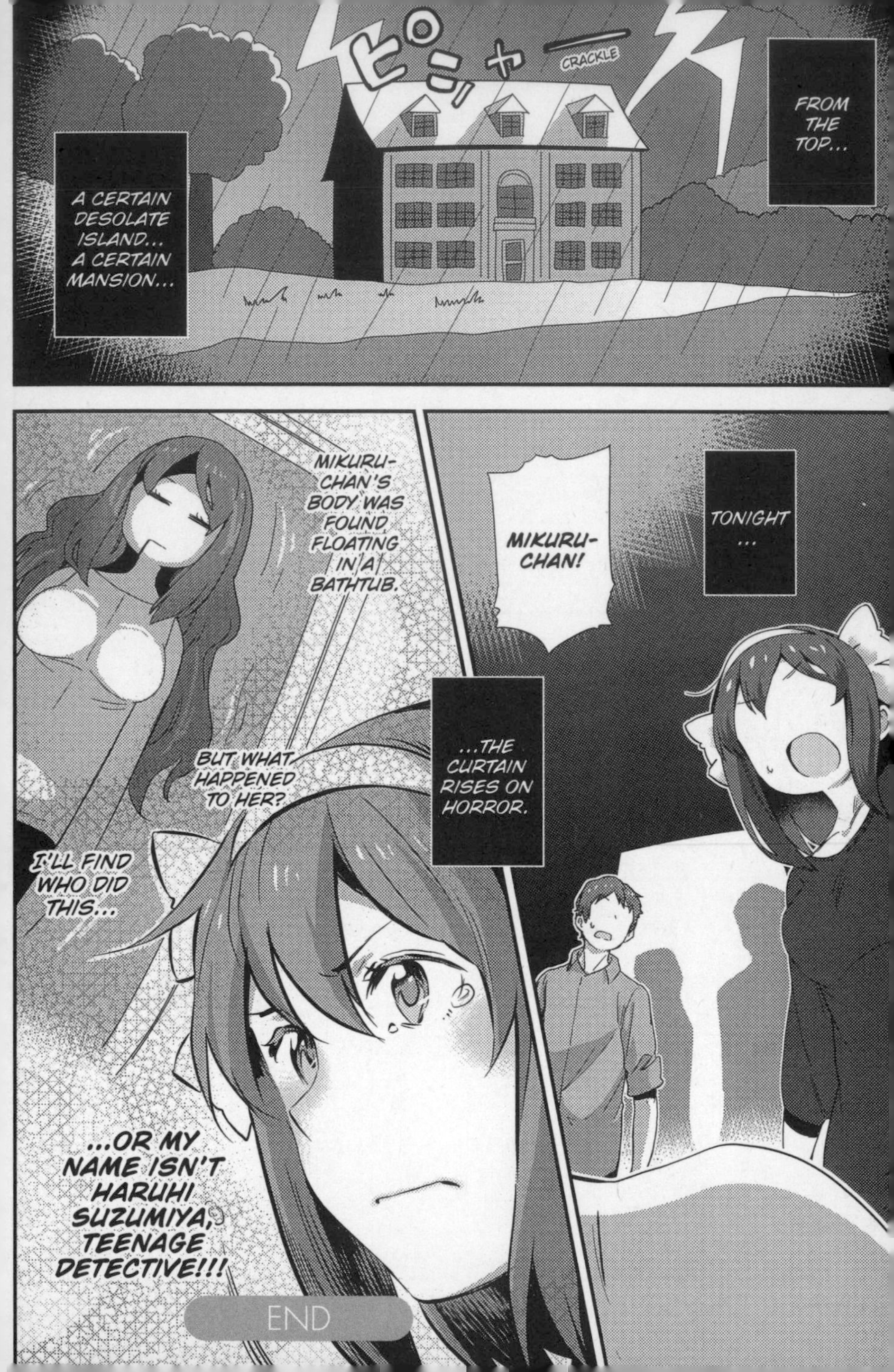
FROM THE TOP...
CRACKLE
A CERTAIN DESOLATE ISLAND... A CERTAIN MANSION...
TONIGHT ...
MIKURU-CHAN!
...THE CURTAIN RISES ON HORROR.
MIKURU-CHAN'S BODY WAS FOUND FLOATING IN A BATHTUB.
BUT WHAT HAPPENED TO HER?
I'LL FIND WHO DID THIS...
...OR MY NAME ISN'T HARUHI SUZUMIYA, TEENAGE DETECTIVE!!!
END

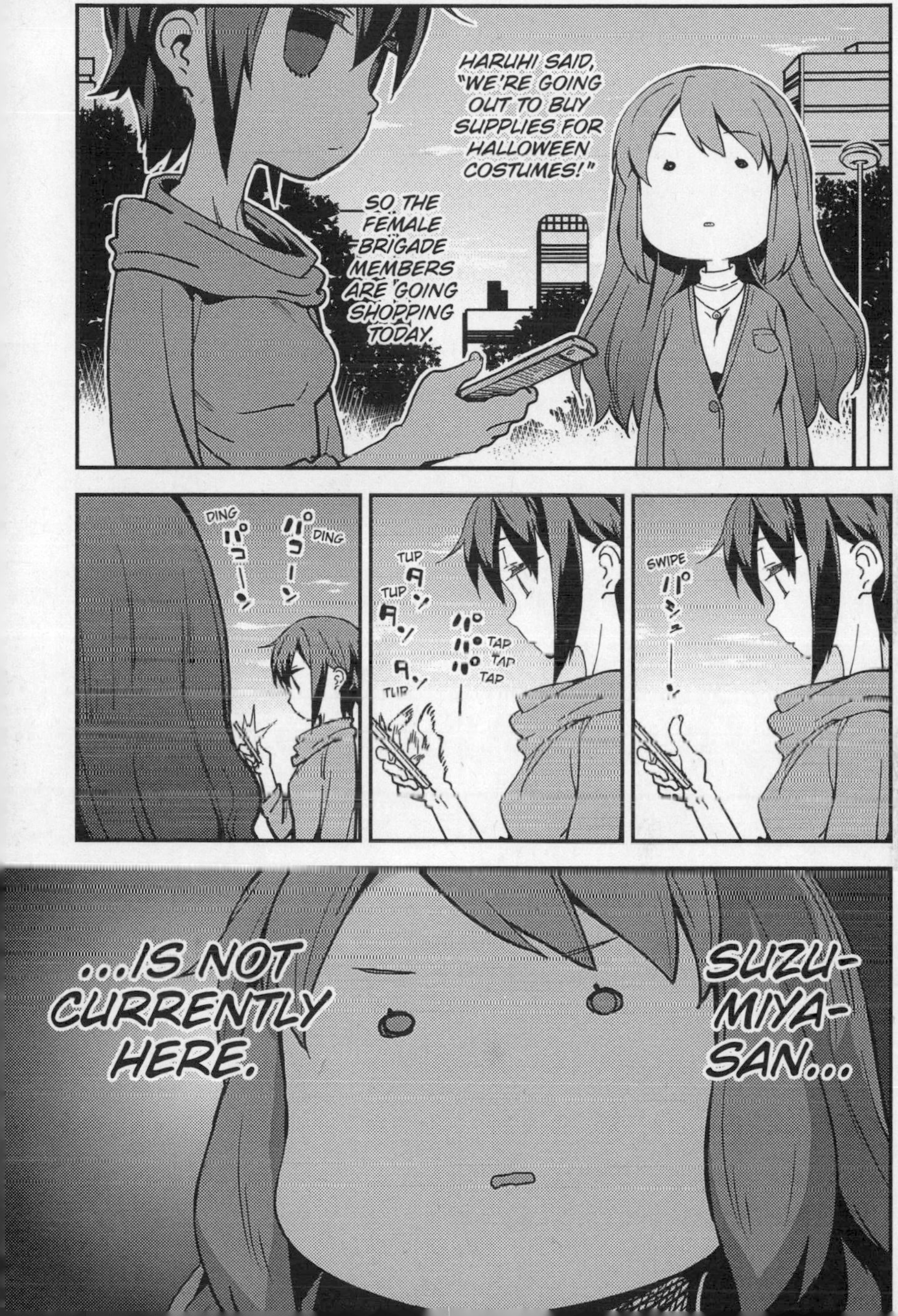
HARUHI SAID, "WE'RE GOING OUT TO BUY SUPPLIES FOR HALLOWEEN COSTUMES!"
SO THE FEMALE BRIGADE MEMBERS ARE GOING SHOPPING TODAY.
SWIPE
TUP
TUP
TAP
TAP
TAP
TUP
DING
DING
SUZU-MIYA-SAN...
...IS NOT CURRENTLY HERE.

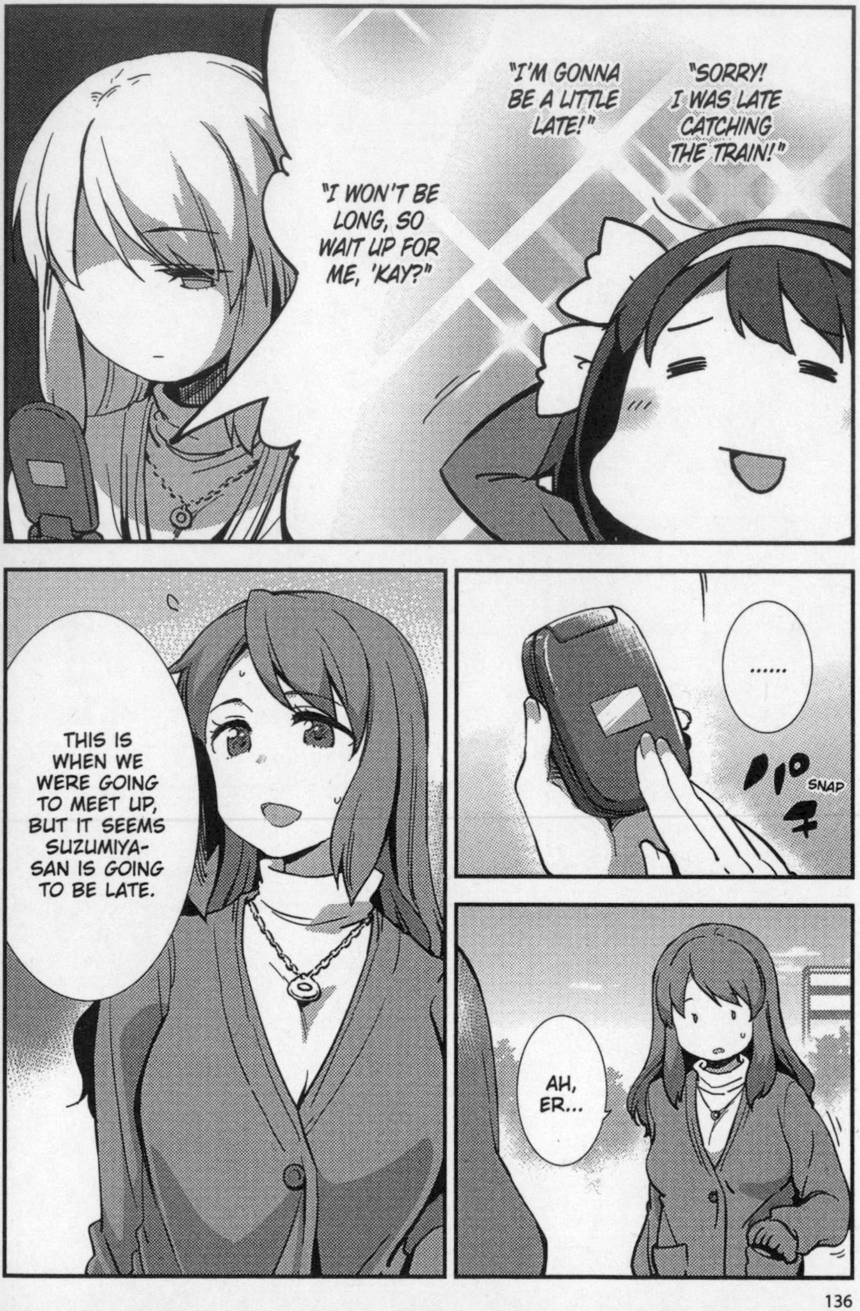
"SORRY! I WAS LATE CATCHING THE TRAIN!"
"I'M GONNA BE A LITTLE LATE!"
"I WON'T BE LONG, SO WAIT UP FOR ME, 'KAY?"
......
SNAP
AH, ER...
THIS IS WHEN WE WERE GOING TO MEET UP, BUT IT SEEMS SUZUMIYA-SAN IS GOING TO BE LATE.

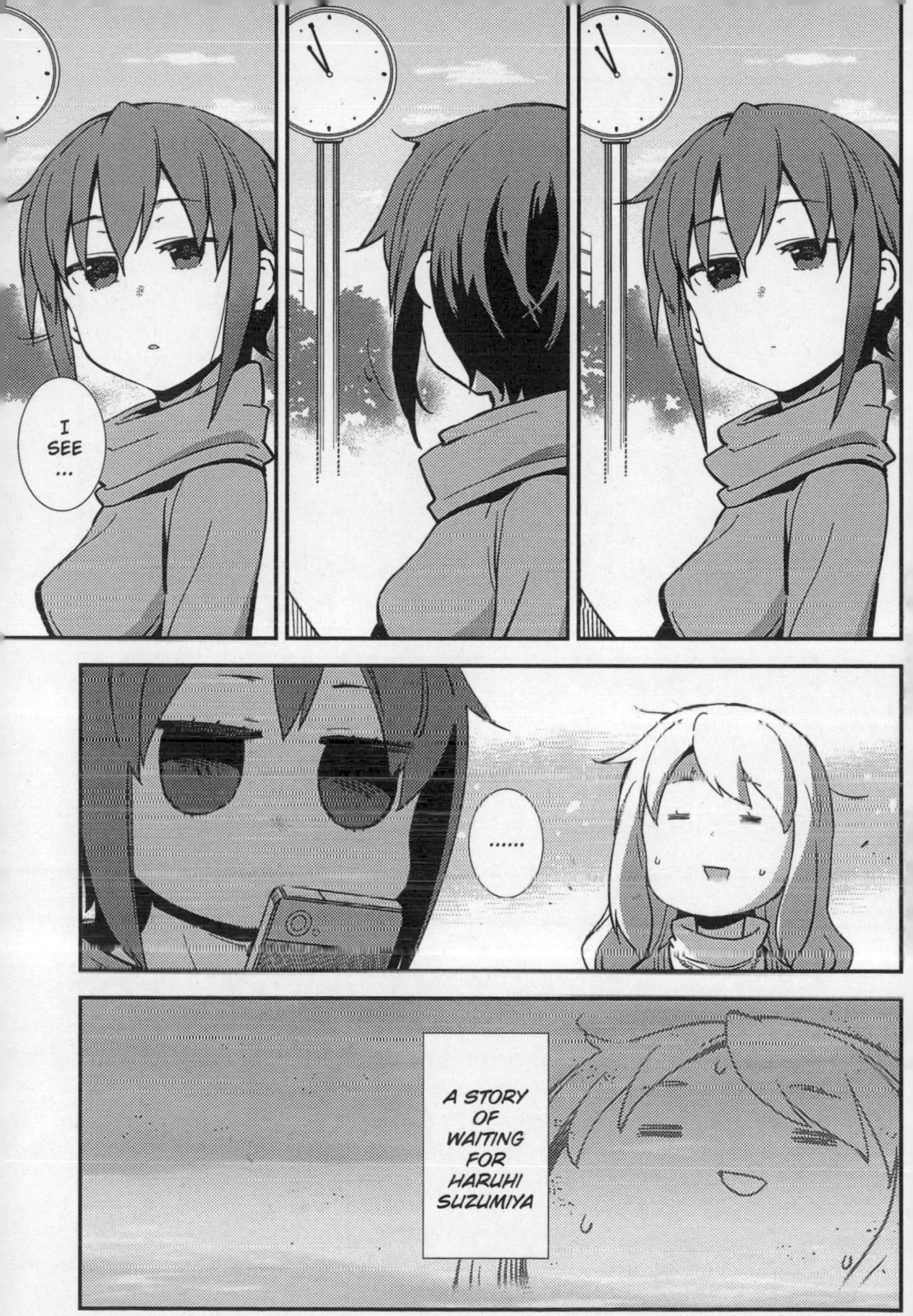
I SEE ...
......
A STORY OF WAITING FOR HARUHI SUZUMIYA

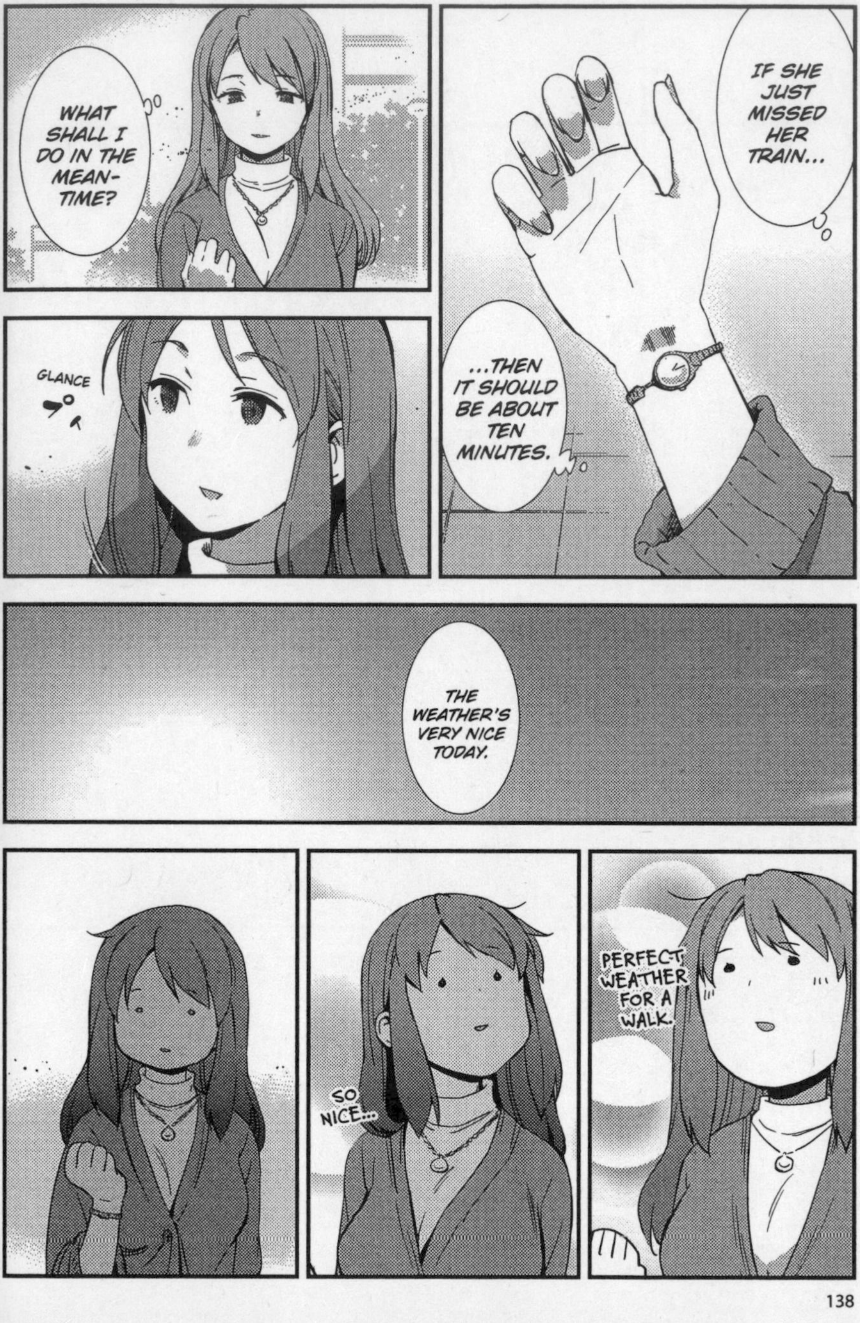
IF SHE JUST MISSED HER TRAIN...
...THEN IT SHOULD BE ABOUT TEN MINUTES.
WHAT SHALL I DO IN THE MEAN-TIME?
GLANCE
THE WEATHER'S VERY NICE TODAY.
PERFECT WEATHER FOR A WALK.
SO NICE...

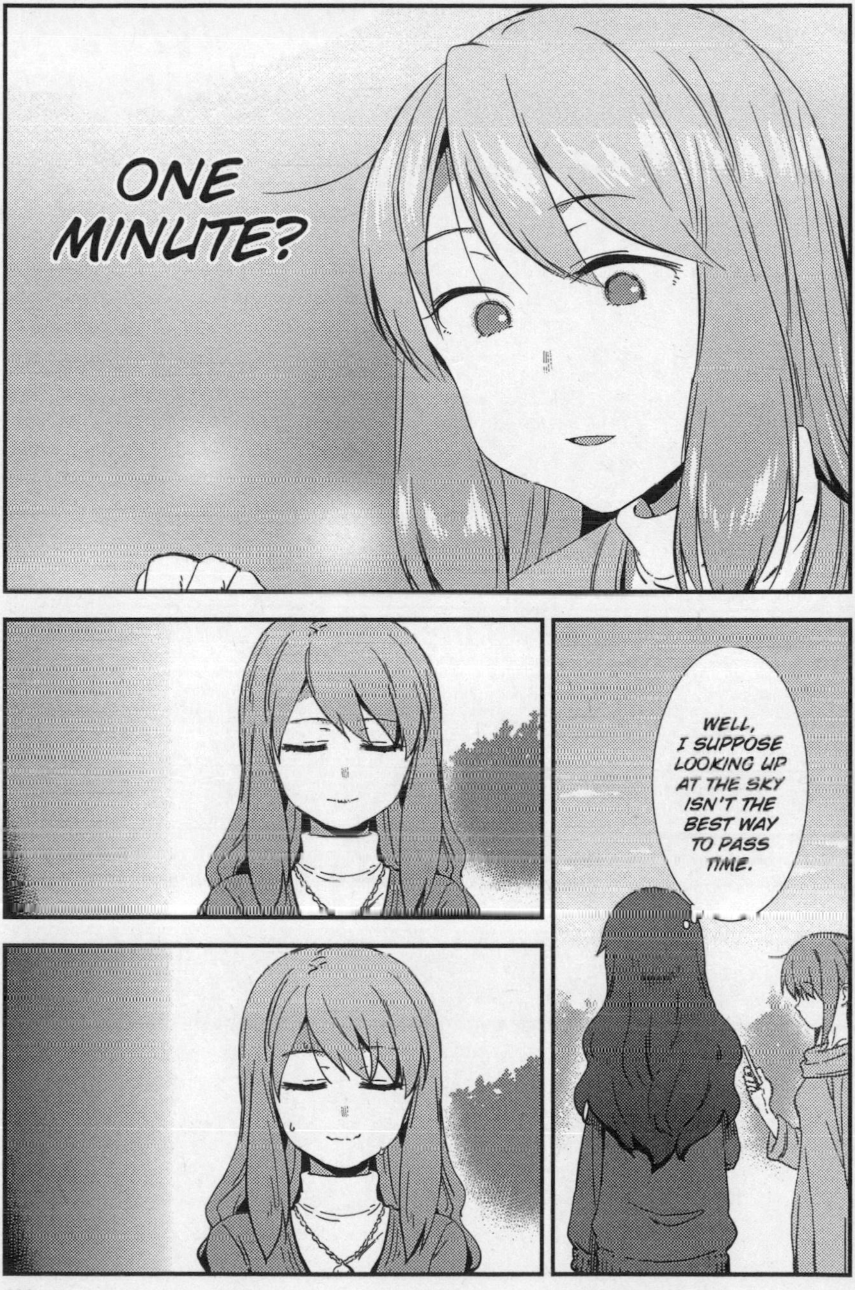
ONE MINUTE?
WELL, I SUPPOSE LOOKING UP AT THE SKY ISN'T THE BEST WAY TO PASS TIME.

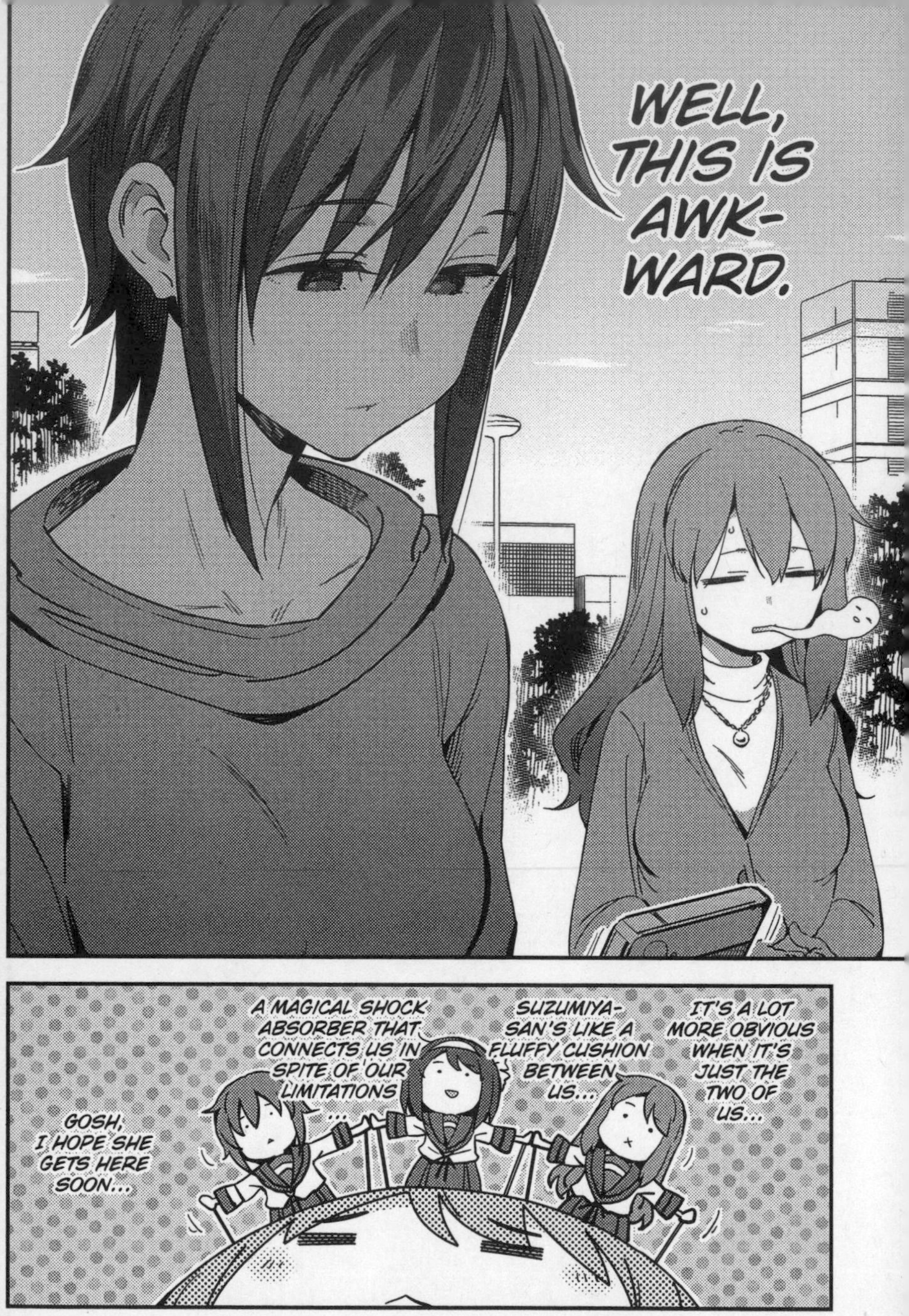
WELL, THIS IS AWK-WARD.
IT'S A LOT MORE OBVIOUS WHEN IT'S JUST THE TWO OF US...
SUZUMIYA-SAN'S LIKE A FLUFFY CUSHION BETWEEN US...
A MAGICAL SHOCK ABSORBER THAT CONNECTS US IN SPITE OF OUR LIMITATIONS ...
GOSH, I HOPE SHE GETS HERE SOON...

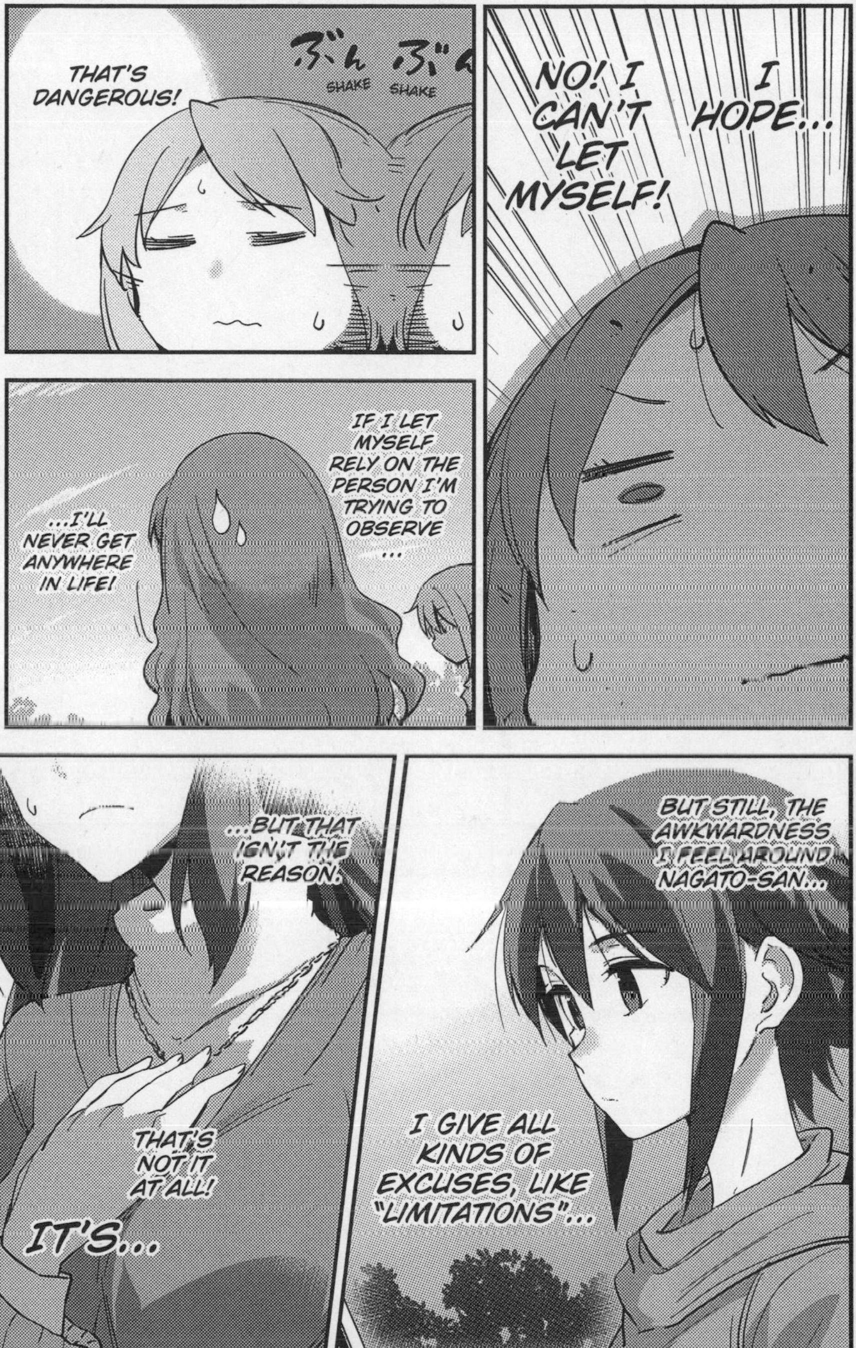
I HOPE...
NO! I CAN'T LET MYSELF!
ぶん ぶん
SHAKE SHAKE
THAT'S DANGEROUS!
IF I LET MYSELF RELY ON THE PERSON I'M TRYING TO OBSERVE...
...I'LL NEVER GET ANYWHERE IN LIFE!
BUT STILL, THE AWKWARDNESS I FEEL AROUND NAGATO-SAN...
I GIVE ALL KINDS OF EXCUSES, LIKE "LIMITATIONS"...
...BUT THAT ISN'T THE REASON.
THAT'S NOT IT AT ALL!
IT'S...

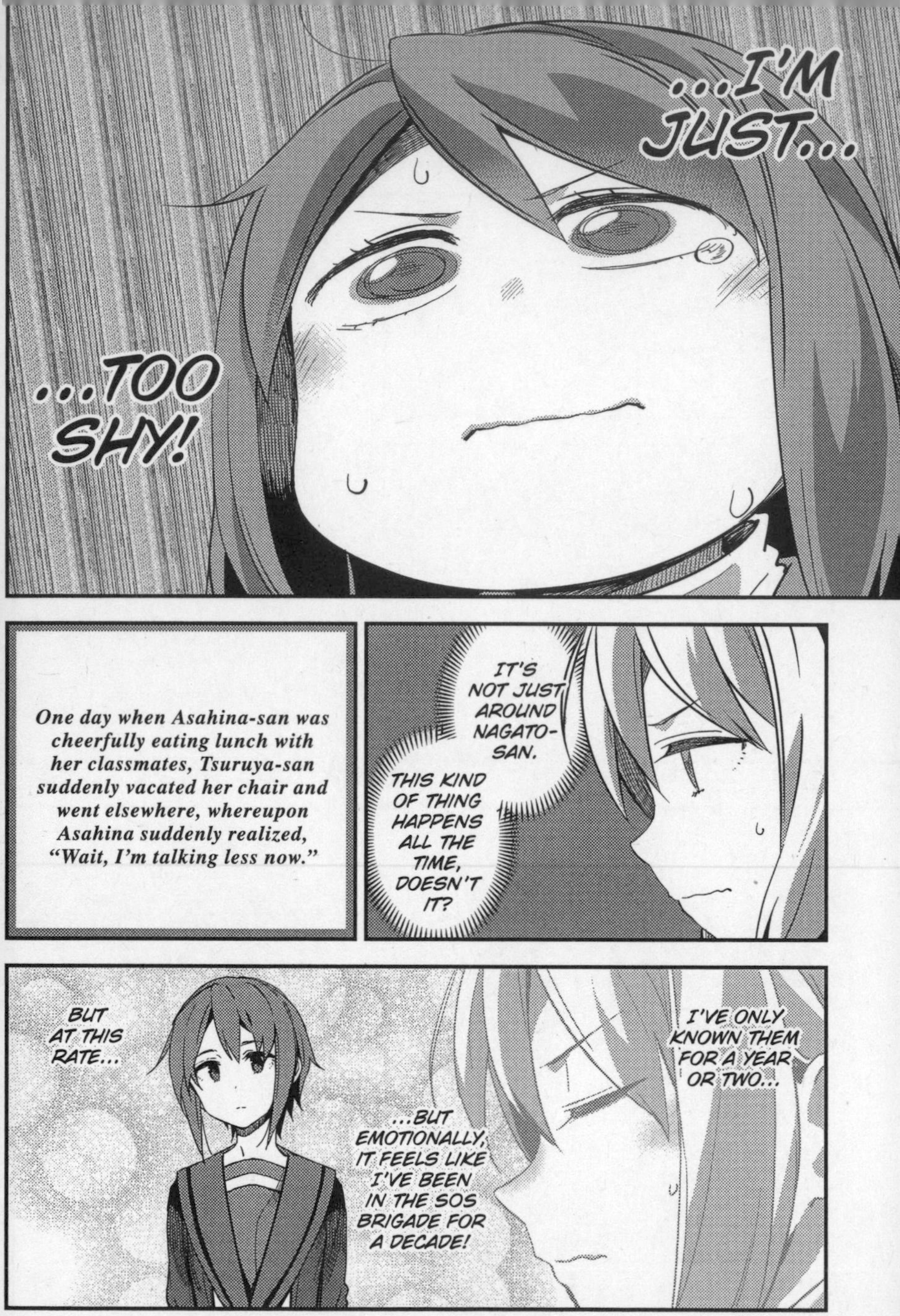
...I'M JUST...
...TOO SHY!
IT'S NOT JUST AROUND NAGATO-SAN.
THIS KIND OF THING HAPPENS ALL THE TIME, DOESN'T IT?
One day when Asahina-san was cheerfully eating lunch with her classmates, Tsuruya-san suddenly vacated her chair and went elsewhere, whereupon Asahina suddenly realized, "Wait, I'm talking less now."
I'VE ONLY KNOWN THEM FOR A YEAR OR TWO...
...BUT EMOTIONALLY, IT FEELS LIKE I'VE BEEN IN THE SOS BRIGADE FOR A DECADE!
BUT AT THIS RATE...

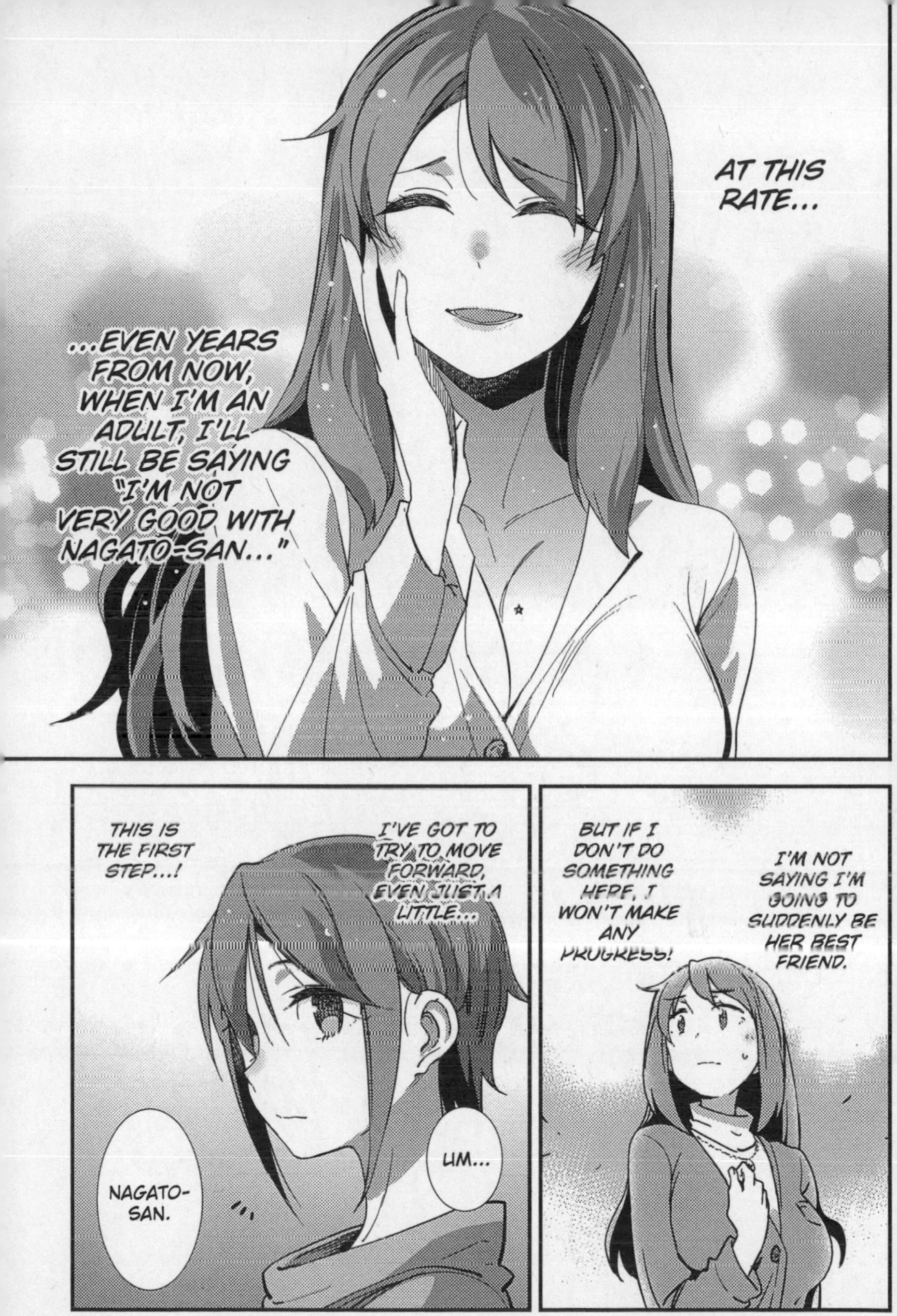
AT THIS RATE...
...EVEN YEARS FROM NOW, WHEN I'M AN ADULT, I'LL STILL BE SAYING "I'M NOT VERY GOOD WITH NAGATO-SAN..."
I'M NOT SAYING I'M GOING TO SUDDENLY BE HER BEST FRIEND.
BUT IF I DON'T DO SOMETHING HERE, I WON'T MAKE ANY PROGRESS!
I'VE GOT TO TRY TO MOVE FORWARD, EVEN JUST A LITTLE...
THIS IS THE FIRST STEP...!
UM...
NAGATO-SAN.

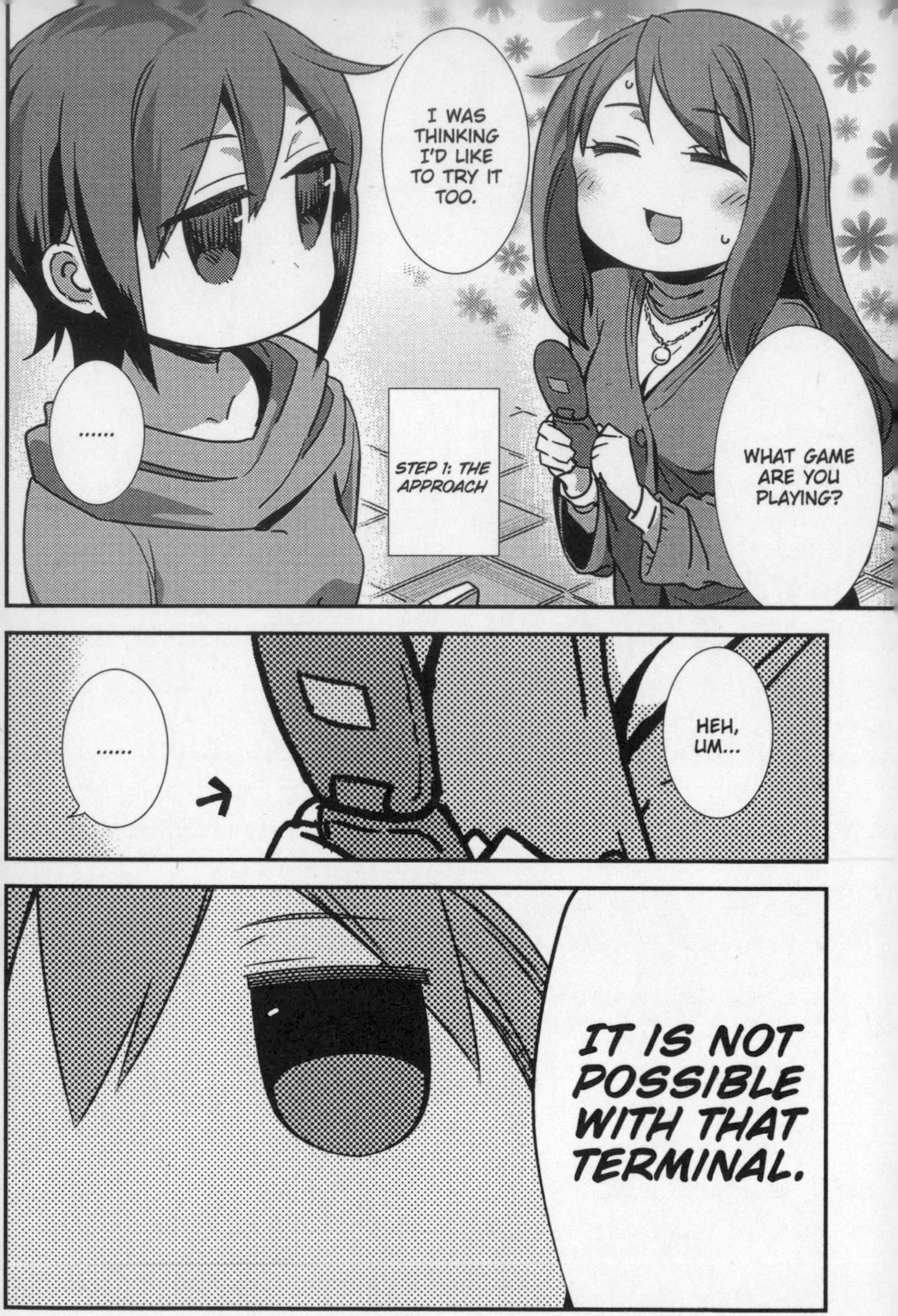
WHAT GAME ARE YOU PLAYING?
I WAS THINKING I'D LIKE TO TRY IT TOO.
STEP 1: THE APPROACH
......
HEH, UM...
......
IT IS NOT POSSIBLE WITH THAT TERMINAL.

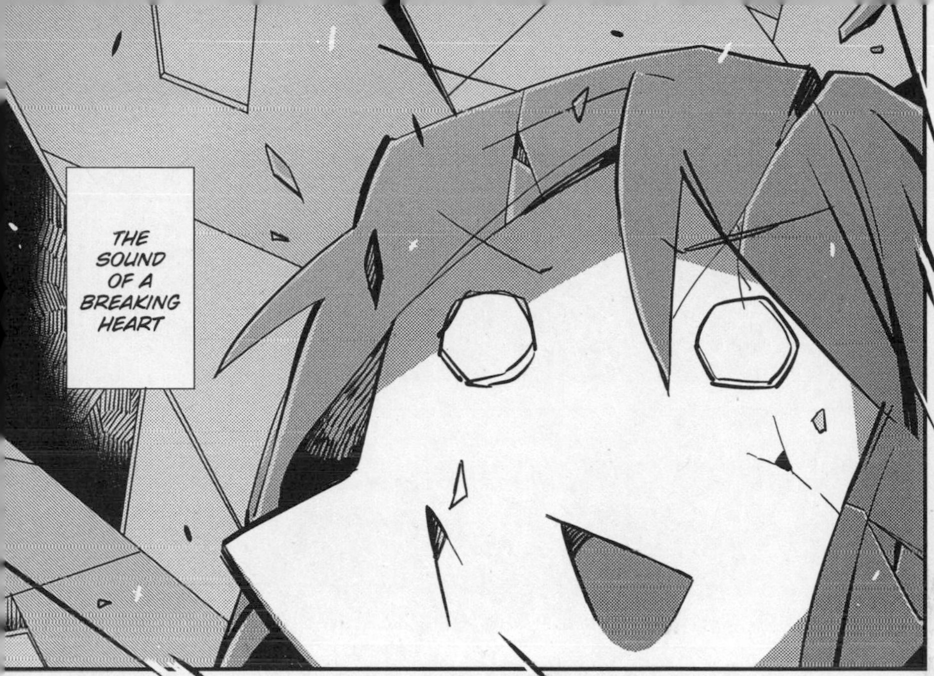
THE SOUND OF A BREAKING HEART

TEN MINUTES LATER

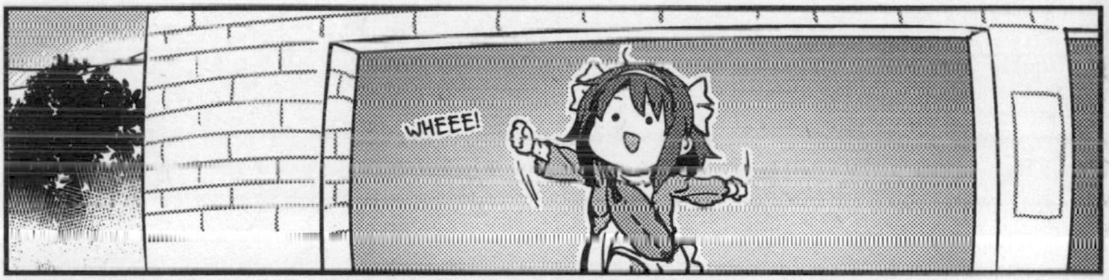
WHEEE!

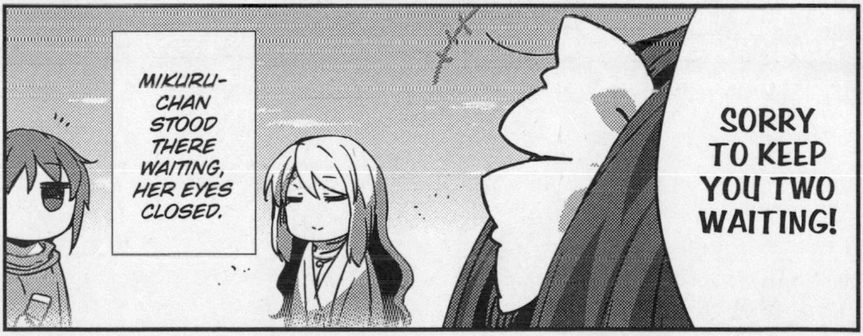
SORRY TO KEEP YOU TWO WAITING!
MIKURU-CHAN STOOD THERE WAITING, HER EYES CLOSED.

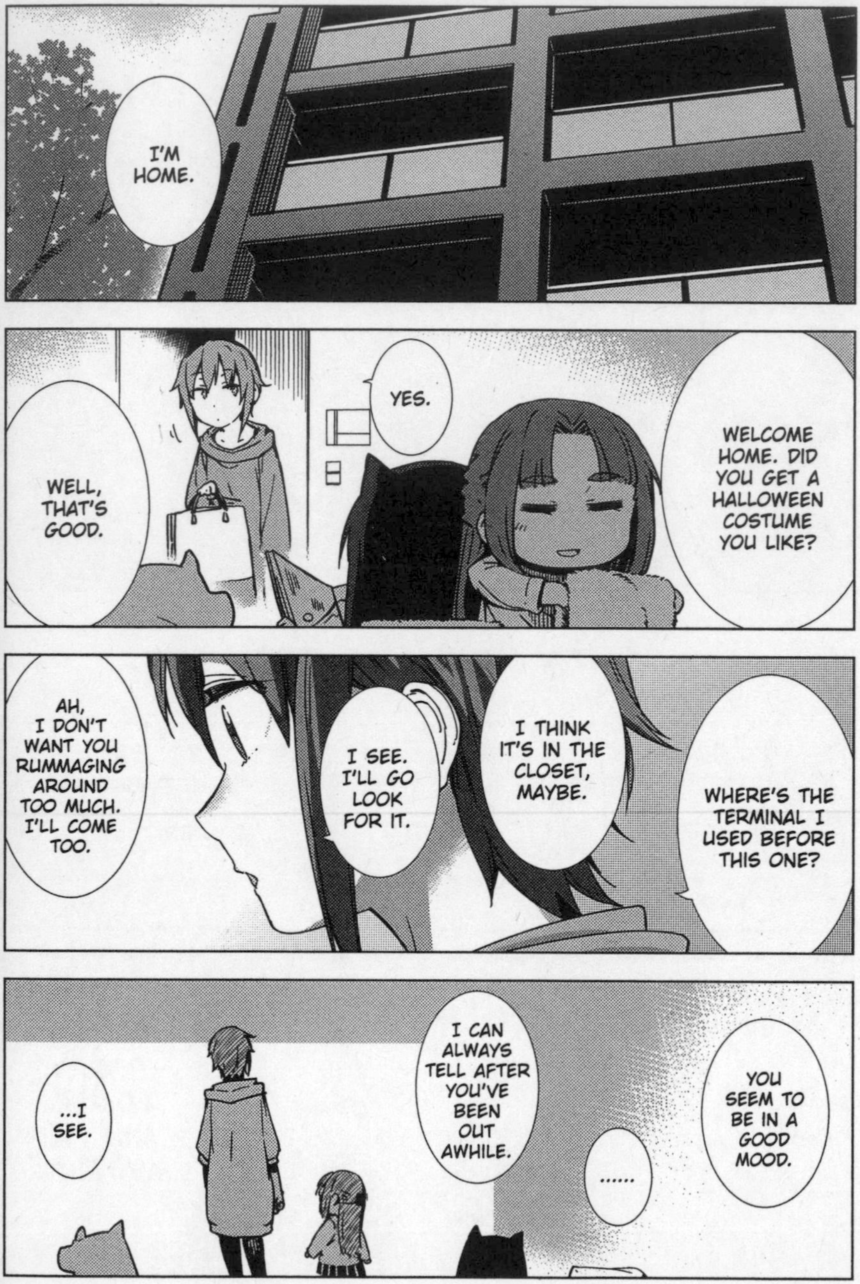
I'M HOME.
WELCOME HOME. DID YOU GET A HALLOWEEN COSTUME YOU LIKE?
YES.
WELL, THAT'S GOOD.
WHERE'S THE TERMINAL I USED BEFORE THIS ONE?
I THINK IT'S IN THE CLOSET, MAYBE.
I SEE. I'LL GO LOOK FOR IT.
AH, I DON'T WANT YOU RUMMAGING AROUND TOO MUCH. I'LL COME TOO.
YOU SEEM TO BE IN A GOOD MOOD.
......
I CAN ALWAYS TELL AFTER YOU'VE BEEN OUT AWHILE.
...I SEE.

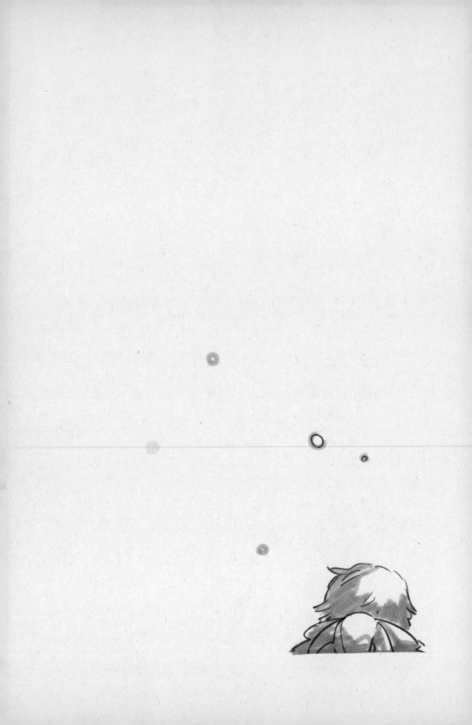

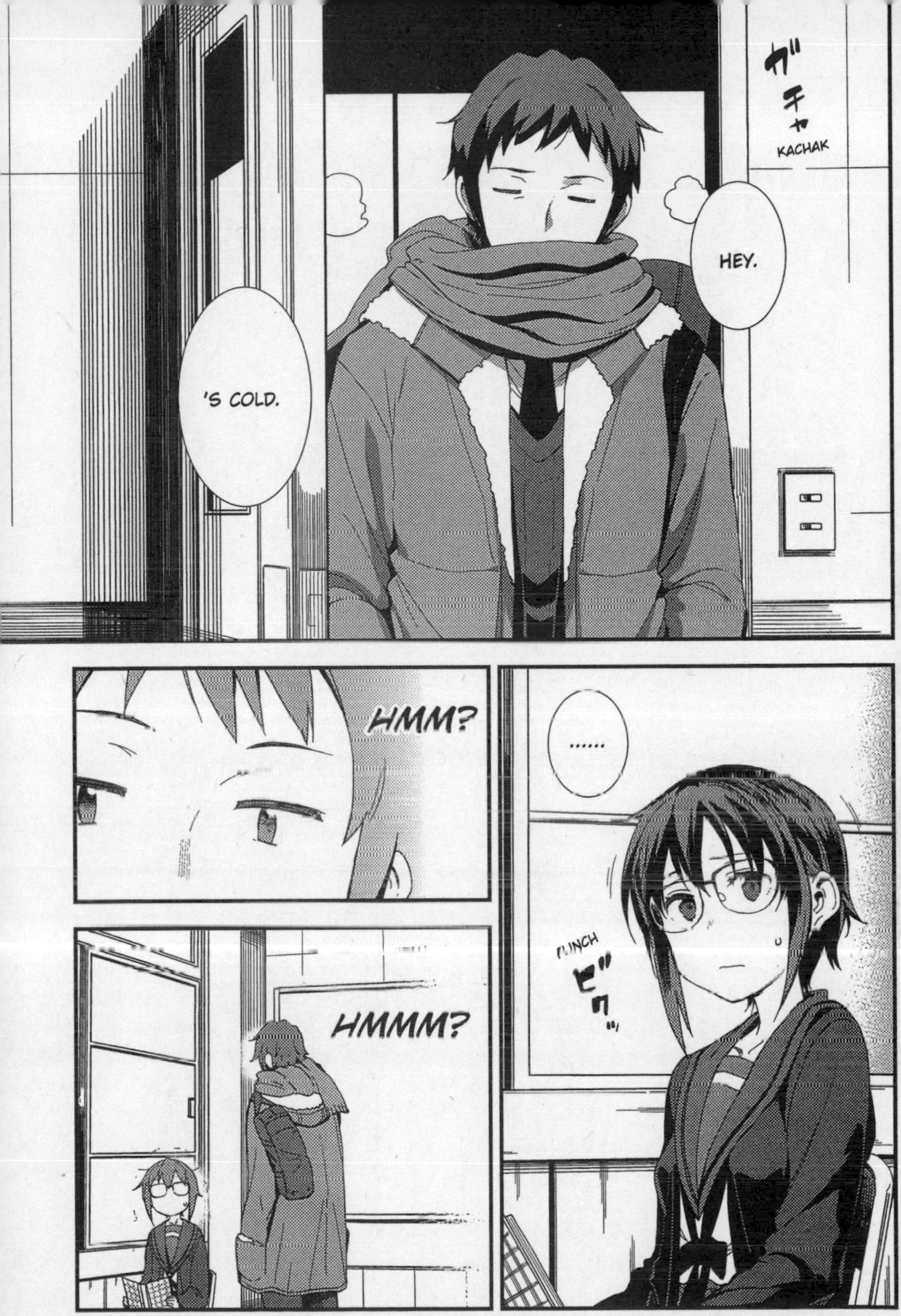
ガチャ
KACHAK
HEY.
'S COLD.
......
FLINCH
ビクッ
HMM?
HMMM?

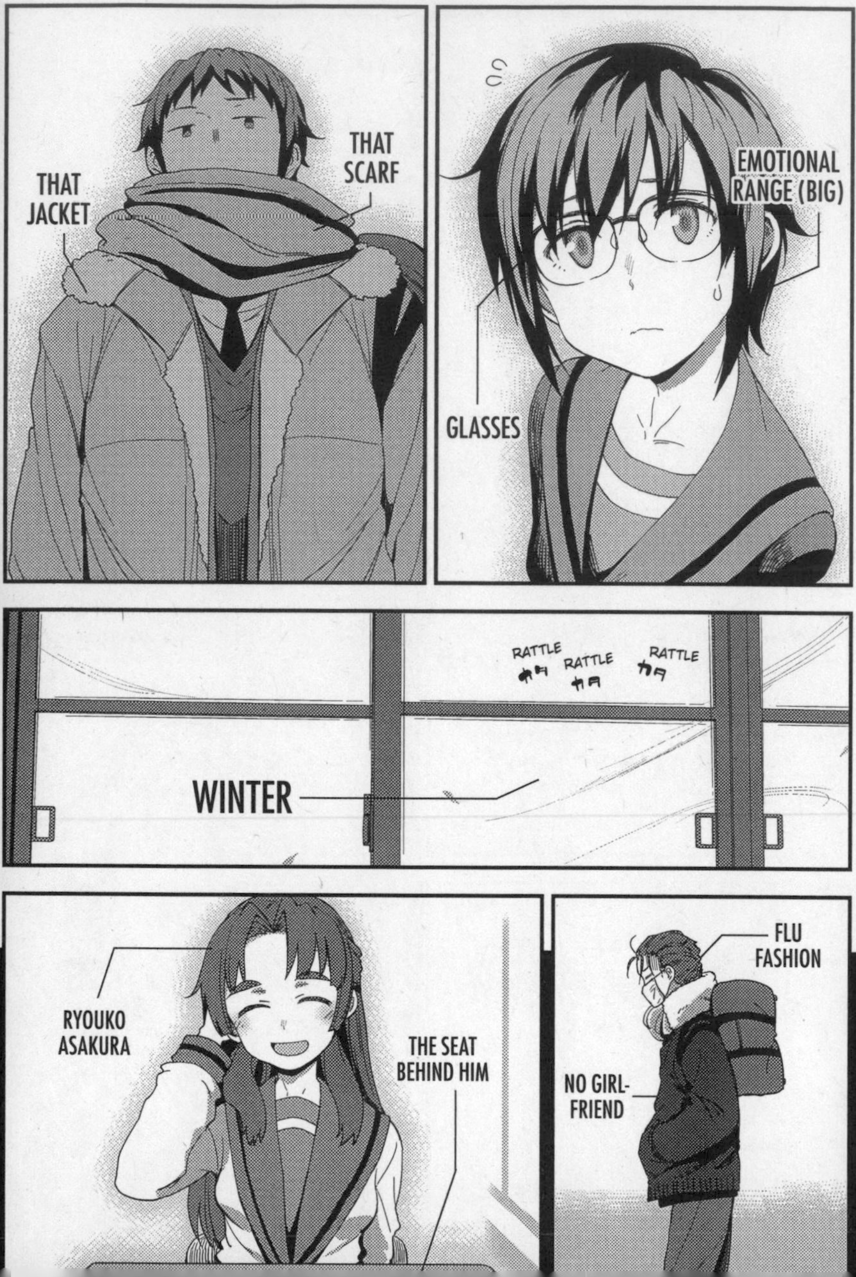
EMOTIONAL RANGE (BIG)
GLASSES
THAT SCARF
THAT JACKET
RATTLE
カタ
RATTLE
カタ
RATTLE
カタ
WINTER
FLU FASHION
NO GIRL-FRIEND
THE SEAT BEHIND HIM
RYOUKO ASAKURA

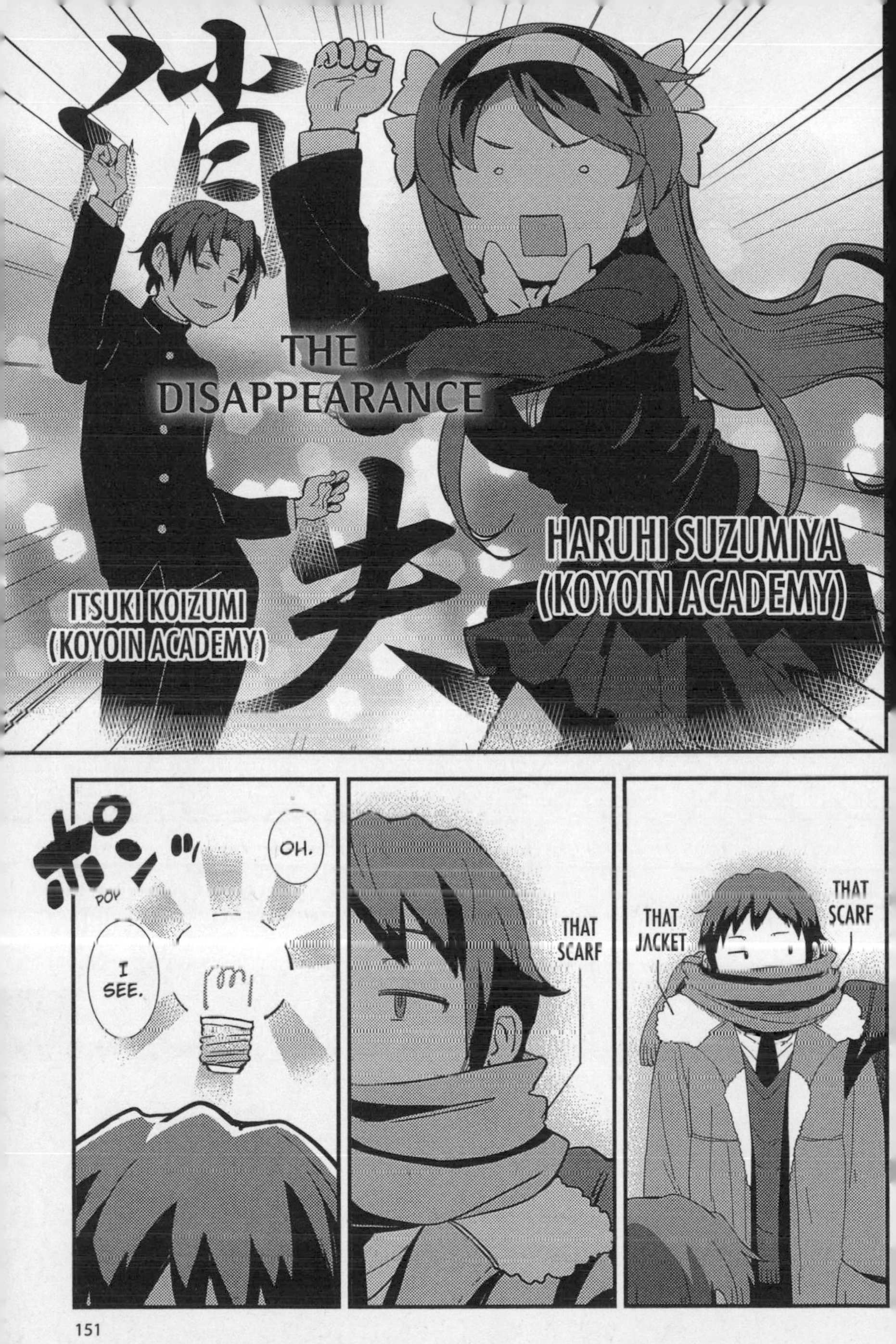
THE DISAPPEARANCE
HARUHI SUZUMIYA (KOYOIN ACADEMY)
ITSUKI KOIZUMI (KOYOIN ACADEMY)
THAT SCARF
THAT JACKET
THAT SCARF
OH.
I SEE.
POP

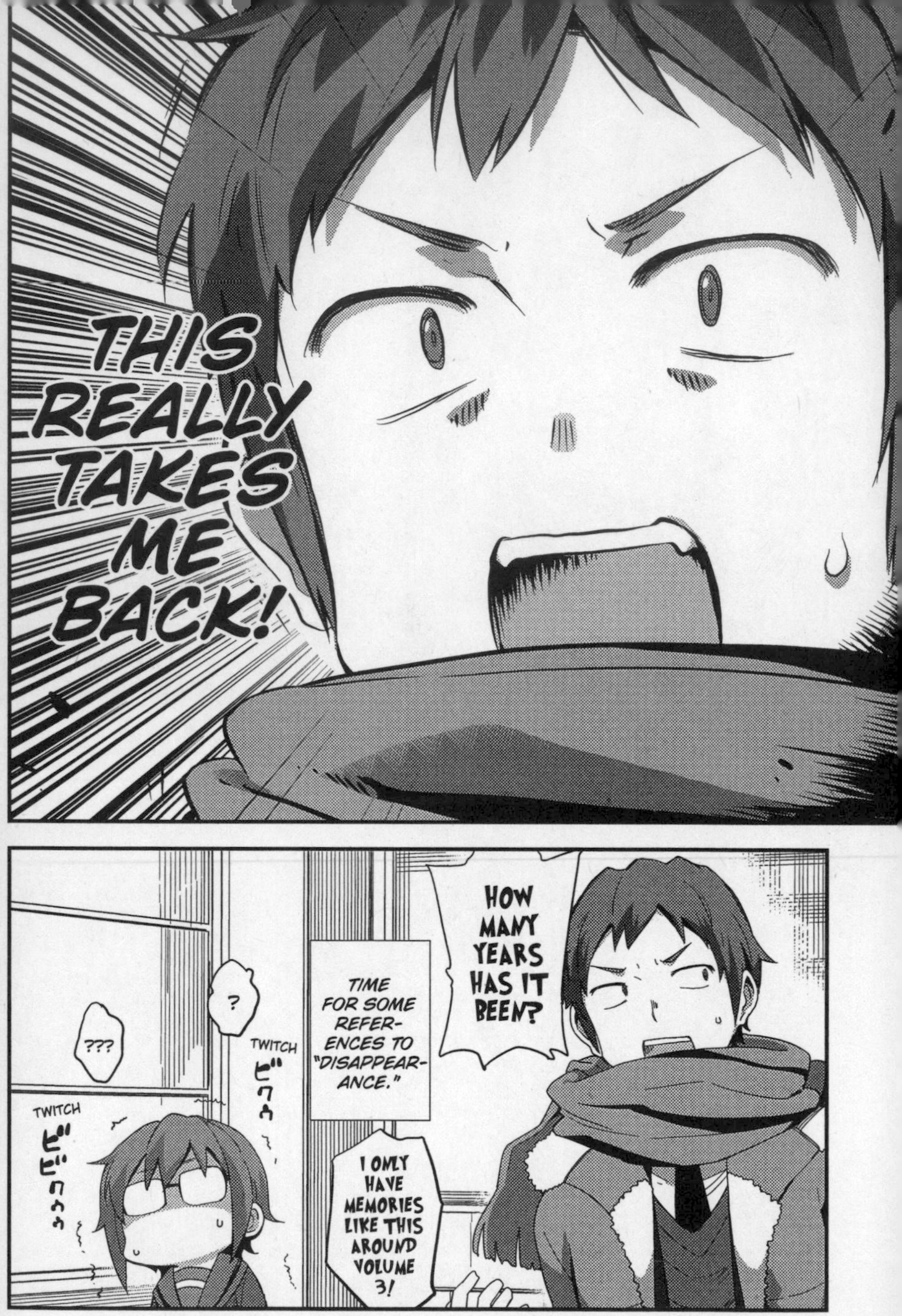
THIS REALLY TAKES ME BACK!
HOW MANY YEARS HAS IT BEEN?
TIME FOR SOME REFER-ENCES TO "DISAPPEAR-ANCE."
I ONLY HAVE MEMORIES LIKE THIS AROUND VOLUME 3!
TWITCH ビクゥ
?
???
TWITCH ビビクゥゥ

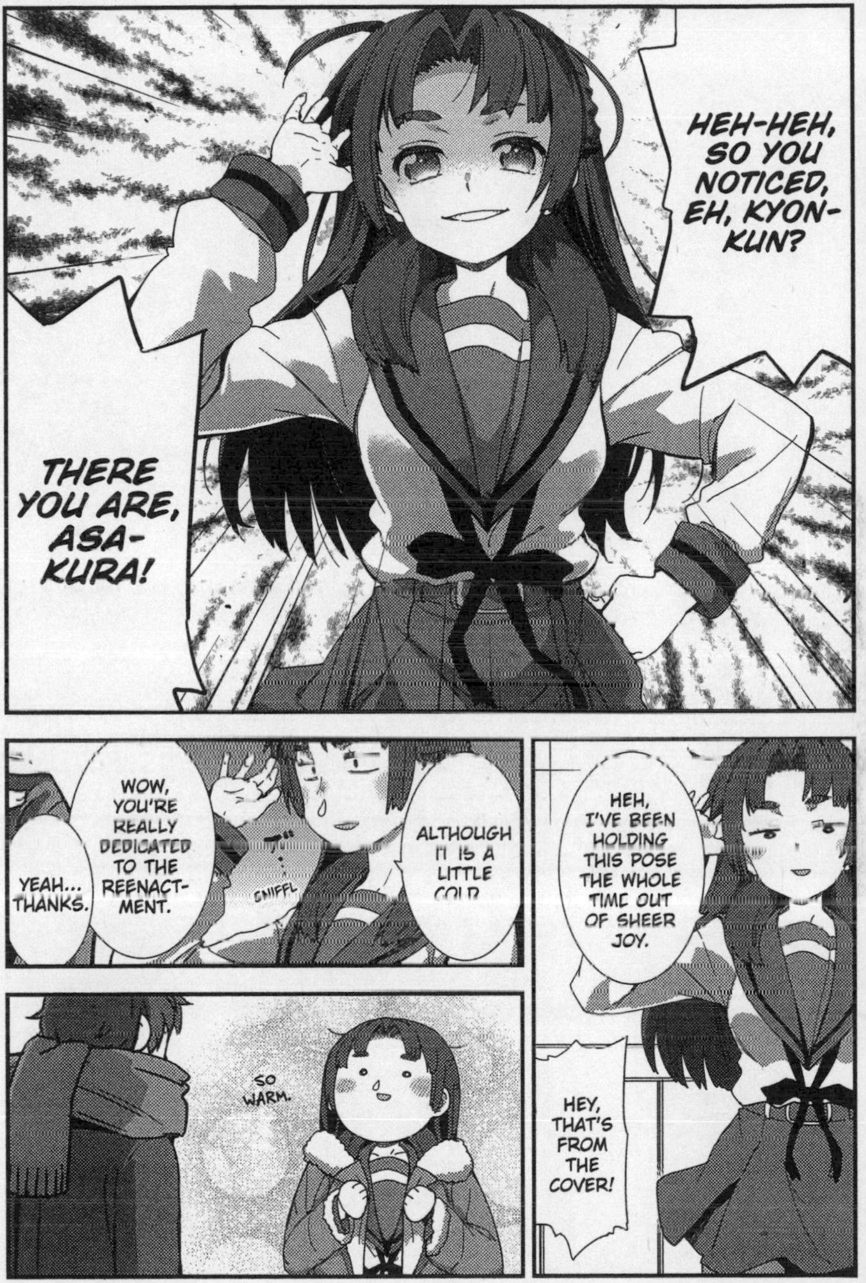
HEH-HEH, SO YOU NOTICED, EH, KYON-KUN?
THERE YOU ARE, ASA-KURA!
HEH, I'VE BEEN HOLDING THIS POSE THE WHOLE TIME OUT OF SHEER JOY.
HEY, THAT'S FROM THE COVER!
ALTHOUGH IT IS A LITTLE COLD...
SNIFFL
WOW, YOU'RE REALLY DEDICATED TO THE REENACTMENT.
YEAH... THANKS.
SO WARM.

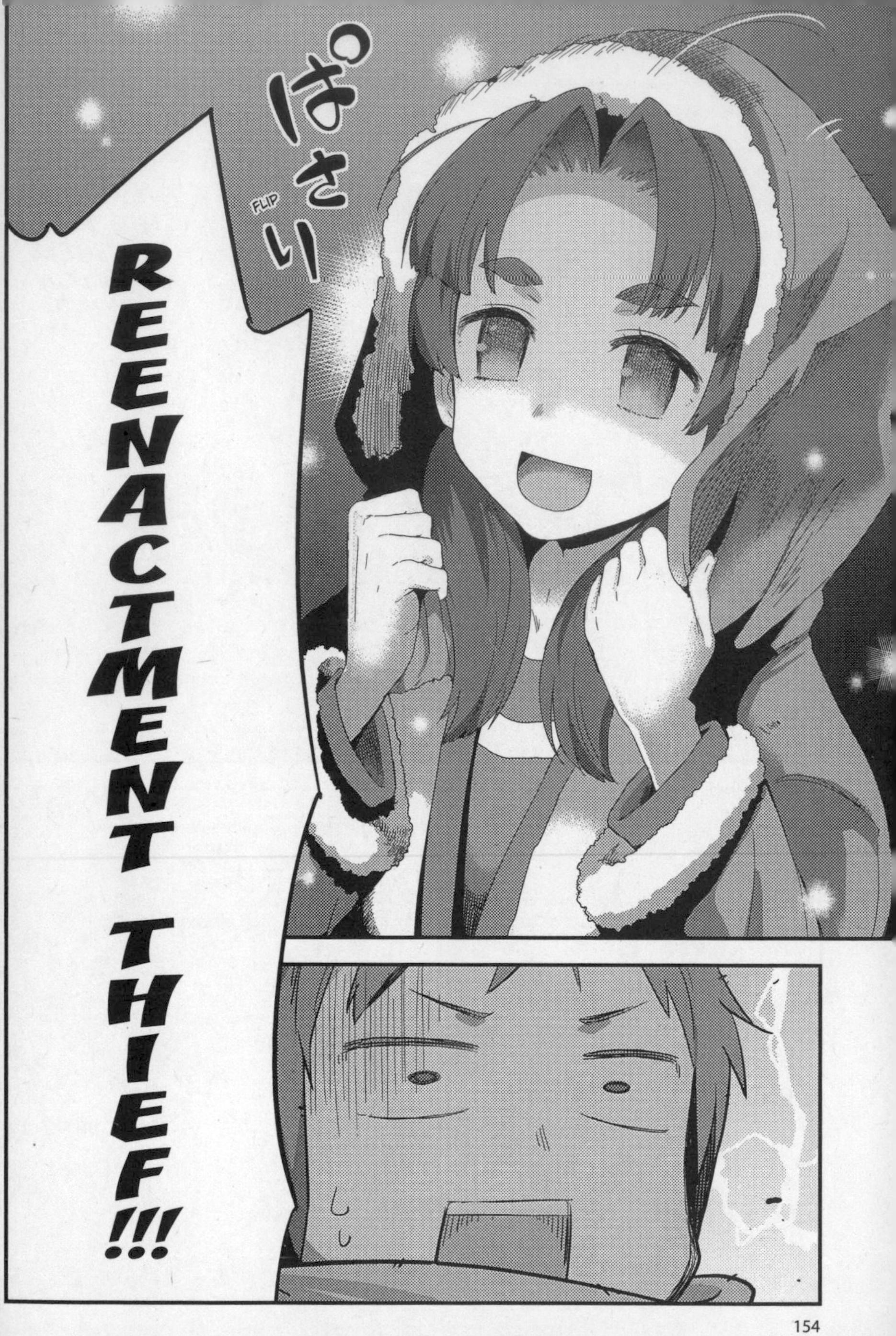
ぱさり
FLIP
REENACTMENT THIEF!!!

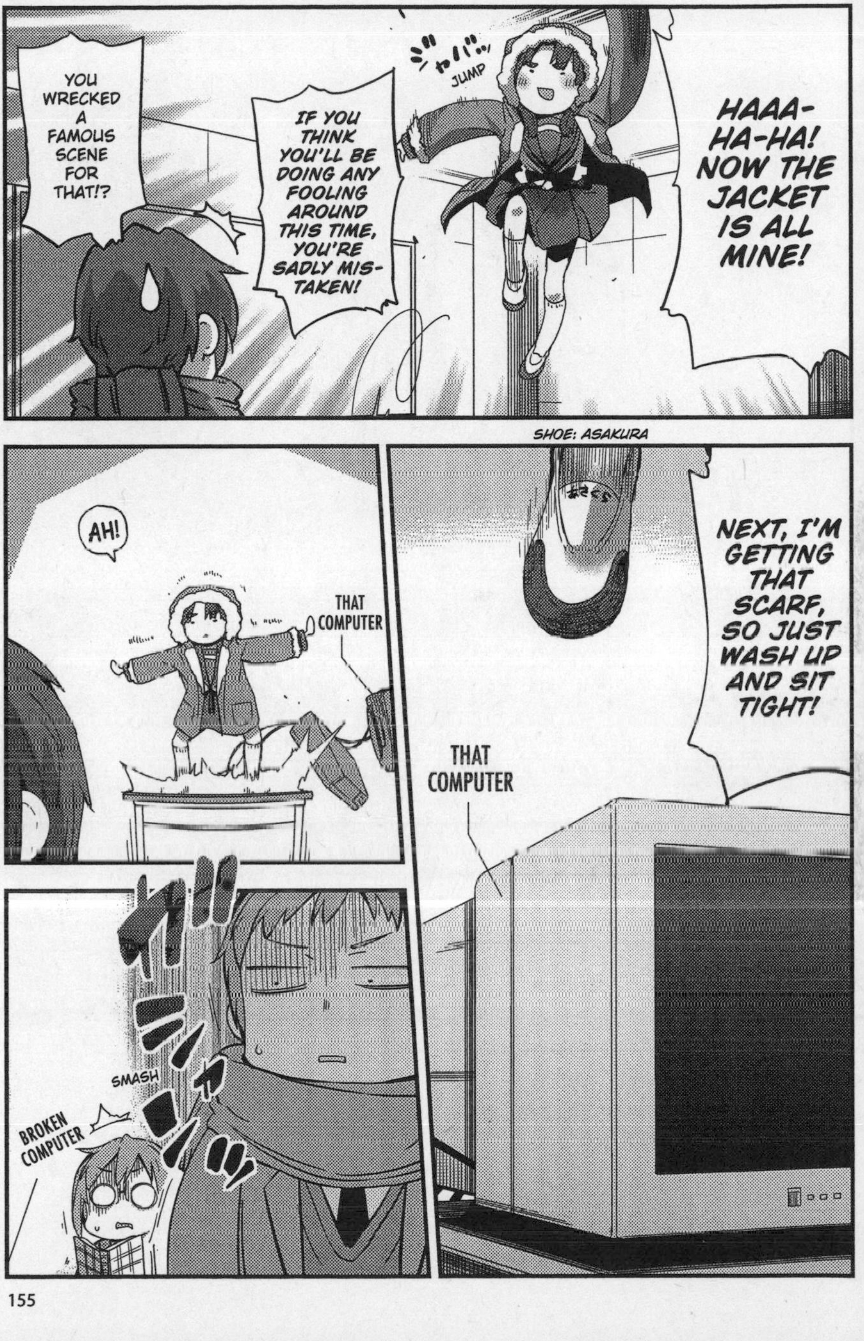
HAAAA-HA-HA! NOW THE JACKET IS ALL MINE!
JUMP
IF YOU THINK YOU'LL BE DOING ANY FOOLING AROUND THIS TIME, YOU'RE SADLY MIS-TAKEN!
YOU WRECKED A FAMOUS SCENE FOR THAT!?
SHOE: ASAKURA
NEXT, I'M GETTING THAT SCARF, SO JUST WASH UP AND SIT TIGHT!
THAT COMPUTER
AH!
THAT COMPUTER
SMASH
BROKEN COMPUTER

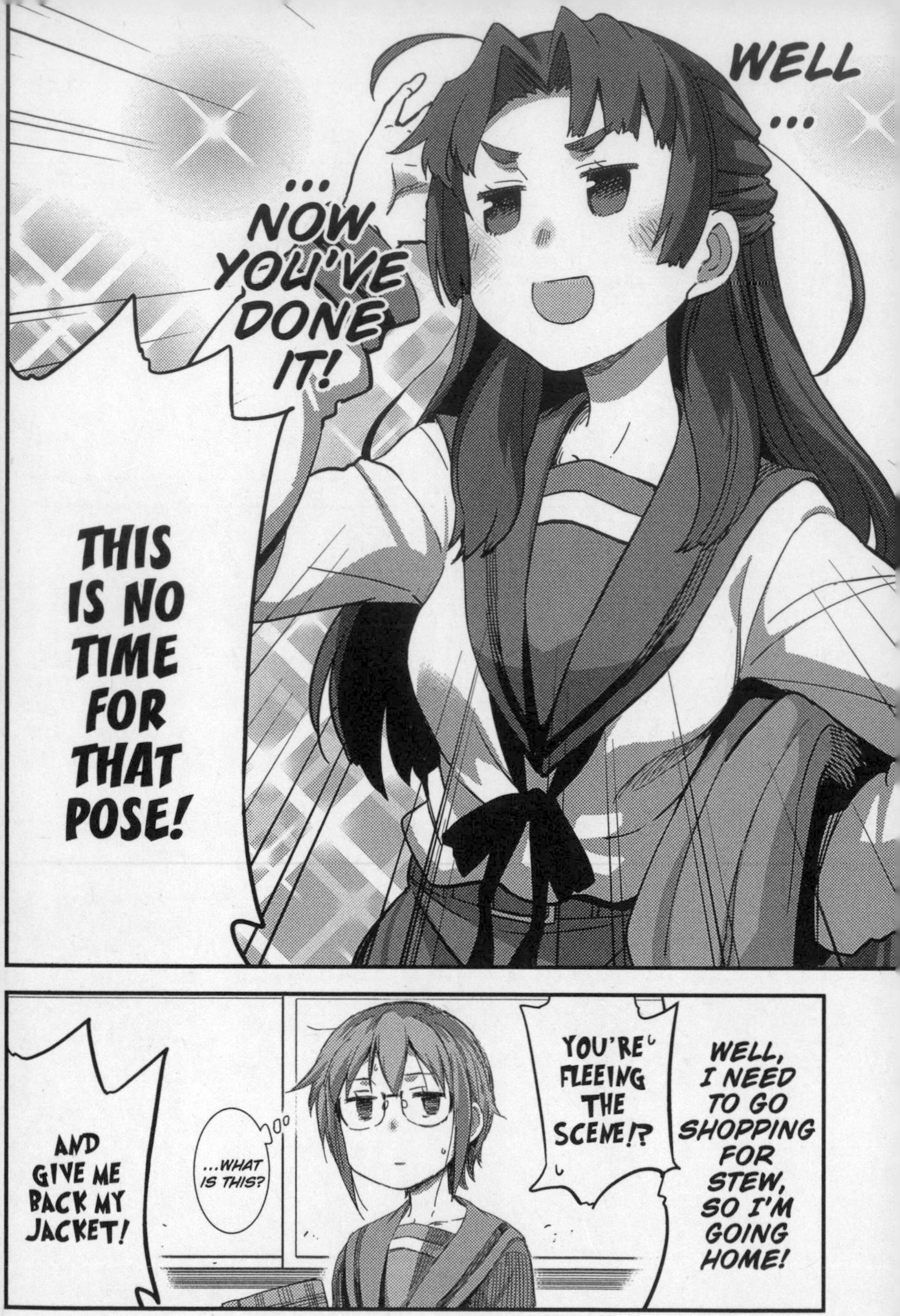
WELL...
...NOW YOU'VE DONE IT!
THIS IS NO TIME FOR THAT POSE!
WELL, I NEED TO GO SHOPPING FOR STEW, SO I'M GOING HOME!
YOU'RE FLEEING THE SCENE!?
...WHAT IS THIS?
AND GIVE ME BACK MY JACKET!

YUKI.N>
See you next volume...

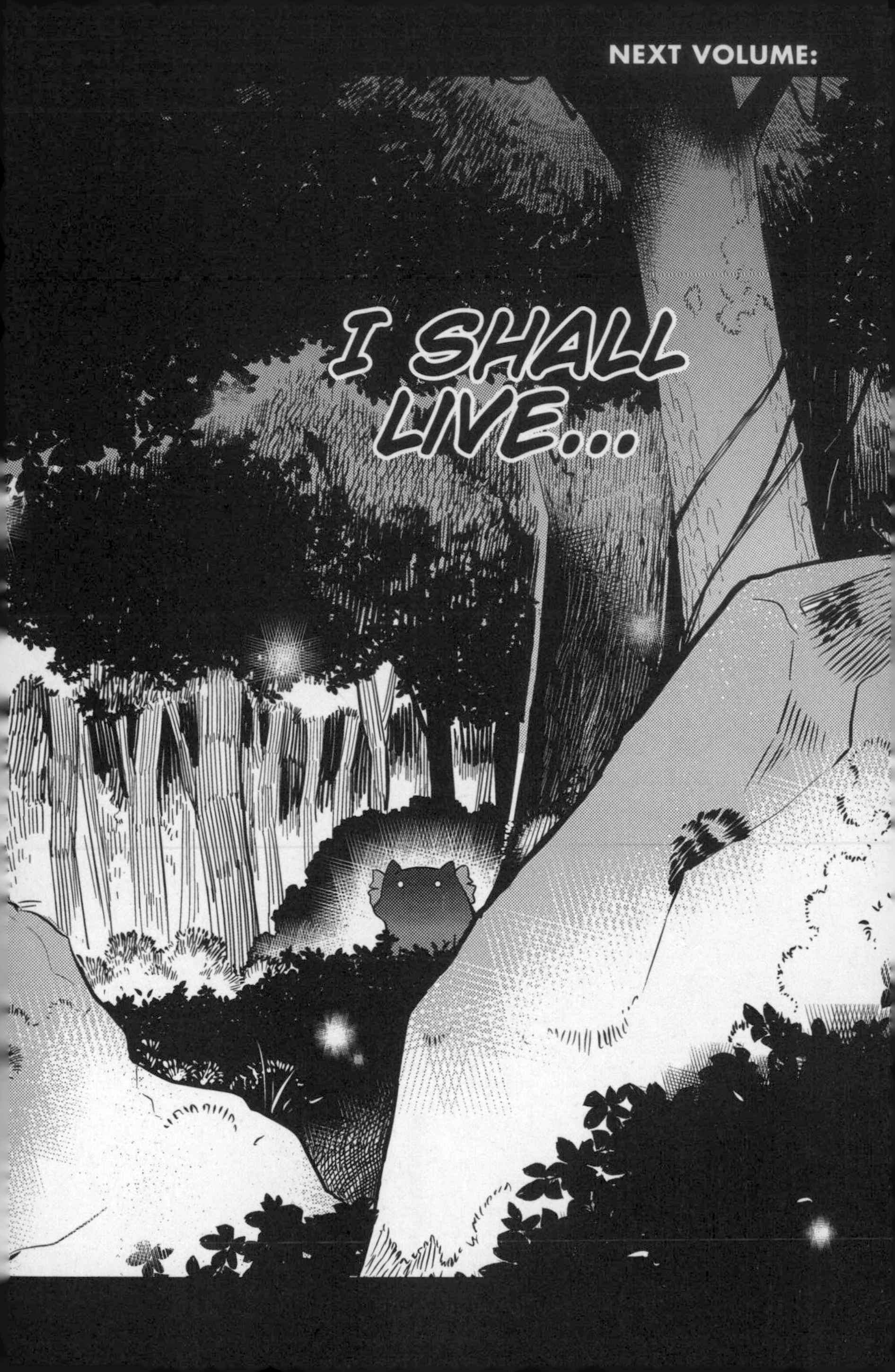
NEXT VOLUME:
I SHALL LIVE...

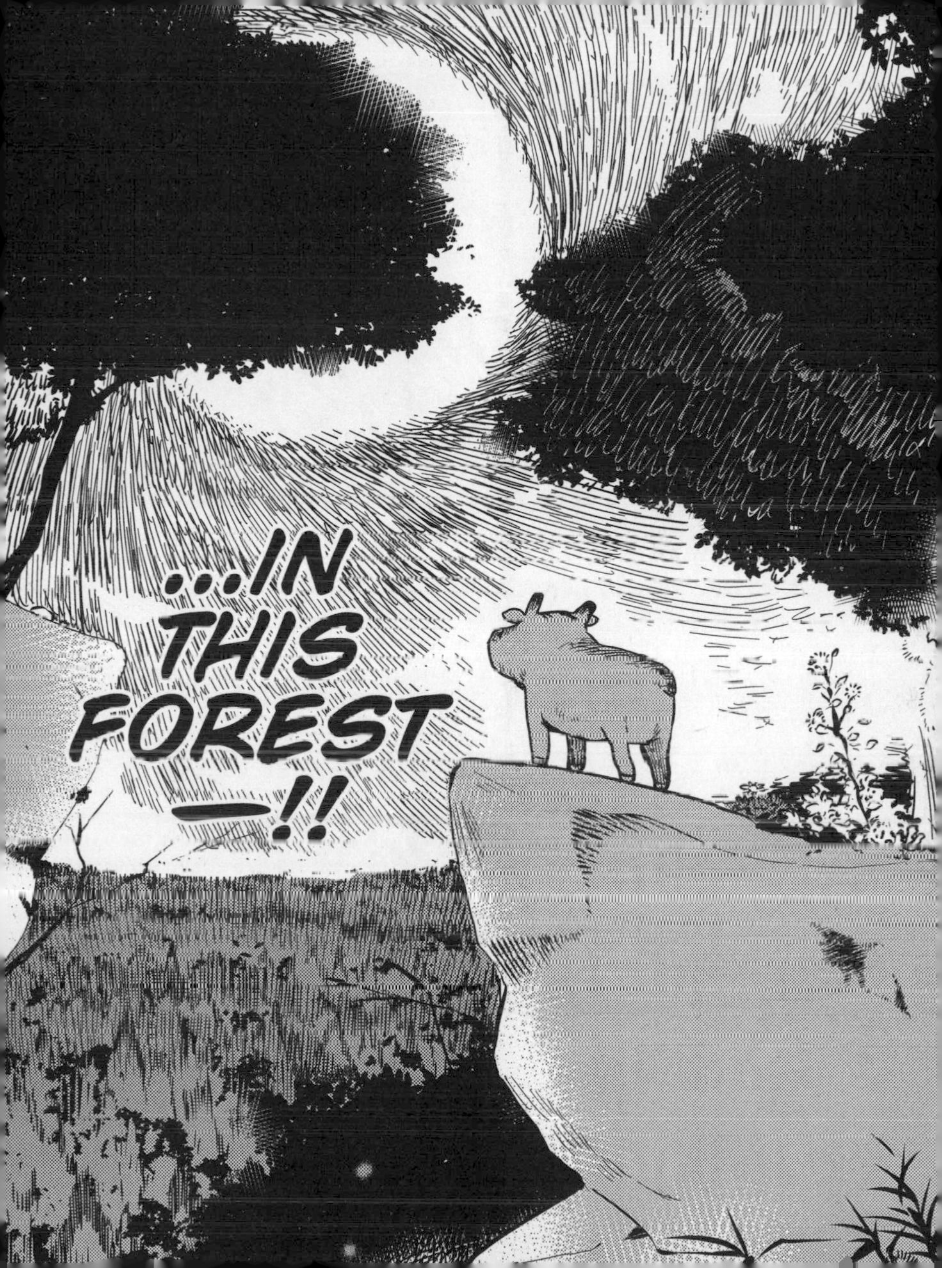
...IN THIS FOREST—!!

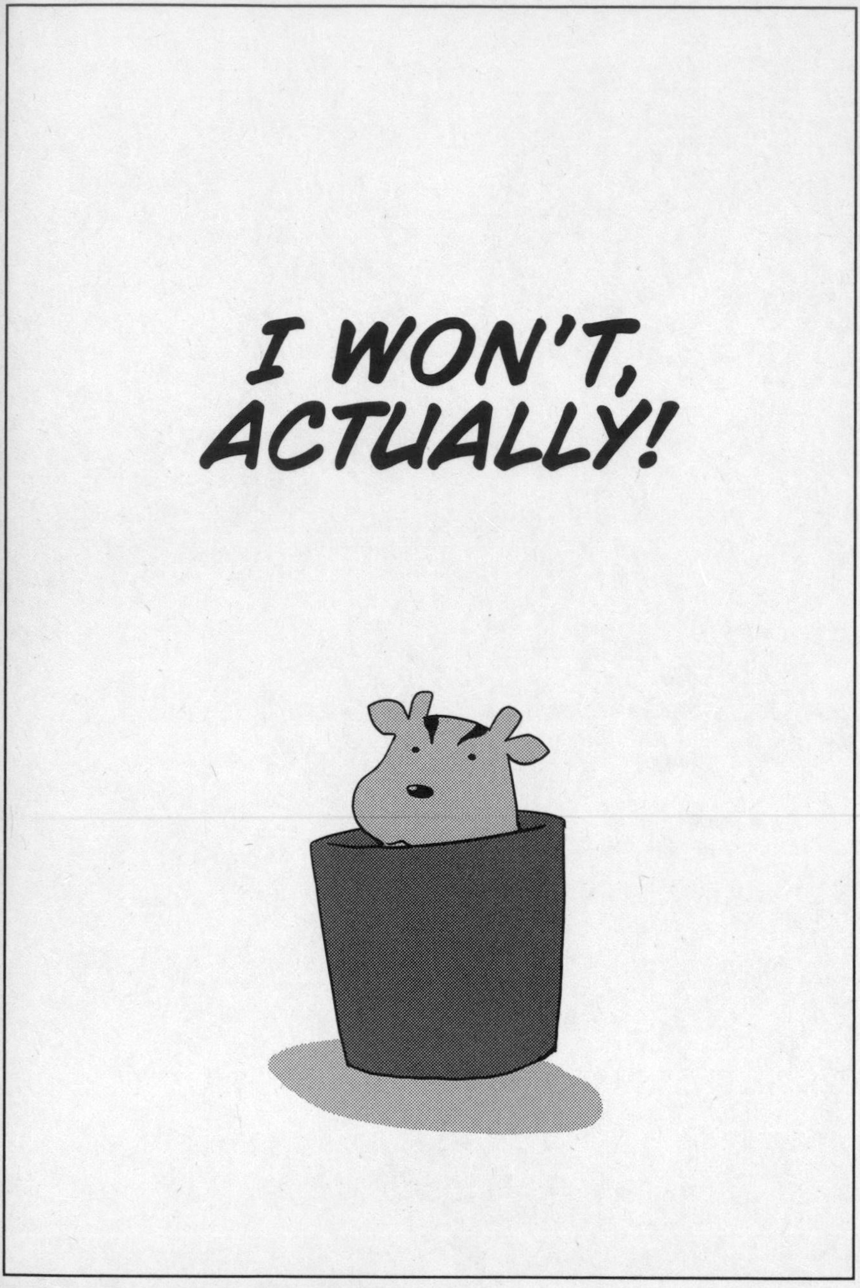
I WON'T,
ACTUALLY!

SEE YOU NEXT VOLUME!!

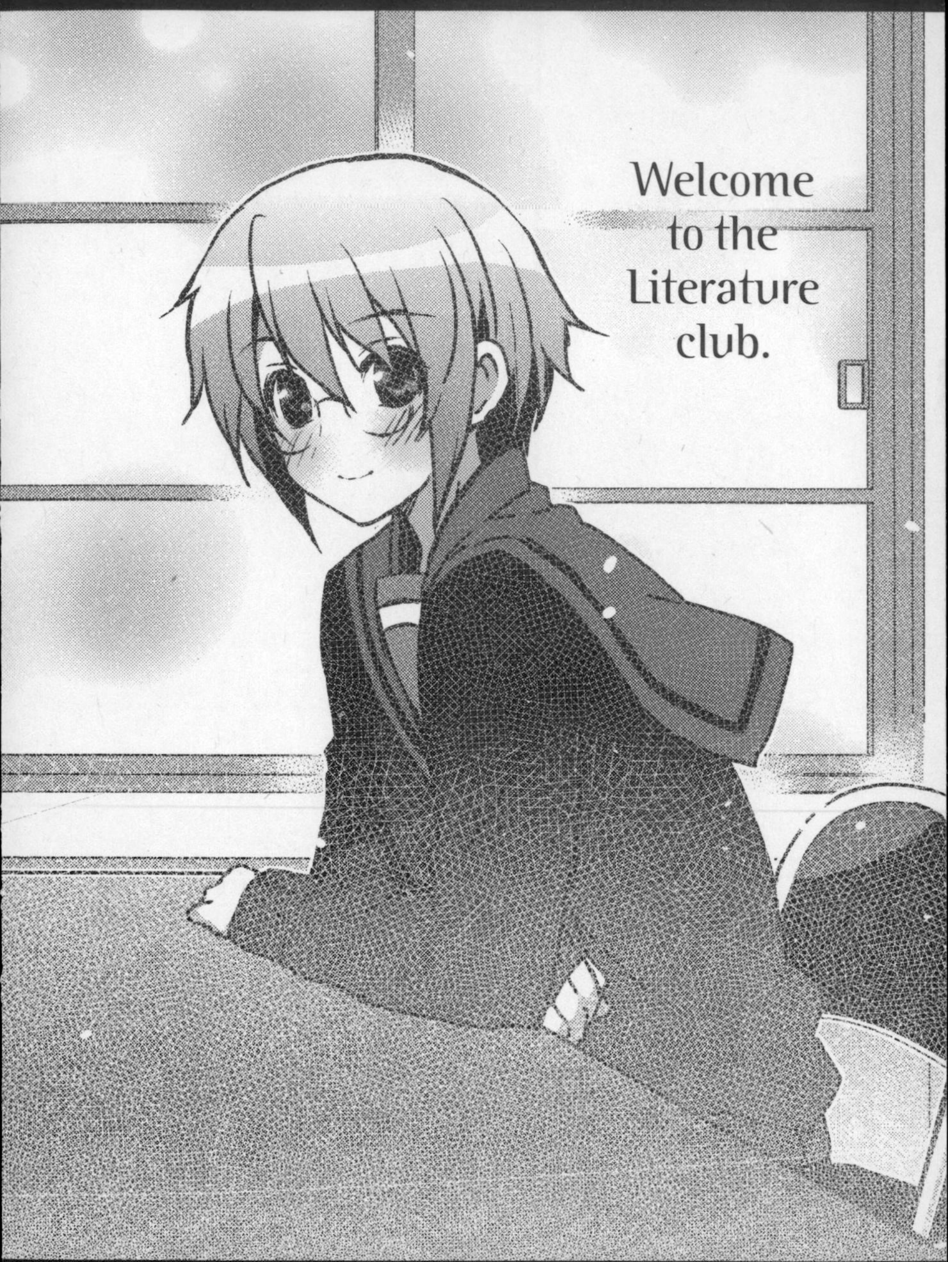
Welcome to the Literature club.

THE MELANCHOLY OF SUZUMIYA
HARUHI-CHAN
⑪

Original Story: Nagaru Tanigawa
Manga: PUYO
Character Design: Noizi Ito

Translation: Paul Starr
Lettering: Abigail Blackman

The Melancholy of Suzumiya Haruhi-chan Volume 11
© Nagaru TANIGAWA • Noizi ITO 2017 © PUYO 2017. First published in Japan in 2017 by KADOKAWA CORPORATION, Tokyo. English translation rights arranged with KADOKAWA CORPORATION, Tokyo, through TUTTLE-MORI AGENCY, INC., Tokyo.

English translation © 2017 by Yen Press, LLC

Yen Press
1290 Avenue of the Americas
New York, NY 10104

Visit us at yenpress.com
facebook.com/yenpress
twitter.com/yenpress
yenpress.tumblr.com
instagram.com/yenpress

First Yen Press Edition: December 2017

Yen Press is an imprint of Yen Press, LLC.
The Yen Press name and logo are trademarks of Yen Press, LLC.

Library of Congress Control Number: 2012450071

ISBNs: 978-0-316-41405-0 (paperback)
        978-0-316-47917-2 (ebook)

10 9 8 7 6 5 4 3 2 1

BVG

Printed in the United States of America

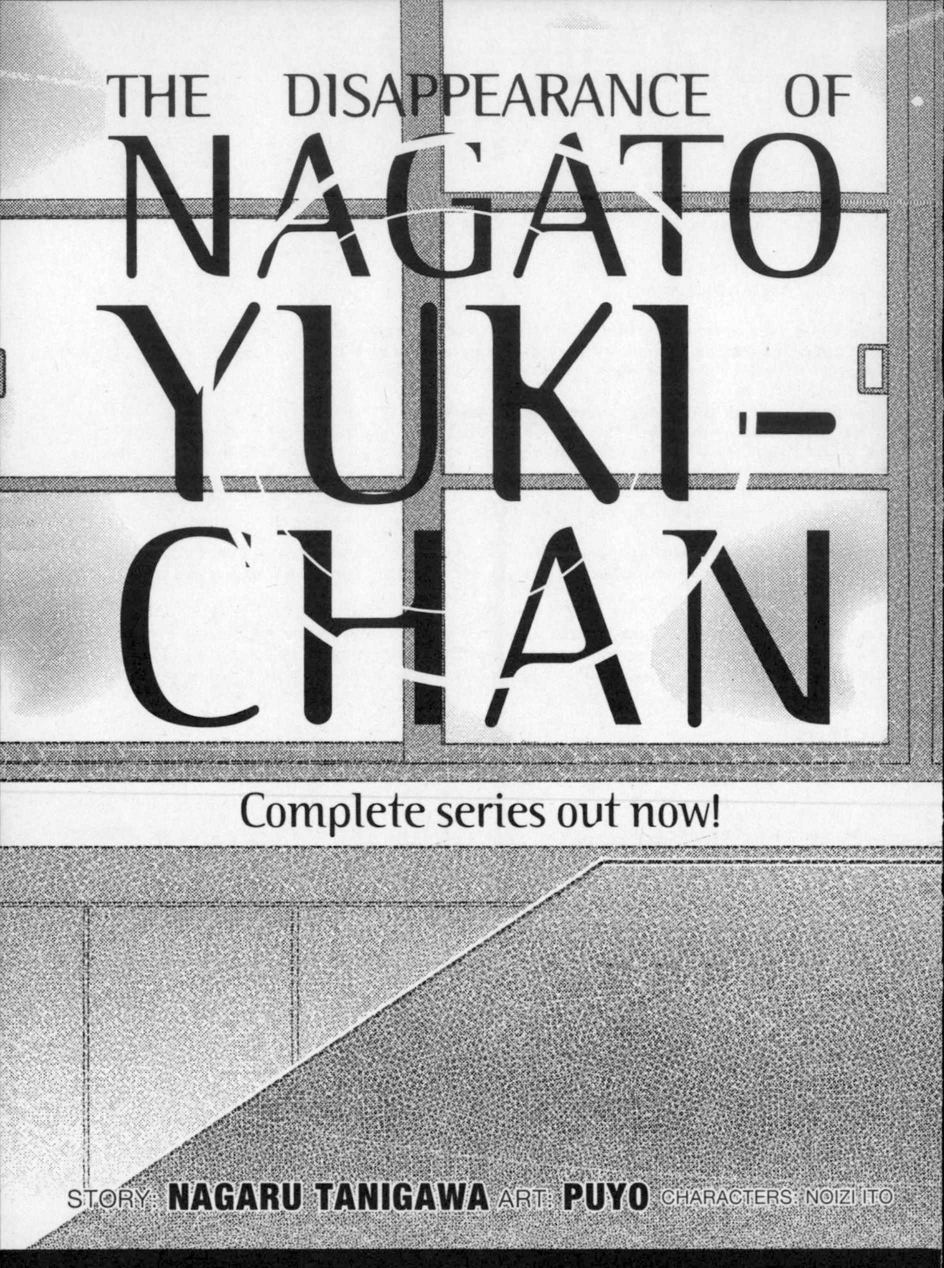
THE DISAPPEARANCE OF
NAGATO
YUKI-
CHAN
Complete series out now!
STORY: NAGARU TANIGAWA ART: PUYO CHARACTERS: NOIZI ITO